Clarmont J. Daniell

The Industrial Competition of Asia

An Inquiry into the Influence of Currency on the Commerce of the Empire in the

East

Clarmont J. Daniell

The Industrial Competition of Asia
An Inquiry into the Influence of Currency on the Commerce of the Empire in the East

ISBN/EAN: 9783744755337

Printed in Europe, USA, Canada, Australia, Japan

Cover: Foto ©Suzi / pixelio.de

More available books at **www.hansebooks.com**

BY

CLARMONT J. DANIELL, F.S.S.

LATE OF HER MAJESTY'S INDIAN CIVIL SERVICE

AUTHOR OF
"THE GOLD TREASURE OF INDIA," AND OTHER ECONOMICAL ESSAYS

LONDON
KEGAN PAUL, TRENCH, TRÜBNER & CO., Lt̠ᴅ̠
1890

PREFACE.

As this work to a great extent deals with current discussions, I desire to state that it was finished about the middle of the year 1889, with the exception of the three last chapters, and a few scattered passages which were added in the following December and January, when it was laid aside until a suitable occasion might arise for its publication.

Measures about to be taken with a view to increase the use of silver money in the United States have again drawn attention to the connection between currency and commerce, and encourage the expectation that the importation of certain commodities from silver into gold using countries, will in consequence be checked. Whatever the result of this experiment in legislation may be, it is certain that a convergence between the values of gold and silver will facilitate the reintroduction of gold into use as legal-tender money in British India, and the establishment of gold as the standard of value in the commerce between Great Britain and that country. If, on the other hand, the gold price of silver declines to a lower point than it has yet reached, the necessity of placing the commerce and the finances of India upon a gold basis, will become more than ever apparent.

The present, therefore, seems to be the proper time for pressing upon public attention the advantage to the Empire in general, of that reform in the Indian currency which is set forth in the following pages.

C. J. D.

May, 1890.

CONTENTS.

CHAPTER I.

INTRODUCTORY.

Objects of appointment of Gold and Silver Commission—India in the Report—Subjects treated in this book—Causes of changes in precious metals—Bounty on exportation theory—Trade and double standard—Effect of rupture of bimetallic tie—Competition of Asia due to cheapness of production; bimetallism no cure for this—Commercial causes regulate flow of silver to the East and rates of exchange—Relation of credit and money to prices—Insufficiency of bimetallism to fulfil its objects, or maintain circulation of dual money at a fixed ratio—Bimetallism at a varying ratio in India 1

CHAPTER II.

THE COMMERCIAL FACTOR.

Objects and methods of the bimetallic party—The monetary and the natural law of values—The issue involved in the silver question commercial rather than monetary—The bimetallic system broke down under pressure of commercial causes—Theory of bounty on exportations from silver-using countries, Professor Marshall's opinion—Value of silver in gold depends on its value in commodities; fixed ratio system hinders free sales, does not insure circulation of both kinds of money—Commercial ratio controls monetary ratio—Fixed ratio restricts supply of money—Fixed ratio to be effective must be universally accepted—Fundamental economic error in the system—Bounty on Indian exportations attributable to cheapness of production, not to cheap silver—Low gold price of silver does not lower silver price of commodities—Professor Marshall's, Mr. Fowler's, Mr. Cernuschi's, Mr. Nisbet's views on the connection between cheap silver and gold prices—Views of Mr. Bythell, Mr. Fielden, Mr. Barclay, on cheap silver protecting Indian industry—Complaints of Lancashire 15

CHAPTER III.

CHEAP SILVER AND TRADE.

Use of silver conceals real causes of trade competition—Can be reduced only by increased value of Eastern productions—Both these and silver take their value from gold—Illustration—Single monetary unit partial remedy for varying exchanges—*A priori* argument in favour of commercial theory—Bimetallist theory that cheap silver acts as a bounty on exportations from India examined—The system will not raise the value or diminish the exportation of cheap produce of Asia—Argument to the same effect in the report of the Commission—Reason why cheap silver has not gone to India—Criticism on these reasons in Report—Defect in this criticism—Argument founded on comparative gold and silver prices of commodities fallacious 51

CHAPTER IV.

COMMERCE AND THE BIMETALLIC PAR.

Bimetallism does not ensure an unlimited circulation of both kinds of coin—The bimetallic par commercial, not legal—A premium on gold under fixed-ratio system amounts to collapse of the system—Illustration of commercial theory from Indian trade and exchanges—Ratio for gold and silver depends on their ratio of value to commodities—Dilemma involved in the bimetallist theory of the exchanges—Defect in the theory of the effect of fixed ratio on value of silver in the East illustrated—Proving the supremacy of the commercial over the legal valuation 77

CHAPTER V.

MONEY AND PRICES.

Origin of the connection between money and prices—Definition of price—Action of money on industry illustrated—How abundance and scarcity of money act on trade—Views of Commissioners on the effect of money on prices—Statistics of the decline of prices and increase of trade—Statistics of the use for, and the supply of, gold—Opinion of the Commissioners on influence of the fixed-ratio system on gold and silver values controverted—Accepted theory of prices questioned—Professor Marshall's opinion—Definition of money—Mr. Macleod's opinion—Mr. Fowler's opinion—Credit and money, their influence on prices—Reasons why they affect prices differently—Wealth of a nation depends on increase of production, not on increase in credits—Mr. Macleod's view of the rise of prices in the last 200 years disputable—Influence of the use of money in initial and final processes of industry on prices—Reasons why abundance and scarcity of money raise and lower prices—How credits and money affect the volume of the loan fund—Theory that the supply of money depends on prices examined—Causes which constitute money the regulator of price—If money depends on prices, what do prices depend on?—Another view of the quantitative theory of money—Abundance of money a real stimulus to production—Conclusion in favour of the necessity of an expanding currency 94

CHAPTER VI.

BIMETALLISM AND THE SUPPLY OF MONEY.

Claim of bimetallism to increase volume of currency and raise prices examined—Alleged universal influence of bimetallic valuation of gold and silver money disposed of by the facts of 1873—Influence of the system confined to use of one, not of both kinds of money—Causes and occasions of replenishment of a bimetallic currency—Opinions about the action of the bimetallic tie on the exchanges—Had the system been maintained silver monometallism would have resulted, supply of gold to bimetallic countries could not have been secured—View of the action of the monetary law in the "Theory of Bimetallism" examined—Relative value not dependent on relative production—Effect of annual production on relative value of precious metals—Which has but little effect on their value in commodities, and therefore on their exchange value—Manner in which the system fails to secure sufficient supply of money—Restricts supply in correspondence with the supply of the dearer metal—Real rise of values only accompanies rise of prices in terms of the dearer metal—When both kinds of money are supplied at commercial rates of exchange no such limitation exists—Conclusion, that the alleged universal influence of the fixed-ratio system over the values of gold and silver cannot be proved—The strength of the bimetallic tie depended on the quality of legal tender it gave to money, not on the fixation of the ratio 133

CHAPTER VII.

GROWTH OF THE RATIO.

Mons. de Laveleye's opinion on the control of the ratio by law as opposed to commerce examined—History of the use of money proves that the real ratio of value is solely commercial—Silver and gold values in ancient times—The ratio in mediæval times—The ratio in modern times—Equalizing effect of commercial exchanges on the relative values of gold and silver money 165

CHAPTER VIII.

SUMMING-UP.

Until commercial ratio of exchange is ascertained fixed ratio cannot be established—The system of the fixed ratio will not create a correspondence between supply and demand of the precious metals, nor will the supply correspond with the wants of commerce, but will be

affected by external systems of currency—For the
objects of bimetallism the monetary law must be
universal in its application—Difficulties of obtaining
universal acceptance for monetary law stated; arising
from variations in supply acting on prices of commodities, which subjects monetary to influence of commercial ratio—India and the East—Objections from point
of view of Asiatics—Risks involved by including India
in a bimetallic arrangement—Case for bimetallism as
stated by either party, burden of proof lies with bimetallists—Initial steps towards reviving bimetallism described—Discretion with the bank to refuse to pay gold
not admissible—Practical result of system on bank
reserve stated, its conversion into a silver reserve—
Theory that bimetallic ratio will impose itself on the
world examined—Remonetizing gold in India secures a
natural ratio of exchange—Conflict of eastern and
western ratios will limit supply of money to western
currencies—Commercial supremacy of England affected
—Process of apportionment of stock of money to
bimetallic countries—Its results on bank reserves foretold by past events—Commissioners' opinion on possible
results of fixation of ratio—Some practical objections
to system extracted from the Report—Bimetallists unable
to prove their case—Mr. Goschen's opinion and Mr.
Gladstone's opinion support preceding arguments ... 179

CHAPTER IX.

Antiquity of the trade of India and of use of coined money—
Descriptions of merchandise supplied by Indians—
Balance of trade in favour of India settled by treasure—
Trade between India and Palestine—Trade with Phœnicia and Egypt and shores of Mediterranean—Drain of
gold to India from the West in historic times—Sources
of supply in Asia—Asiatic trade of India—European
trade with India in Middle Ages—Estimate of gold
treasure now existing in India; accumulations up to
1835—Accumulations since 1835—Estimate of coin
current in British India—Statistics of coinage—Exportation of coined money—Effect of trade by land into
Asia on stock of coin in India, tale of coin *per capita* in
use in India 224

CHAPTER X.

SCHEME FOR REMONETIZING GOLD IN INDIA.

India most concerned in silver question—Amount of loss by exchange in ten years—The present time most suitable for resuming use of gold money—Cost of purchasing gold an increasing burden on India—Financial risks incurred by India averted by use of gold money—Evidence of the predilection of the people of India for gold money—Evidence of injurious effects on trade produced by disuse of gold money—Propensity to hoard gold would have no effect on supply of the metal for money—Use more profitable than hoarding—Inducements to hoard diminishing under British administration—Gold money as necessary to India as to England—Consequent rise of prices beneficial to India—The country can supply ten times the gold required for the currency—Reasons why prices are stationary in India—Silver currency inadequate; use of gold would not check coinage of silver—The disuse of gold acts as a restriction on industry—Silver purchased abroad with gold bullion less efficient as money in India than gold—Results of modern monetary legislation on trade—Silver token currency unsuitable to India—Dual currencies of gold and silver common in India—Plan for circulating gold money, and its effects—Similar methods considered on previous occasions—Opinion of the Duke of Wellington 260

CHAPTER XI.

PRACTICAL APPLICATION OF THE SCHEME.

This plan secures unrestricted supply of money to commerce—Use of gold will stimulate use of silver and improve the exchanges—Consequent stability of gold and silver prices and of the gold price of silver—Reasons why gold money will not be hoarded—Alleged hoarding of silver exaggerated—Causes of diminished hoarding of silver apply to gold—Effect on Indian commerce of double full-value standard—The £1 sterling and international currency—The Indian currency will secure ascertainment of relative values of gold and silver for all the World—Necessity for gold money being legal tender—State rate of conversion fixed by innumerable trade dealings—Alterations in the State rate of conversion will seldom occur—Conditions of maintenance of true value of the two kinds of money in one another—Indian system would be unaffected by any addition to either kind of coin—Instances of State valuations of gold and silver money—Facility of ascertaining the commercial value—Objections to a varying rate of exchange—Case of gold falling against silver—Case of silver falling against gold—Alleged loss of common measure of value—Indian system provides a better common measure than French system—Case of effect of system on retail dealings—Variations in exchange rate involve no loss on use of either money—Case of double accounts—Case of "cornering" gold could not occur—Apprehension that India will be drained of gold groundless—Theory that gold coin would be of no more use in India than gold bullion; its unsoundness shown—Indian gold money a support to British commerce—Levy of a gold revenue; objections thereto considered—Comparative advantages of a gold and silver revenue—Beneficial to all classes alike—Necessity for strengthening our commercial connection with India—Dependent on continued prosperity of India—Proposed currency reform especially suited to India—Beneficial results summed up—Diminished taxation—Substitution of silver by gold as financial basis—Returns to investments attainable in most profitable form—Indian currency the test of gold and silver values will cause a general diffusion of money and promote cash transactions in trade—Will raise prices of Indian productions abroad—Fallacy involved in the theory that high prices are injurious to Indian industry—Influence of system on foreign exchanges leaves silver currency of India unaffected, avoids differentiation of values in respect of either metal—Excludes influence of law and promotes free trade in the precious metals—Is especially beneficial to commercial and financial business of England 306

INDUSTRIAL COMPETITION OF ASIA.

ADDENDA ET CORRIGENDA.

P. 7, line 13, for "metals" read "two kinds of money."
P. 9, line 11, for "cause" read "causes."
P. 61, line 13, after "89—91)" read "by the author."
P. 77, line 2, for "circulate" read "*circulate*."
P. 83, line 5, for "economics" read "economies."
P. 90, line 10, after "legal-tender quality" read "at a certain rating."
P. 115, line 1, for "used up her" read "used her."
P. 147, foot-note after "Chap. X." read "by D. Barbour."
P. 155, line 12, for "8 to 23" read "8 to 28."
P. 219, line 13-14, for "number of coins" read "Silver money."

THE
INDUSTRIAL COMPETITION OF ASIA.

CHAPTER I.

INTRODUCTORY.

Objects of appointment of Gold and Silver Commission—India in the Report—Subjects treated in this book—Causes of changes in precious metals—Bounty on exportation theory—Trade and double standard—Effect of rupture of bimetallic tie—Competition of Asia due to cheapness of production; bimetallism no cure for this—Commercial causes regulate flow of silver to the East and rates of exchange—Relation of credit and money to prices—Insufficiency of bimetallism to fulfil its objects, or maintain circulation of dual money at a fixed ratio—Bimetallism at a varying ratio in India.

ANY investigation, into the economical conditions which influence the competition of India and other countries in Asia, with England in her own markets; into the connection existing between the supply of money and trade; into the action of the currency systems of England and of India on the commerce of both countries; as well as into the advantages, both fiscal and commercial which would be secured to the people of India and to the mercantile classes in every nation with which they trade, from that country employing a full value monetary unit both of gold and silver in its commerce with gold-and-silver-using countries respectively;—must first be

B

directed to an examination of the claims which bimetallism makes to surpass in efficiency any other existing system, and therefore to obtain for commerce in general more beneficial results than can accrue either from the monometallism of the English system, or from that of the exchange of gold and silver at varying commercial ratios which prevails universally, elsewhere than in those parts of the commercial world which are occupied by nations of European descent. The system of the Latin Union has been so long the subject of general discussion, and takes so large a share of the interest which the public feels in such matters, without any decision on its utility, either as applied to the requirements of Europe and America or to the pressing necessities of the Government and of the inhabitants of India, being even remotely in prospect, that the scientific basis upon which it is alleged to rest, as well as the actual effects which it has hitherto produced, cannot be overlooked. In this examination an endeavour will be made to regard the system as far as possible from some new points of view, and to make a forecast of the practical consequences of its application either in England or in India; and thence to show how a reform in the currency of India may be brought about, which has had the support at different times during the last thirty years of men of the first rank as Indian administrators, and the way in which it will achieve all the objects which bimetallism proposes as its aim, without exposing that country or the commerce of the Empire to a single one of the many risks which furnish such weighty objections to that system of currency.

The Royal Commission on the Depression of

Trade and Agriculture, over which the late Lord Iddesleigh presided, recommended that an investigation, separate from and independent of that which they were conducting, should be made into what is commonly known as the "silver question," which, from its complexity and extent, they hesitated to undertake. The Royal Commission, appointed in accordance with this advice, was especially directed to ascertain whether the changes in the relative values of the precious metals which have occurred since 1873, arose from a depreciation of silver, an appreciation of gold, or from both causes, and to inquire into the effect which an increase or decrease in the supply, or an increase or decrease in the demand, of either kind of metal, may have had on these alterations of value, and into their bearing upon the financial administration of the Government of India, as well as on the interests of those making remittances of money from India in gold; on the interests of producers merchants and taxpayers in India, and on those of merchants and manufacturers at home.

The Commissioners' inquiry was also to extend into the effect of those changes upon the foreign trade of the United Kingdom, both with silver-using and gold-using countries, and upon our internal trade and industry. They were instructed to suggest any remedies they might consider calculated to remove or palliate such evils or inconveniences of permanent or important character as their inquiries might show these interests to be exposed to, which at the same time would not cause other evils or inconveniences equally great. On some preliminary points the opinion of the Commissioners was unanimous. They agreed generally as to the statement of the facts relating to the subject of their inquiry, and the arguments advanced in connection with them, and also in the opinion to be found in part i. sects. 192-198, of the Final Report, that the primary cause of the recent changes in the relative value of precious metals was to be traced to the abandonment by the Latin Union of the bimetallic system of currency; but between six of the Commissioners on the one hand and six on the other, a divergence of opinion arose regarding the extent of the evils resulting from this step, as well as the possibility of removing it, and also in respect of those inconveniences which might arise if no remedy were applied at all. The Commissioners thus became divided into two groups of six each; the one we may call, for convenience' sake, the monometallist, and the other the bimetallist party; the latter advocating the adoption by this country, in concert with the chief commercial nations of the World, of a system of currency essentially the same as that which the Latin Union abandoned fifteen years ago.

The compilation of the Special Commissioners' Report has been justly commended on all sides as being admirably done. The argument, however, in some places loses force from terseness of expression and insufficient amplitude of explanation. Many of the papers contributed, at the request of the Commission, by specialists on particular parts of the subject are of permanent value, and the translation of Dr. Ad. Soëtbeer's work on the " Materials for the Illustration and Criticism of the Economic Relations of the Precious Metals and of the Currency Question," which is given in the appendix, makes accessible to English readers a statistical record of the highest importance. Sir Louis Malet's note (in the Final Report) is a remarkable specimen of logical exposition, while the Report generally is distinguished for the skill and the judicial impartiality with which the evidence—ample, conflicting, and dealing with so great a number of subjects—has been summed up, and all that is relevant to the matter in hand concentrated upon it. It is nevertheless to be regretted that the interests of India, and the peculiar connection between those interests and the currency system of the Empire, were comparatively neglected in the Commissioners' inquiries. Statistics of the absorption by India of the precious metals in recent years, of the use of council bills, of the coinage of silver, are not wanting; and some description is given of the complaints made by mercantile men of the inconvenience which they are put to for want of a monetary standard, common to both England and India, and of the expedients they resort to, to minimize risks arising from this cause. The arguments for and against the theories that cheap silver puts the English trader in the East at some disadvantage to his Indian rival, and that the present condition of the exchanges interrupts the flow of capital to India, are impartially stated; but when the reader seeks for any suggestions towards a remedy for the injurious effects which the changes in the values of the precious metals have had upon producers and merchants, as well as upon taxpayers of all classes and English residents in India generally, upon merchants and manufacturers in our own country who trade with India and other silver-using countries in the East, he finds the Report to be almost totally silent.

The gravity of the embarrassments in which the Government is placed, the great hazard of financial calamity, and the impossibility of any improvement in the fiscal, as distinguished from the commercial condition of the country, are dwelt upon with a due sense of their importance; but while the Special Commissioners consider that the present constitution of the monetary system of India involves real and very serious evils, which may be increased and the difficulty of dealing with them augmented by a further depression in the value of silver, the only help towards extrication which they can offer is to say that these evils and inconveniences which the situation involves are so serious that it would be well worth an endeavour to remedy them, if a remedy could be devised and adopted without injustice to other interests, and without causing other evils and inconveniences equally great;* but no attempt is made to provide a remedy, nor is any suggestion made as to the quarter in which a way out of them may be found.

The Commissioners deprecate the application of bimetallism to India, pointing out that its advocates are not agreed as to the inclusion of India in an international Convention; and that while the exclusion of India from such an arrangement would be a singular anomaly, its inclusion would provoke fresh and grave difficulties.† As affording any relief to the difficulties attending the financial administration of the Indian Government, the bimetallism of the Latin Union must therefore be held of no account;

* F. R., part ii. § 102. † *Ibid.*, § 104.

and of other remedies directly touching India, the most practical is considered by the Commissioners to be the establishment of a gold standard for India.* To this end two propositions were made—one † for raising the value of the rupee artificially to a certain price in gold, and making gold legal tender for all payments due to Government concurrently with the rupee at the fixed rate, which was for very good reasons disapproved by the Commissioners; and another‡ for making gold legal tender, and exchangeable with silver money at a rate to be declared by Government from time to time in conformity with the market price of the two metals in one another.§

No investigation into this proposal was made. The difficulties in the way of a return to the use of gold money in India are considered by the Commissioners to be "formidable;" but that is no reason for passing over *sub silentio* the single remedy which the investigations of the Commissioners show to have survived the process of elimination which all others offered to them, had undergone. The inquiries of the Commissioners for all practical purposes resulted in nothing more than a drawn battle between bimetallism and monometallism. This intermediate proposal was subjected to no examination adequate or inadequate, it had no adherents in the commission, it could not be made to fit into the scheme of either contending party, and although it combines all that is of material value in both systems, and avoids the defects of either, and is within certain limits complete, and is absolutely free from risk of involving either those who use gold or those who use silver

* F. R., part ii. § 133.   † *Ibid.*, § 175.
‡ *Ibid.*, § 177.   § *Ibid.*, and appendix iii. p. 91.

money in any loss or hindrance in their business, and possesses other manifest advantages, not the smallest effort was made to ascertain how far such a system would benefit the commerce of India, would be an aid to the material progress of the people by facilitating production and thus increasing wealth and plenty, or assist in establishing the financial system of the country on a sounder basis than a monometallism of silver affords, and lessen or remove those effects of the recent alterations in the relative values of gold and silver which have proved in any way prejudicial to the people of India, or to Englishmen engaged in public or private business in that country, or to the commerce of England with the East; subjects which the Commissioners were especially directed to take into their careful consideration.

As it is necessary to clear the ground for the discussion of a system of currency for use in India, which proceeds on principles diametrically opposed to the bimetallism of the Latin Union, the first part of this book will deal with the principal objections, both economic and practical, to which that system is open, and with an exposition of the reasons why a dual currency worked on the principle of the *fixed ratio* is wholly impossible of acceptance either by England or by India. The latter part will be given to showing that the proposed reform in the currency of India, with its gold and silver money exchanging in one another at a varying ratio, is not only practicable in that country, but is sanctioned by custom of immemorial antiquity, that it would be found highly advantageous to the people, and prove a remedy for the evils and risks of the existing monetary situation; or if this cannot be at once realized, that it will at least afford an immediate mitigation of their effects, and become a means towards their final removal, and thus directly contribute to the solution of those difficulties which was intended to be the object of the Commissioners' investigations.

It is not proposed to follow the inquiry into more than a portion of the subjects with which it deals; but it may here be stated that the general view taken by the Commissioners of the cause of the changes in the values of the precious metals is that the supply of gold has run short of the use to be found for it, and that on the other hand silver has to a large extent become redundant as money while the supply available for that purpose remains undiminished. The production of commodities has simultaneously increased enormously. These three causes acting together are obviously sufficient to account for the altered relations of value which have arisen between gold and silver money, and between gold money and merchandise in general.

The theory that the low value of silver in gold has acted as a *bounty* would act on exportations from India does not receive support, and, as will afterwards be shown, is, though specious, devoid of foundation in fact. Under a similar mistake, the competition of India in the market for Lancashire manufactures, both in India itself and in other parts of the East, will be seen to have been erroneously attributed to cheap silver.

The investment of capital in silver-using countries is shown to be hindered by uncertainties in the exchanges, and, as will afterwards appear, would be greatly promoted were the mechanism of commerce, *i.e.* the money of trade, one and the same in the eastern and western parts of the Empire. The inconvenience of a double money and of a varying exchange is much reduced by the use of the telegraph, but the disadvantage still remains to the investor in the East, of receiving his returns in the less instead of in the more valuable money-metal; in the money which is falling, instead of in the money which is rising, in value.

The Special Commissioners seem to be of opinion that the rupture of the bimetallic tie has been the principal cause of the fall in the value of silver as against gold, and therefore its maintenance, while it was maintained, to be that which kept up the par of exchange at $15\frac{1}{2}$ to 1, and also (which of course follows) that the influence of the bimetallic system extended far beyond its territorial limits in Europe, and affected the values of the precious metals in the most distant parts of the East and of the West alike. Both of these positions we shall show to be untenable. For the rest the general tendency of the evidence for bimetallism is to show that its advocates have failed to make out their case, or to justify its adoption by this country in supersession of our own.

As that part of the controversy between the two parties which is of most practical importance to the trade and industry of this country and to the administration of the government of India, turns upon the efficacy of legislation to redress the mishaps of trade ventures, and to raise the value of the silver currency and the values of the commercial productions of that country by the standard of English money, it will be shown that the stress of competition which the agriculture of this country in our own markets, and which the cotton industry of Lancashire in the markets of the East has been exposed to since the decline in the value of silver set in, arises from industrial and not from currency causes, and that the remedy for this state of things is to be found in the industrial and material progress of countries whose cheap productions compete with our own.

It will be shown that the bimetallism of the Latin Union, if the system were revived, would not assist this progress, as it depends on commercial, and not on currency causes; and that the maintenance and working of that system are involved in its compliance with commercial conditions. Also that the competition of Eastern with English produce, both in our own and Eastern markets, has arisen from cheapness of production, and not from a low value of silver in gold, and that cheap silver does not act as a bounty on exportations from the East, nor will those exportations cease until their value rises in gold, whatever the value of silver in gold may be; and that the expected flow of silver to India as a result of its cheapness in gold has not taken place, because in that country silver is not correspondingly cheap by the standard of commodities.

That the conclusion to be drawn from the evidence taken by the Special Commission, as to the influence of the system of the Latin Union on the relative values of gold and silver money, is that the actual rate of exchange was dependent on the courses of commerce, and not on the monetary law in force throughout the Union.

With regard to the action of metallic money on prices, it will be shown that the theory that credits and money have the same effect on prices is unsound. The influence of an abundance or scarcity of money on prices, and of high and low prices on industry is explained; and the question is raised whether the bimetallism of the Latin Union can, under all circumstances, provide sufficient capital to commerce to ensure its healthiest activity? The conclusion arrived at is, that the system fails to produce the results claimed for it, because it involves the fundamental economic error that a monetary law can supersede and regulate the natural law of values.

It is also proved, that if the system were revived, it must embrace all silver-using countries, as well as the principal gold-using countries of the Western world; that Eastern nations will not accept a legislative valuation of their gold and silver money, apart from that evolved out of commercial conditions; and that if those nations remain outside the Convention, their practice of exchanging the two kinds of money at their natural values, will prevent the continuous and certain working of a fixed-ratio system in the West; that the burden of proving their case lies on the bimetallic party, and that it is incumbent on them to show how certain practical objections to their system, which the evidence taken before the Special Commission disclosed, are to be overcome.

A bimetallic system, with a fixed ratio of exchange, being scientifically unsound and impracticable in European and Asiatic communities alike; and the true economic basis of a dual currency of full-value money being such a valuation for gold and silver in one another, as a free exchange at market values may determine, the conclusion of this paper is occupied with an argument directed to prove that it is to India we must turn in order to establish a true bimetallism. Immemorial custom in that country has habituated the people to the use of money on those terms; and such objections, on the score of inconvenience, as might be made to a varying rate of exchange for current money in England, apply either not at all, or to a very small extent in India.

It will be shown that all the beneficial effects which are asserted to have arisen from the bimetallic system of the Latin Union in past times, will be obtained by the trade and industry of the world in general from the local use in India of a currency of full-value gold and silver money exchanging into one another at their market values; that the commerce of the British empire, and that of India in an especial manner, will be largely benefited by the re-introduction of gold money into the Indian system, both by providing the producing classes of that country with a common basis of trade, with all gold-using and all silver-using countries alike, as well as by restoring to commercial employment the vast treasure of gold bullion, which India has been accumulating for many centuries, but which during the last fifty-five years has been discarded from circulation as money; that the effect of such a use of gold money in India, will be to diminish if not to stop the drain of gold to the East, to cause gold money to depreciate in respect of commodities, to induce a convergence in the relative values of gold and silver, and secure greater permanence to the exchange rate than is otherwise possible; and by promoting the internal as well as the foreign trade of India, and the general prosperity of her people, to give their industrial productions a higher value than they now hold in those of other countries, and thus alleviate the severity of the competition between the cheap labour of the East, and the dear labour of the West.

It is contended that such a system will provide the Government of India with a resource from which gold can be procured for the conversion of a part, greater or less, of its silver revenue into a gold revenue, and thus allow the fiscal system of the country to be placed upon the most secure foundation; that the tendency of the system will be to lighten taxation, to facilitate the collection of revenue, to enhance the financial credit of the administration, and to lighten the burden of the public debt; that as the Home charges of the Indian Government will be provided for in gold at a lower cost to the people than is now possible, a considerable portion of the taxation of the country will become free to be applied to more profitable purposes than the purchase of gold money in England at scarcity prices; that a general use of gold money will attract capital to India in unprecedented quantities as the returns to investments of all kind will be made in gold, and that this will act beneficially on the development of industrial enterprise, give increased employment and higher wages to the working classes, and insure a general diffusion of prosperity among the people far beyond anything which they have hitherto experienced.

CHAPTER II.

THE COMMERCIAL FACTOR.

Objects and methods of the bimetallic party—The monetary and the natural law of values—The issue involved in the silver question commercial rather than monetary—The bimetallic system broke down under pressure of commercial causes—Theory of bounty on exportations from silver-using countries, Professor Marshall's opinion—Value of silver in gold depends on its value in commodities; fixed ratio system hinders free sales, does not insure circulation of both kinds of money—Commercial ratio controls monetary ratio—Fixed ratio restricts supply of money—Fixed ratio to be effective must be universally accepted—Fundamental economic error in the system—Bounty on Indian exportations attributable to cheapness of production, not to cheap silver—Low gold price of silver does not lower silver price of commodities—Professor Marshall's, Mr. Fowler's, Mr. Cernuschi's, Mr. Nisbet's views on the connection between cheap silver and gold prices—Views of Mr. Bythell, Mr. Fielden, Mr. Barclay, on cheap silver protecting Indian industry—Complaints of Lancashire.

BIMETALLISTS expect that if throughout the civilized world generally, gold and silver money are coined in such quantities as under the limitations imposed by their system may be possible, and laws are at the same time passed fixing the rate at which the coins shall exchange for one another at one and the same figure everywhere, the industrial depression, and the financial difficulties which have come into existence simultaneously with a low level of gold prices, will disappear. They attribute to the collapse of their system the low gold price of commodities which, during recent years, has exposed English manufacturers and producers to a more severe competition with America, India, and some of the Continental states, both in our own and foreign markets, than they had before experienced. They ask, in fact, that a fixed price for silver should be imposed by law on gold, in order that in the trade with silver-using countries, gold may be reduced in value, and thereby be disabled from buying more and more rupees or dollars, and that as a consequence of the diminution in the equivalent sum of silver money, less and less corn or other Indian produce will be procurable for any given sum of gold money, and that the returns to the sale of Manchester goods in the East which are taken on the spot in silver coins, should be enabled to procure more sovereigns when they are spent in purchasing bills of exchange on England.

In order to achieve these results, they require legislative aid, and also a powerful combination of commercial countries, directed to fixing the money values of the precious metals in one another; and without this adventitious support they admit that they can effect nothing. This amounts to a serious admission of the weakness of their plan, since the necessity of such an arrangement proves that there is some force at work which interferes with its operation and will defeat its ends, if its appeal to the interference of law in the regulation of values is unsuccessful.

This force is the natural law regulating values through the free action of commerce.

Bimetallists do not ignore the existence of this natural law, but they assert that their monetary law will, from the extent of its range, coerce the natural law into acquiescence in its provisions.* The natural law, however, if left to itself, would be evolved out of the free course of commerce, the demand and supply of silver and gold, and the necessities and inclinations of mankind to use either metal in varying quantities. The value of one metal in the other, or of either, or of both, in commodities is thus fixed in one way by natural causes, at an equivalence varying from time to time, while bimetallists wish to fix it in another way, by force, so to speak, at an equivalence which shall be permanent. The question in dispute is whether their system can avail to do this, and if it can, whether any country using their plan will be the better for doing so.

The main issue upon which the controversy between the monometallist and the bimetallist parties turns is for all practical purposes industrial rather than financial. If it could be shown that our corn is undersold by American and Indian grown corn, and that the yarns and cotton goods of Lancashire are being driven out of the markets of India, Japan, and some other places in Asia, by cheaper goods of the same class supplied from the former country, as a result and in consequence of silver having fallen in value against gold, and also that the bimetallism of the Latin Union is calculated to reverse these conditions of commerce in favour of the United Kingdom, then there would be some reason in the demand that we should adopt this currency system. Unfortunately

* "Theory of Bimetallism," Cassell and Co., p. 42, 2nd paragraph; p. 45, 3rd and 5th paragraphs.

the arguments which are addressed to the public to convert them to this belief are the same as those which were used before the Special Commission brought them to the test of an elaborate criticism applied from the other side, and their weak points, which have now been exposed, are either passed over or inconclusively dealt with in bimetallist orations. The discussion, unless it is carried on by the light of the evidence produced before the Commission, is likely to become interminable, and at the same time, if that evidence is carefully examined, it will be found to be heavily against the acceptance by the World in general of the discarded bimetallism of the Latin Union. It will not be difficult to show, that it is not by the exchange of gold and silver money in terms fixed by law that the desired relief can be obtained; that under the French system such a fixation was nominal rather than real; that the currency of France, and subsequently of the Latin Union, was usually a close approximation to a monometallic system with a shifting standard; that the system prevented the use of both kinds of metals as money indifferently and in unrestricted quantities; that such an equation of value between the gold and silver money of the Union as was set up was the result of commercial causes; that so far as the bimetallic law exerted any influence over their relative values, it was felt in the restraint rather than in the promotion of the free operation of the trade between the precious metals and commodities, and necessarily in the determination of the metallic par between gold and silver by the action of commerce; that in consequence, if a rate of exchange could have been maintained by law, the currencies of bimetallic countries would have been artificially limited, and the production of the precious metals and their free employment in commerce rather hindered than assisted. It followed as a necessary result of this condition of things, that under a great development in the production of gold and silver, and a still greater expansion of industrial production throughout the commercial world, occurring simultaneously with some political events of an unexpected kind, these forces became too strong for the system to resist, which in consequence broke down.

The industrial competition of countries where labour and other elements of production are cheap, the uncertainties of trade speculations, the losses of the Indian Government on their payments of gold in England, are the effects of the same causes which snapped the bimetallic tie. How little the advocates of this description of currency are likely to succeed in restraining these forces or diminishing their strength, by attempting to bind them again in the chains which they have effectually burst, such an examination into the facts of the situation as the Commissioners have completed makes abundantly evident.

Professor Marshall being asked whether in his opinion a fall in the gold price of silver gives a bounty to exporters of produce from silver-using countries (Q. 9735), replied, "My own view is that it is à priori impossible;" and he explained the law that the volume of the exports of a country depends on the relation it holds to the value of the merchandise imported to pay for it, by the following illustration. "If Spain is sending oranges to England in exchange for cutlery, the question whether the English market will be flooded with oranges depends upon the relative values of oranges and cutlery in England and Spain." So if India can produce corn cheap and sell it dear in Europe, it will go there as long as that cheapness lasts. Silver in the trade with India is only a commodity used intermediately to carry through the exchange of Indian for English productions. The silver money of India regarded as the equivalent in value of Indian merchandise is cheap in British goods because the productions of India are cheap in those goods also. British goods being priced in gold, we do not talk of Indian silver being cheap in machinery, hardware, cottons, and so forth, but in the gold money which is the equivalent of their value. When therefore silver becomes dearer in gold than it is now, its cheapness in commodities will diminish correspondingly, because the rise in its value will follow on a rise in the value of Indian productions in British goods, or which is the same thing, in English gold money. Upon this supposition we should expect Indian goods to rise higher in their silver price in India, as silver rose in the gold valuation. But for the same reason that Indian goods have not fallen in correspondence with the fall in the gold price of silver, this expectation would not be immediately fulfilled. The reason for this will be explained more fully further on. It will be found partly in the fact that gold and silver money are not in use together and therefore are not exerting their respective influence on prices in India, and partly in the primitive methods of production employed in India, and on the scarcity of currency in the country, which prevent fluctuations in gold and silver values having so rapid an effect on prices as they have in Europe. That which determines the value of silver money in gold money (where both are circulating at full value) is the value of the goods in commerce in silver and in gold at the same time. Thus, if a given weight of wheat (supposing, for the sake of illustration, that trade were confined to wheat) fetched in India 16 ozs. of silver money, and being exported to London sold for 1 oz. of gold money, the ratio of value between silver and gold would be as 16 to 1, and if at another time the same weight of corn fetched 18 ozs., in fact had risen in India, and still sold for 1 oz. of gold money, the ratio would be altered in favour of gold. For the same reason, if the value of Indian wheat were to rise, the ratio would become that which might correspond to the value of English-grown in Indian-grown wheat. If, for instance, at one time the following equation of values were to exist, viz., one quarter of Indian wheat = 20 rs. = one quarter of English wheat = £2 (then £1 = 10 rs.), and if subsequently the value of the first factor rose to 25 rs., and the theory we are advancing is erroneous, then the equation would stand at, 6 bushels of Indian wheat = $18\tfrac{3}{4}$ rs. = 1 quarter of English wheat = £2. But as 6 bushels of one kind of corn cannot (*ceteris paribus*) be equal to 8 bushels of another kind, the real parity of values would become, 6 bushels of Indian wheat = $18\tfrac{3}{4}$ rs. = 6 bushels of English wheat = £1 10s. (and £1 = $12\tfrac{1}{2}$ rs.); that is to say, that the relative value of the two kinds of produce would fix the ratio of exchange between rupees and sovereigns. To simplify the illustration, we have assumed trade to be confined to one commodity, but if the argument is good in this case, it is equally good where, as in practice, the determination of the ratio is complicated by the number of commodities concerned and their varying values in one another. This principle acts in precisely the same manner in a country where both gold and silver money circulate together at a rate fixed by law, as in a gold-using and a silver-using country trading together. If, for example, a given quantity of French wine sells for 15,500 francs, or for 1000 gold pieces each worth $15\frac{1}{2}$ francs, the value of the wine in silver and gold money respectively fixes their value at $15\frac{1}{2} : 1$; but if, owing to the price offered for the wine in England, the same quantity sells for the metallic equivalent in English gold money of 1100 French gold pieces the equivalence of value as between gold and silver then becomes $15\frac{1}{2} : 1\frac{1}{10}$. This ratio of value would arise from the wine being sold in England for the equivalent in English money of 1100 gold pieces, with which English manufactures would be bought and being imported into France would sell for a larger tale of franc pieces than 15,500. This condition of prices, it may be argued, would be corrected by the silver price of wine rising 10 per cent., but then the gold price would rise 10 per cent. also, and, *ex hypothesi*, the wine being only obtainable for the English market from France, its price would rise in England another 10 per cent., and the advantage would still be with the exporter of English manufactures. The currency relation of French gold and silver money to one another would be concealed in the commercial exchange of French wine for English goods and of these for silver francs. The apparent effect on the French currency would be the withdrawal of gold from circulation in France. Gold would, perhaps, continue to be coined in the proportion prescribed by law, but none of it would be procurable, the bimetallic rate of exchange would become merely nominal, the ratio of value would prove to have been determined by the relative value existing between the imported goods purchased in England for the metallic equivalent in sovereigns of 1100 French gold pieces and of the wine or other French productions selling for 15,500 francs.

Let us state the case in another way, and suppose that 1 oz. of gold, and 17 ozs. of silver, and 1 parcel of silk, are all of the same value in China; the silk must sell in France under the bimetallic law indifferently for 1 oz. of gold money or for $15\frac{1}{2}$ ozs. of silver money. The Chinaman wants silver to take away to his own country; but he can only get $15\frac{1}{2}$ ozs. instead of 17 ozs. for his silk, and he can get no gold, as other traders know as well as he does that an ounce of gold will buy more silk that $15\frac{1}{2}$ ozs. of silver. Bimetallism gives him the choice of selling his silk, which is worth 17 ozs., for $15\frac{1}{2}$ ozs. of silver or not selling it at all. The silk is undervalued in silver, and no sale takes place, and trade is correspondingly hindered. He can, however, buy an ounce of French gold money with $15\frac{1}{2}$ ozs. of Chinese silver, and take it away to his own country; but that is not his object, he wants to sell his silk and to procure 17 ozs. of silver for it. The silk and the gold being alike worth 17 ozs. of silver, the gold is undervalued as well as the silk, and for the same reason that the silk is withdrawn from sale, other traders withdraw gold from circulation. As silver is, in the case supposed, overvalued in gold, all commodities which sell for silver are overvalued in gold also, and at the equation of 1 : 17 by about 9 per cent. Any one therefore buying goods in France on the terms of the fixed ratio, with gold, loses a little over 9 per cent. Gold is in consequence sent abroad to buy silver at 17 ozs., and is coined into the French currency to buy goods at 15½ ozs., at a profit of 9 per cent. above that which would be made by using gold. Bimetallism gives commerce the option of selling goods for silver at a lower price than is the equivalent of their gold value or of not selling them at all. Commerce chooses the latter alternative. Commerce offers to bimetallism to sell goods at the equivalence of value in gold and silver which its processes have evolved (1 : 17); but bimetallism, by its coinage law, is practically prevented giving that price in silver for the article; it can only give less, 15½ instead of 17 ozs. And because the silk is withdrawn from sale, being worth 17 ozs., gold is withdrawn from exchange with silver at 15½ ozs. because it is worth 17 ozs. also. Of the alternatives thus presented, of buying goods with both gold and silver money indifferently at the commercial rate, or of a disuse of gold, bimetallism is compelled to choose the latter.

One of these two results is produced, affecting either commodities or money to the value of tens of millions of pounds every time a divergence between the commercial and the legal rate of exchange occurs. Goods are withdrawn from sale, or the undervalued metal is withdrawn from circulation; and, if money of this metal is sought for, a higher price has to be paid for it than that fixed by the legal rate of exchange; if it happens, as in the illustration, to be gold, then an *agio* is put upon gold; and if gold is wanted for remittance abroad, then a gold bill, say on London, costs more than 25·0088 francs to the £1 sterling, *i.e.* more than the metallic par which exists between the gold money of the two countries, would fix as its value. It is difficult, then, to understand what the ratiocinative process can be, by which, under these circumstances, any one can persuade himself that the commercial values of gold and silver do not fix the exchanges, but that the rate of exchange ordained by the monetary law controls the commercial value of the money-metals in one another; and that the bimetallic system promotes freedom of trade in all kinds of commodities; in all cases secures, by an abundance of both kinds of money in the most desirable form, the fullest supply of currency to commerce; and is otherwise wholly beneficial in its influence on trade and industry.

The unsoundness of the bimetallism of the Latin Union, regarded as an economic system, is exposed by the arguments used to support it, being in disagreement with the facts of its history, which are notorious. One of its advocates argues that the price of gold and silver coins in one another follows a specific monetary law which supersedes the regulating influence of supply and demand. Another believes that, as the value of the metals is controlled by the continued absorption of them at the mints, at a rate fixed by the law, and as the demand which rules the market is that which acts at the mint, the market value of the precious metals is the mint price; the State, therefore, which creates the demand can fix the price. A third asserts that as no one will exchange gold for silver at any other ratio than that fixed by a powerful monetary convention, the price which the ratio prescribes will become universal.

The first theory we need not discuss as a serious proposition. The others have more reason in them, because they do at least imply that the market rate, and the legal rate for exchanging gold and silver money will be one and the same. The second theory assumes that because a bimetallic mint, say at Paris, will deliver a kilogramme of gold coin for 3100 francs (which is the weight of $15\frac{1}{2}$ kilogrammes of silver), those metals will exchange at no other ratio anywhere else. Herein lurks the fallacious assumption, contradicted by the evidence of a long array of facts, that the coining of the money ensures its circulation; and another equally questionable, that no other price than that of the bimetallic ratio will prevail elsewhere. The third argument is of the same kind as the second. They both assume that the mint or the law under which it works can make the market, that is to say, can regulate the demand and create the supply required to meet it, inducing the presentation of no more or no less gold and silver than it chooses to supply to commerce. That which militates against these theories is, that the system never succeeded in doing this continuously or with certainty during the seventy years of its existence; but, on the contrary, another price was ruling elsewhere, continually operating to make one metal more or less valuable in the other than the law of the fixed ratio decreed that it should be, and this resulted in the more or less complete disappearance from the bimetallic circulation of the undervalued metal.

The Bank of France was in consequence invested with a discretionary power to refuse gold in payment for notes drawn in terms of silver. There were, on the occasions when it exercised this right, in some other parts of the world than France, those who were ready to give a higher price in silver for gold than the French legal price, and if the desired payments had been made, all the gold in France might have been taken out of the country for sale elsewhere, at a better price than that paid for it. It follows from this that on these occasions there was found to be in operation a commercial law abroad, in conflict with the monetary law at home; and also that when the latter was in full working order and one kilogramme of gold money exchanged for 3100 francs, this equation of value arose from a temporary coincidence between the market value of gold in silver outside the system, and that prescribed by the law in force within it.

This being the case, the conclusion is unavoidable that if the expectation that all men will agree to exchange gold and silver at a rate fixed by a convention of nations is to be realized, then the agreement must include in its scope nearly all the gold and silver metal throughout the world; so large a proportion of it, in fact, that the remainder shall be too small in value to allow those who own it to find any profit in exchanging it on other terms than those fixed by the Convention. The Latin Union was, the bimetallists say, too limited in the number of its members to make the action of the system certain. In this way they account for its collapse, and they therefore desire to obtain the co-operation of England, Germany and the United

States of America, and of any other countries who will join in a new Union, before they make their next experiment. The only object they can have in this extension is to limit the competition of countries using systems of currency which would conflict with their own, by reducing their stock of the precious metals to an insignificant fraction of the world's supply. That the establishment of such a proportion in favour of a new Convention must be an antecedent condition of the resuscitation of the system has been placed beyond doubt, by the fact it was the lower commercial value in gold of the silver of Germany and America when brought into competition with that held at the valuation of the Latin Union, which wrecked the system in 1873-78. Until, therefore, this is accomplished, it is impossible that the prediction will be fulfilled that—no one will exchange gold and silver at any other ratio than that fixed by the Convention, and that the price it prescribes will universally prevail.

Seeing then, that the price of gold and silver in one another are fixed by the same causes which fix that of commodities in either metal, it is a weak point in these bimetallic theories that they involve the contrary assumption; and assert that it is law which by creating a market for the money-metals can fix their value in one another. If this contention were true it would necessarily follow (because the supply of money would be limited to that amount which could be produced and brought into exchange on the terms fixed by the law,) that law would be efficient to fix the values of money and commodities in one another also. The supply, for instance, of both gold and silver would be large if the legal rate of exchange were always identical with the best market rate, that is to say, if the law allowed the rate to vary from a fixed rate in correspondence with the market rate; but the supply of money made from one of the metals would be small or none at all if it were rated at a value differing from its real value in the other; if gold, by way of example, cost by the ounce 18 or 20 ozs. of silver, at a time when the legal exchange rate fixed the value of an ounce of gold at 16 ozs. of silver.

Under the fixed-ratio system, such a restriction of the volume of money in circulation and therefore of the mass of the standard by which prices are fixed, arising from a deficient supply of one or other of the money-metals, is certain sooner or later to occur, however extensive the combination may be which is directed to maintain the system, unless it can control all but an insignificant fraction of the world's stock of the precious metals. Upon the ability of the system to include within its range so vast an area of the surface of the globe and nations so many and numerous as this condition implies, depends its power of regulating the demand and supply of money and arranging the prices of commodities in trade. Unless bimetallism is able to do this much, that enlargement of the standard of value and that stability of prices which is to result from its revival can by no possibility be attained. When the system succeeds in these aims, it may succeed in raising the price of corn and other farm produce and manufactured goods when sold for gold, and it may give a higher purchasing power to silver and cause rupees to buy more sovereigns and sovereigns fewer rupees, than is now the case.

We hope to show what little reason there is in such pretensions, or in the expectation that even a few of the principal commercial nations of the world, much less the numerous semi-civilized populations who use silver money, will join in working the scheme of the fixed ratio; and that at every turn the system is met by practical objections and difficulties of detail which can for the most part be more or less directly traced to two circumstances. One of these is the impossibility of bringing within a system which fixes by law an exchange rate for money, more than a small portion of the metallic money in use throughout the world, and the other is that the bimetallism of the Latin Union proceeds upon a fundamental economic error in assuming that a monetary law (except it be universally accepted and obeyed), can control the commercial law of values. The relative value of gold and silver money when circulating together in quantities unrestricted by law, depends on their relative efficiency as media of exchange, and that again depends on the quantity of either kind of money in use contrasted with the amount of merchandise of many different kinds and of varying relative values, which may be, at the same time, under exchange in the markets. A currency system which runs counter to the imperative regulations imposed by commerce upon value and price, is foredoomed to failure.

If the fact were fully recognized that it is the value of commodities in silver and in gold respectively, which prescribe the ratio of exchange for the precious metals in one another, and not the ratio of exchange, under a legal fixation, which prescribes the value that one kind of merchandise holds to any other kind, the delusion that law can fix values either in the case of the precious metals or in any other case would cease to impose upon men's minds, and with it would vanish the belief that the rate of exchange decides whether a particular class of goods shall be exported from a silver-using to a gold-using country or not. Trade is carried on as well under one rate of exchange as under another, because profits depend on the relative values of commodities, and not upon ratios of metallic value. The value of silver in gold money being then fixed in this way, it is evident that it cannot be fixed by law until the values of commodities in one another are fixed by law also; and this no bimetallist would assert to be possible.

Professor Marshall proceeds to show that a fall in the Indian exchanges may be so brought about as to have exactly the opposite effects to those that are commonly attributed to it and give a bounty to the Indian importer, and impose a penalty on the Indian exporter. He says: "I contend therefore that the bounty which is caused one way or the other by a fall in Indian exchanges depends merely on the question whether the change in the price of silver takes place first in Europe or first in India. If it happens that silver falls in value in Europe before it falls in India, I admit that in proportion to the differences between prices measured in silver in Europe, and prices measured in silver in India, to that extent there will be a bounty to the Indian exporter, but that this bounty is due not to the fall in the exchange itself, but to the particular cause which produces that fall is shown by the fact that if the silver had been discovered in India, and if silver prices had risen in India before they had risen in Europe, then the difference between them would have been a penalty on the Indian exporter and a bounty on the Indian importer."

What has happened is that silver prices, or, to speak more exactly, the value of silver in gold has fallen in Europe, while its value in the exportable products of India has not fallen correspondingly, or at all in that country. These products, which cost no more or no less silver than before silver fell against gold, appear to have fallen against gold as a consequence of the decline in the gold price of silver. The fall in the value of silver, and the fall in that of Indian commodities by the standard of gold, are concurrent incidents in the trade and do not stand to one another in the relation of cause and effect. If Indian goods become more costly, which will be shown by a rise in their silver price, or which is the same thing by silver falling in value against them, as it has fallen in value against gold, they will be seen to be more costly in gold also, and there will be no apparent advantage to the Indian trader in a low gold price of silver. That it is only apparent and not real will be shown by the low gold price for silver remaining unimproved, while the gold price of commodities has risen; an eventuality which the relation of the currencies of England and India respectively to the commerce of India makes by no means unlikely. The efficiency of gold to purchase goods either in English or Indian markets depends on the relation of value existing between the same produce of either country. To speak in round terms, if the presentation in the markets of India of 100 quarters of corn cost the producers less of the necessaries and conveniences of life than a similar quantity offered for sale in England cost its producers, gold money will buy more of the former in the Indian market than it can buy in the English market; but as Indian silver money cannot buy corn in both markets, but only in the Indian market, its relation of value to corn is regulated by the circumstances of the markets of India only, and silver money may fall against Indian produce without falling further in its gold price. When there is a free circulation of gold and silver money at their natural values in the markets of India, then the gold and silver prices of her commodities will vary together, and it will be more clearly seen than it is now, that it is not the rate of exchange but the low value of Indian as compared with the English commodities which gives the advantage to the richer country.

Professor Marshall repeats in various forms his argument (Qs. 9755, 9759, 9775), that the relative values of gold and silver do not lower the value of wheat relatively to other commodities. He contends that the importation of Indian wheat into England is due exclusively to the development of the railway system and the lowering of freights, and to a series of very favourable harvests, that if the cause of this exportation had been the rate of exchange, we should have found Indian wheat coming a long time ago. In 1876, the price of silver was low, but India exported then only one million sterling in value of

D

wheat as against eight millions now. "The difficulty," to use Professor Marshall's words, *i.e.* the competition of Indian with English wheat, "exists without any reference to silver, and would be the same if India had a gold currency." This way of putting the case of course neglects for the moment any consideration of the tendency which a gold currency if used in India might have, for more reasons than one, to raise the price of Indian productions. Using the argument merely to prove that it is not the metal out of which the coin of India is fabricated which *bonuses* her exports,—it is unanswerable.

Mr. W. Fowler expresses a similar opinion (Qs. 8388, 9077) that "price depends much more upon the supply and demand of the article than upon any condition of money," and that "prices, which are the governing factor in exports and imports, have much less to do with the question of the money than we suppose in our ordinary ideas about these things."

The hypothetical case stated by M. Cernuschi, in illustration of the theory that the present state of things acts like a protective tariff against goods imported from the West into the East, and as a bounty upon goods exported from the East to the West, was put to this witness. He was asked to suppose a bale of goods worth £10,000 selling in India for 100,000 rs. when the rupee is at 2*s.*, and for 133,000 rs. with the rupee at 1*s.* 6*d.*, and to assent to the conclusion that it could not be sold at a profit unless the price of the goods had risen 33 per cent. To this Mr. Fowler replied, "English merchandise has fallen so enormously that you are able to sell in return for the exports what you could not otherwise have sold." This objection to M. Cernuschi's illustration may be enlarged somewhat in this manner. The bale has become 30 per cent. bigger than it was fifteen years ago, and the larger bale costs no more than the smaller one did before. As prices have remained stationary in India, it exchanges for 30 per cent. more rupees than the smaller bale could have exchanged for, and these purchase 30 per cent. more of Indian commodities, and thus 30 per cent. of the 33 per cent. of increased price to which it is assumed that prices must rise to secure a profit is met. If the Indian commodities purchased for export with the proceeds of the bale of English merchandise are properly selected, they should sell in England for 5 per cent. or 10 per cent. more than they cost; this disposes of the remaining 3 per cent. of the increased price, and converts the loss which it is contemplated as occurring in the absence of a rise in prices into a gain (Q. 9070). Mr. Fowler says very truly, "If you are allowed to take a certain supposition and leave out all the other facts you may prove almost anything," and the simple answer to the theory of which the quotation from M. Cernuschi is an illustration, is—that it does not square with the facts of the case; that in spite of the theory, we are sending more things to India than ever; and Mr. Fowler gives figures to show that during the five years, 1880-85, when the exchange was low, the exports from India had increased by nearly 45 per cent., and the imports into India by more than 50 per cent. upon the figures for the trade carried on during the five years, 1870-75, when the exchange was better.

Another illustration, taken from one of M. Cernuschi's pamphlets, was presented to Mr. Fowler. It is as follows: Assuming that wheat is selling in England at 33*s*. per quarter, and can be sold in Bombay at 27*s*., which at 1*s*. 6*d*. to the rupee are equivalent to 18 rs., then 18 rs. is the Indian price which competes with 33*s*. the English price. If, to quote the words of the illustration, the bimetallic par still existed, 36*s*. instead of 27*s*. would be the equivalent of these 18 rs., and the difference, 9*s*., would have to be obtained in the selling price. The inference intended to be drawn is, that the exportation with a price of 33*s*. prevailing in the English market would not have taken place. Mr. Fowler mistrusted the soundness of the illustration; being unprepared on the spur of the moment to explain the fallacy it contains, he contented himself with saying, "I cannot make it square with what I see going on in the imports and exports. The reason being, I apprehend, that all the facts are not taken into account" (Qs. 9103-4). This is the reason. The illustration altogether overlooks the circumstance that Indian wheat being at 27*s*. in gold in India, silver is also at 27*s*. in gold in India; and for that reason the bimetallic par, if it had been maintained instead of having been lost as it has been in the collapse of the system, would not have been at 2*s*. to the rupee or at 15½ : 1, *except in name*, and gold would have disappeared from the French currency. The relative value of wheat and of other commodities in the trade, in Indian silver and in gold respectively, would fix the value of the money of one metal in the money of the other, and if that worked out at 1*s*. 6*d*., and France had maintained a legal rate of exchange at 2s., then, for the reason above given, in the case of the sale of wine for French francs and English sovereigns, France would have become a monometallic silver country. Indian-grown corn would not have risen to the price of 18 rs. + 9s., *i.e.* to 22 rs. 8 an. per quarter; and if it had been imported into France, the price it would have sold for would have been the metallic par in francs of 18 rs. (cost of transport and trade profit apart), and in the sale in France no gold money would have passed at all.

The fallacy lurking in the theory, which the hypothetical case thus stated is intended to explain, consists in the assumption that the bimetallic par can stand at $15\frac{1}{2} : 1$ when the commercial par stands at about $20 : 1$, and the inability of some economists to recognize this fact arises from their putting the cart before the horse, and arguing that the fixation by law of the value of silver in gold will regulate the values of different kinds of merchandise in one another, whereas it is the value of the stock of merchandise in commerce by the gold standard, and the value of the same stock at the same time in silver, in a free market, which fixes the rate of exchange at which the gold and silver money actually circulating therein, in unrestricted quantities, shall exchange into one another.

Mr. Nisbet, member of a firm of corn-factors in London and Liverpool, says, with reference to bi-metallism and monometallism, "I fear that as regards British agriculture there is really not much in it. . . . I believe very little in bimetallism or monometallism as far as regards the supply of produce. If produce is wanted, it will come" (Q. 10,054). This witness is of opinion that Russia, the river Plate, India, and America, are our most formidable competitors, and that Adelaide, Melbourne, and New Zealand, will in the future export corn largely to this country also. The export of corn he considers to be induced by such countries as Russia and India producing such heavy crops that they must and do export them; that the construction of railways from the wheat-growing districts to the seaboard of India, and the opening of the Suez Canal, have made it inevitable that corn would be exported. Mr. Nisbet adds much more to the same effect, proving that it is the abundance of Indian and other foreign corn which supports the competition rather than the low gold price of silver. "I do not," he says, "for one moment believe that bi- or mono-metallism has any effect on imports of wheat, for this grain each year comes in from all parts of the world, and it is the natural course of affairs that it should do so." Being asked whether the Indian producer can still maintain his export, even if his price were not so good, this witness replied, "I think so. We have always had a pretty good supply from India when they have had it. When the price was 32s. to 34s. a quarter, we have always had large quantities, but when the price was 28s. to 30s. a quarter, we found there was a falling-off." Again; (Q. 10,059) "No doubt India shows a tendency to produce and to export more wheat because, if you make fresh railways through the wheat-growing districts, naturally the wheat must come to the seaboard, and of course the wheat would be exported." Again; (Q. 10,035) "If Italy ceases importing Indian wheat,

England must import more Indian wheat, for India will not keep her wheat. She will sell. Comparatively speaking, she has an open market at all times at a price." Being questioned about the competition from the Argentine Republic, Mr. Nisbet gave his opinion that if that country were to produce twice as much as she does "that would keep down the prices in the market all over. It is the overproduction which causes low prices; all the roubles and rupees in the world will not do it" (Q. 10,078). As to the effect of the exchanges on the exportation of wheat from India, he says (Q. 10,066), " Supposing the rupee changes, and you get less from India, you will simply get more from America and Russia, or from the Colonies, or from the river Plate; if, again, the opposite occurs, then India is put in a position to do more, and those other countries would do less" (Q. 10,067). That given the export in a particular year, supposing that during that year the rupee were to fall, Indian wheat would be sold at a lower price, if the wheat existed. "Given the wheat existing as the silver market becomes worse, so it helps India to export." Again; (Q. 10,100) "I do not think that any exchange will produce more wheat in India on its present basis, but if you go on extending railways through parts of the country where we know wheat can be grown, no matter what your exchange is, wheat will be grown, and will have to be exported. The exchange alone is a secondary affair, in my opinion, to the extension of railways in India for the production of wheat."

That the exchanges have an influence on the export of wheat from silver-using countries as an occasional and passing incident in the trade may be admitted, but even the rather qualified opinion that Mr. Nisbet gave on this point in speaking of the correspondence between downward movements in the gold price of silver, and upward movements in the exportation of corn from India, is found on examination to go further than the facts of the case warrant.* Professor Marshall supplied the Commissioners with a table giving the movements in the price of silver and the contemporaneous movements in the price of wheat, and this showed that so far from the movements corresponding, the occasions during the years 1886 and 1887 when they went together were 84 in number, and when they went apart 1035. Speaking of Mr. Nisbet's evidence, Professor Marshall says, "I do not imply that he or any one else has suggested that the price of wheat, in a year in which the harvests of the world had been bad, would be low merely because the price of silver was low. But I fail to see the drift of his evidence, unless he means at least this much, that the minor movements upwards and downwards of the price of wheat, those extending over a few weeks, have been accompanied, and, in a great measure, caused by parallel and, roughly speaking, proportionate changes in the price of silver. On such a matter as this, the opinion of experts, infinitely more important as it is than the opinion of those who are not experts, has yet to be received with some caution. For it is the natural tendency of the human mind to be impressed by striking coincidences, and even though they are few in number, to attach to them a greater importance than to many other cases in which there has been

* Appendix, pp. 51, 52.

no coincidence; and therefore we ought in all such cases to check the results of general impression by the aid of arithmetic, when that can be brought to bear. And it fortunately happens that we have thoroughly trustworthy statistics of the price of silver and the price of wheat." Professor Marshall then gives figures of which the result has just been stated. There can be no doubt that he is right in holding that the theory that cheap silver *bonuses* Indian exportations is derived not from the facts of the case, but from the propensity of the human mind to be impressed by striking coincidences.

The conclusion then to be drawn from these facts, is that the importation of Indian or other foreign wheat depends on the low cost of its production, and on the gold price it will fetch in London, and not on the rate of exchange subsisting between silver and gold. If the exportation were to depend on the rate of exchange, then it would follow that the Indian exporter would send more and more corn to England for the same gold price, or, in other words, that he would give to the English consumer the same quantity of corn in exchange for a lower real value than before, that is, that he would be trading at a loss. There must, as Sir Thomas Farrer put it, be in this case a loss to the producer somewhere (Q. 10,112), but the growing expansion of the trade shows that the Indian ryot is making a profit, not a loss, and this circumstance proves that the theory is unsound. Mr. Nisbet suggested that the loss falls on the English landlord (Q. 10,110); but to shift the loss from the Indian to the English corn-grower does not help the argument, unless it can be shown that the English landlord's loss goes into the pocket of the Indian cultivator. But it does not, it goes into the pocket of the English consumer of English-grown corn. The Indian cultivator gets no higher price for his own than he did before, nor does he get any part of the 10s. a quarter, by which his competition is said to have beaten down the price of English wheat. It therefore is not the exchange which is answerable for the exportation from India, but the general level of cheapness prevailing throughout the industries of the East, added to the special facilities which India possesses in railroads to carry corn to the seaboard, and low charges for transportation to the Mediterranean and to England.

Mr. Bythell (Qs. 1933, 1942, etc.), sometime chairman of the Bombay Chamber of Commerce, speaks lightly of the so-called protection extended to India by the low price of silver. He is of opinion that as regards wheat it is the opening of the Suez Canal which has been a great help to the export trade : that it is always a mistake to attribute too much to the fall of the Exchange. Mr. Bythell also holds the view that the fall in silver has prevented the Indian agriculturist from feeling the full extent of the fall in gold prices; that although for him prices have remained fairly constant, he has been getting 20 per cent. more silver money for his wheat than he would have got if silver had appreciated against commodities to the same extent that gold has (Qs. 2087–2097). That is to say, that the price of Indian wheat is higher than it would otherwise have been, and but for this circumstance the competition between Indian and English-grown wheat in our markets would have been more severe than it has been.

Mr. Bythell, speaking of the so-called protection extended to Indian labour by the low price of silver, says (Q. 2087), that the cotton-mills in Bombay have some advantage in respect of labour and country-made stores, but in respect of raw cotton but little, and in the case of the coal and machinery which they use, none at all, but much the reverse. In coarse goods and yarns they are also aided in the competition with Manchester by the accident that these can be economically made with cotton grown on the spot. The great extension in the export from India of these goods is due to the fact that when the thing was properly started it was found that it was a very profitable industry, that the exchange has helped the exporter a little, but that the trade would have been developed without it on account of the natural advantages which Bombay possesses.

Mr. Fielden, manager of a large mercantile business in Manchester and also director of a company trading with the Straits Settlements, India, and China, holds very strongly the opinion that, owing to the cost of imported coal and machinery, and the much larger number of operatives employed in a Bombay than in an Oldham mill to turn out the same quantity of cotton goods, it is not the cheap labour of India which is beating Lancashire; but that the Indian cotton trade has grown out of monetary dislocation which is of the same character as protection, and that it will go out whenever this currency question is settled (Qs. 8021, 8024). He gives figures to show that with the rupee at 2s. the Bombay mill-owner secures a margin of 13·21 rs., and the Lancashire mill-owner 25s. 5d., to cover cost of spinning and profit; that with the rupee at 1s. 6d. the Bombay man secures the same margin, while the margin for the Lancashire man is cut down to 19s. 9¾d., which sweeps away all profit and involves a loss. This calculation is another instance of what Mr. Fowler describes as "leaving out some of the factors in your calculation." Mr. Fielden's figures deal with 116 lbs. of cotton, out of which 100 lbs. of yarn are manufactured. The capital employed in the first calculation, based on 2s. to the rupee, is 53s. 3¼d., *i.e.* the cost of the raw cotton. In the second calculation, based on 1s. 6d. to the rupee, the capital employed is put at 39s. 11½d. These figures are doubtless correct as far as they go, but they say nothing as to what is done with the difference between the two capitals, amounting to 13s. 3¾d. This capital represents the advantage which the Lancashire manufacturer gains from buying American cotton with appreciated gold. With the 53s. 3¼d. employed in buying 116 lbs. of cotton in the first case, he in the second case not only buys the same weight of cotton in order to spin the same weight of yarn as in the first (viz. 100 lbs.), but he has 13s. 3¼d. over, and if he uses it for this business his gains are proportionately increased on the same investment of capital in the raw material. It appears that about 12s. 6d. should be added to the margin of 19s. 9¾d. which is stated in the second calculation to be so low as to be prohibitive on any trade at all. A manufacturer in Manchester works, it may be assumed with a certain amount of capital: in this case 53s. 3¼d., and uses the whole of it. He does not, when he finds it go further in his business than it did before, only use so much as would bring him in a loss, and lay the remainder aside unused (Q. 9031).

It is, as we said before, chiefly owing to the advantage which the English manufacturer derives from the low gold price of his raw material and perhaps of some other elements in the cost of production, that we owe the fact, that in spite of a low rate of exchange between rupees and sovereigns in the five years 1880-85 the imports into India were 50 per cent. more than in the five years 1870-75, when the exchange was much better (Q. 9069).

Mr. Robert Barclay, an export merchant engaged in the trade between Manchester and India, describes those engaged therein as having suffered very materially from the fluctuations in exchange (Qs. 2234, 2236), because when a fall takes place, the Manchester manufacturer must in order that a transaction may go through, accept a lower price (Q. 2253). But this witness admits that the disadvantage to the English manufacturer arises from the circumstances that wages in England do not follow at once, or perhaps do not follow at all the downward course of other prices, and that India has certain natural advantages which would have produced a great growth in the cotton manufacture quite apart from the fall in silver; and that wages in India have remained constant, or perhaps fallen, while in England they have, from an appreciation of the gold standard, practically risen (Q. 2305). Assuming this advantage to amount to 3 per cent. in favour of India, a purchaser of Manchester goods has to pay 103 rs. where he need only pay 100 rs. for the same quantity of cotton turned out by a Bombay mill. The compensation to the Manchester manufacturer would however be found in his ability to make a profit, in spite of this disadvantage of 3 per cent., because the appreciation of gold which may be said to have raised the wages he pays (because it has increased their purchasing power), has lowered his expenditure in other items, such as the cost of his raw material. As we said before, in examining Mr. Fielden's evidence, but for there being some means of this kind for making a profit, and for the fact that the people of India are every ten years growing richer and better able to purchase foreign goods, the trade could not have increased from both sides to the marvellous extent to which it has increased while the gold price of silver has been falling.

The English manufacturer's capital goes further than it did before the appreciation of gold set in, the capital of the Indian manufacturer goes hardly so far. The possibility of cheaper production is doubtless on the whole somewhat in favour of India; at the same time, while Bombay can spin a hundred pounds of yarn and make a profit, although the gold price of yarn may have fallen 20 or 25 per cent., the same rupee capital has to be put into the business whatever the gold price of silver may be, whereas Manchester can turn out the same weight of yarn with a capital expenditure diminished to the extent of the fall in the gold price of raw cotton.

As a matter of fact, had the English manufacturers during 1888 been compelled to pay for the raw cotton which they worked up in their mills for exportation, the prices which ruled for the article in 1873, it would have cost them over £15,000,000 more than it did cost them.* There were 1206 millions of pounds of cotton goods exported from England in 1888, and if the value of this weight of

* *Economist*, "Commercial History," 1888.

raw cotton at the average price for that year is compared with the value of the same weight of the material at the price of 1873, the figure for 1888 will be found to be £15,000,000 lower than that for 1873. So much less was spent on this item of the cost of producing the cotton goods exported in 1888, than would have been spent if the prices of 1873 had been ruling. The low price of the raw material induced a larger export, and larger sales abroad. Those who tell the Lancashire operatives that £25,000,000 have been kept out of their pockets by the fall in the value of silver, should not omit to tell them at the same time of these and various other less important reductions which have been effected in the cost of bringing the cotton goods to market, and that owing to the increased sales abroad which these savings have made possible, wages to a larger amount have been paid than the manufacture and sale of cotton goods at the high prices of 1873 would have permitted. If the prices of 1873 had been maintained in 1888, the sales of that year would not have been effected, and the £25,000,000 would never have been realized. It is, therefore, both illogical reasoning and an unfair statement of the facts, to allege a hypothetical loss on large sales of goods, arising from a fall of prices, when, but for the low price of the goods, the sales would have been less and the aggregate profits less also. Lancashire manufacturers may urge that with a low price of silver the actual return to the sale of any given quantity of cotton goods in the Eastern trade has been less than it would have been if a higher price of silver had prevailed, and that their turn-over has correspondingly diminished; but they should not at the same time omit from the account the compensations which this condition of the value of silver and other circumstances secured to them, among which has been the increased consumption of Lancashire goods in India. For the five years ending with 1873-74, and for the five years ending with 1884-85, we find that the importations into India of cotton twist and cotton piece goods was on the average as follows:—

Cotton twist in millions of pounds for 1st period   32·4.
„   „   „   2nd period   44·3.
Cotton piece goods, yards for 1st period ... ... 976·6.
„   „   2nd period ... ... 1698·6.

The values for the same periods of these importations were as follows:—

Cotton twist in millions of rupees for 1st period ... 27·5.
„   „   „   2nd period ... 34·5.
Cotton piece goods in millions of rupees for 1st period 147·7.
„   „   „   2nd period 228·5.*

We need not pursue the inquiry so far as China and Japan, and other Eastern ports or countries. The cheapness of silver, which is said to have had so disastrous an effect on the prosperity of Lancashire, is of the same kind and produced similar results, though differing in degree in different places. Furthermore, the decline in the gold price of silver has not prevented Manchester selling her goods abroad for a silver price which is higher than the silver price of the gold at which the same goods were priced in England. The *Economist*† gives figures to show that "grey shirtings" had fallen in

---

* "Theory of Bimetallism," pp. 131-133.
† *Economist*, p. 360, March 23, 1889.

the silver price in India 21 per cent. in 1887 on that ruling in 1873, while the price of the same goods in gold in London had fallen 40 per cent. between those two years; there was thus a variation of 19 per cent. between the gold and silver prices of the goods in each market respectively. In fact, cotton goods sold in Bombay in 1887, 19 per cent. better in silver than might have been expected judging by the gold price of the same goods in London. When it is alleged that the fall in the value of silver, amounting to 25 per cent., is the measure of the diminution of a cotton dealer's profits in this trade, 19 per cent. must be knocked off the account at once; and if the advantage of the low freights which were then ruling is taken into consideration, the net loss will prove to be extremely trifling. If a similar calculation were made for 1886, it would be found to be still more in favour of the export cotton-goods-trade with India. Lancashire, therefore, so far from being hit hard, was scarcely touched at all in those two years by the fall in the gold price of silver. These figures are more or less typical of the condition of the trade in other years during the period of the decline in silver.

Bombay, it is true, has largely extended her trade in cotton goods with the "farther East," but Lancashire has also at the same time done the same in her trade with India, and probably with other parts of Asia also; the losses, therefore, which her manufacturers say that they have incurred from the cheapness of silver in spite of the increased quantities and increased values of the goods sold in silver-using countries, have probably arisen from unskilful trading, or the stress of competition to which all merchants are exposed; and as such they can hardly be expected to move the sympathy of the general public, nor can they be accepted as a good reason for legislative interference, which, to be effectual in aid of Manchester, must be directed to limiting the expansion of the trade of India.

The theory that cheap silver has injured the trade in Manchester-made goods with the East, has no more reason in it than the corresponding theory that the same cause has brought down the price of English-grown corn. It is neither a low value of silver, nor fluctuations in exchange, which support the competition between India and Europe, either in textile manufactures, corn, or anything else; but the low cost at which, owing to the comparative poverty of the inhabitants of Eastern countries, all kinds of productions can be put upon the markets which are accessible to them.*

* The *Economist* for July, November, and December, 1889, contains papers which afford strong corroboration of this view of the effect of cheap silver on the trade of Lancashire with the East.

CHAPTER III.

CHEAP SILVER AND TRADE.

Use of silver conceals real causes of trade competition—Can be reduced only by increased value of Eastern productions—Both these and silver take their value from gold—Illustration—Single monetary unit partial remedy for varying exchanges—*A priori* argument in favour of commercial theory—Bimetallist theory that cheap silver acts as a bounty on exportations from India examined—The system will not raise the value or diminish the exportation of cheap produce of Asia—Argument to the same effect in the report of the Commission—Reason why cheap silver has not gone to India—Criticism on these reasons in Report—Defect in this criticism—Argument founded on comparative gold and silver prices of commodities fallacious.

It will be seen from what follows that the trade loss which is attributed to exchange, arises from the low value of both commodities and silver in gold money. The employment of silver as an intermediary agent in the exchange disguises the real cause of the loss, and makes it appear to be the work of the agent when it is really the work of the principal. If silver were not used at all in the business, but if the exportations of the gold-using country were exchanged for the produce of the importing country directly, and that produce brought home and sold for gold, the true cause of the loss, which is called " loss by exchange," would appear, and it would be recognized as arising from the low value of Eastern produce in the produce, and therefore in the money, of Western nations, and no one would be foolish enough to clamour for currency legislation, to effect an object which statesmen and economists have long since been convinced can only be arrived at by the increasing prosperity of the poorer country, and the diminishing cheapness of its productions. Until the value of Eastern merchandise is enhanced by the operation of natural causes, that is to say, until each item which goes to the cost of its production procures for those employed thereon a greater value of the necessaries and conveniences of life in their own countries than is now the case, cheapness in European markets will be the characteristic of importations from Asia.

The exchange question is a question of the value of the commodities produced in Asia in the gold money of Europe. Among these commodities is silver (although it is, properly speaking, found, not produced, in India); but while silver is bullion in the West, it is money in the East, and speaking of India, its value as money is determined by its scarcity or abundance, viewed in relation to the productions of that country which it serves to exchange with one another. This being the case, a given sum of gold will procure no more silver than may be its equivalent in value in indigo, corn, saltpetre, or any other produce. If these are low in value in gold, rupees will be low in value also in gold; as money, rupees are of no account in England, and the variation in the exchange rate of sovereigns and rupees is of the same character and arises from the same causes as the variations in value between sovereigns and saltpetre. That the standard money of India is cheap in the standard money of England has little or nothing to do with the price of corn or saltpetre in rupees. If rupees were in the future to become dearer in sovereigns than they are now, and if this were the result of a depreciation of gold and not of an appreciation of silver, one sovereign might procure only 10 rs and 20 seers of corn, whereas now it can, *ex hypothesi*, purchase 15 rs. and 30 seers of corn. The equation we will suppose to stand thus. At present £1 = 15 rs. = 30 seers of corn. In future £1 = 10 rs. = 20 seers of corn. The rupee purchases 2 seers of corn in each case, but the £1 sterling purchases 30 seers in the first case and only 20 seers in the other. Indian-grown corn we shall be told (if the theory that cheap silver *bonuses* Indian exportations still survives), will not in that case come into competition with English-grown corn, because the sovereign can only buy fewer rupees than it could before. But the diminished competition will arise not from 10 rs. purchasing only 20 seers of wheat (which it did before), but because one sovereign purchases a third less wheat. If 36s. a quarter is the price of wheat before the fall in gold, and gold has fallen in value from 15 to 10 rs. to the sovereign, then we may expect the quarter of wheat to rise, say, to 50s. or more, and the importation of corn from India will cease, because corn will have risen in the gold valuation in that country likewise. If gold were (as we are supposing it has) to depreciate, then it would depreciate against silver and corn alike, as it has in recent years appreciated against both alike. The gold price of silver and of corn would be attributable in the one case to a diminution, in the other to an enhancement of its intrinsic value. But while gold might depreciate against silver and corn, it does not follow that silver would depreciate or appreciate against corn ; the relation of value existing between gold on the one hand, and these two commodities on the other, might be altered in the same proportion for both without any alteration in the relative values of silver and corn. If the sovereign were to fall from 12 rs. to 10 rs., and buy 20 instead of 24 seers of corn, corn would still stand at 2 seers the rupee as the result of commercial, not of monetary causes. If this argument is good to prove the effect of a depreciation of gold on Indian rupees and Indian-grown corn, it is, *e converso*, good to prove the effect of an appreciation of gold on the same commodities.

Mr. Barclay admits in his evidence (Q. 2493) that provided you have a good mechanism of exchange, it does not matter in the long run what the ratio between gold and silver may be, and he explains that the great difficulty of the present situation is the "shifting mechanism" of trade; that "the two bases of valuation are continually shifting." This view is no doubt sound. As long as one basis of valuation is money, and the other a commodity which takes its value from that money, the mechanism is faulty, because it consists of two parts which are not independent of one another, and working in concert under the impulse of the same force, but the one depends for its movement on the other, and the efficiency of its action diminishes in proportion to the strength of the regulating influence to which it is subject. As long as this is the case, the two bases of valuation can never coincide, and the only means of obtaining the necessary coincidence is to provide both parties to the valuation with one and the same metal for use as money. When this is effected, the industrial competition between East and West will not cease, except in so far as such a secondary aid to commerce as a common currency may advance the prosperity of India; but English corn-dealers, buying Indian-grown corn in Bombay with Indian sovereigns, will then be more easily convinced than they are now, that it is the low value of Indian wheat, and not the low value of silver which enables them to import the grain and undersell the English farmer in his own markets. This is what happens in the Indian trade with China and Japan. We never hear it said that cheap silver *bonuses* Indian cotton goods. When imported into those countries they are described as being cheap or dear in dollars, because they are sold for the metal from which the money both of the exporting and importing country is made; so when we have a dual currency in India of gold and silver circulating at their full value in one another, we shall read in the papers of the price of corn in India having risen or fallen in pounds sterling. We shall cease to hear of loss by exchange, because silver, which will at one and the same time in different hemispheres be token and full-value money, will not come into the account. Indian wheat, indigo, saltpetre, hides, etc., will be priced in sovereigns, without any question of loss by exchange between the rupee and the pound sterling, and variations between the value of the money of India and England respectively will be such as are due to fluctuations in the price of commercial bills, or to the supply and demand of capital for trade in either country.

To the evidence on the facts that the competition between the commercial productions of the East and West is sustained by the operation of industrial as contrasted with monetary causes, must be added the *à priori* argument, that no other than such causes can produce this result. Professor Marshall (Q. 9744) speaks as follows: "It is of course true that India can export wheat or tea more profitably when exchange is at 1s. 4d. than when it is at 1s. 6d., if we suppose that the fall in exchange has not been accompanied by any changes in prices; but it is of the nature of the case that it will be so accompanied, and to suppose that it is not is to assume unconsciously the conclusion against which I am arguing. . . . If wheat is selling at 36s., and a scarcity of gold lowers exchanges from 1s. 6d. to 1s. 4d., it will also lower wheat from 36s. to 32s., and the Indian exporter will be where he was. Of course silver might fall a little faster than wheat, owing to a panic in the bullion market; that would give a bounty to the Indian exporter equal to the small difference between the two falls. There is no reason why the gold price of silver should fall at a different rate from the gold price of wheat, unless there should be a panic in the bullion market; and, after all, such a fall would be temporary, and if it led to silver going to India when it was not wanted there, there would be a reaction. The argument that the fall in the gold price of silver gives a great bounty to Indian exporters assumes that there is great difference between silver prices in India and Europe, after allowing for carriage. That is impossible. To assume that it is possible is the *petitio principii* of which I complain. There can only be a small difference, and the fact that Indian importation of silver is not large shows that the difference is only (as it was before 1873) just enough to pay the freight of the silver. ... If there had been for a short time any considerable premium of this kind on exportation from India, if there had been even for a short time a large fall in the gold price of silver in England, without a large fall in the gold price of commodities, there would have been an enormous export of silver from Europe to India on a scale such as has never been approached, though some faint indication of it was given about the year 1866, when the French bimetallic law prevented silver from rising in Europe relatively to the newly imported gold, and in consequence India imported £20,000,000 of silver in one year."

That the bimetallists consider the competition of cheap corn with English-grown corn in our own markets to be a question of values which a restoration of silver to general use as money by means of a revival of bimetallism will rectify, is not, we presume, denied. They demand that a fixed price should be given for silver in gold, that the price should be fixed by a Convention, in order (to take the case of the Indian competition as a typical case), that the fall in the value of rupees when measured in sovereigns may be arrested, and increasing sums of rupees may not be procurable with the same sum of gold money and that "as a consequence of this diminution in the number of rupees obtainable for a sovereign more and more corn will not be procurable for the same sum of gold, and that less and less corn will in consequence be exported from India to England."*

Let us suppose that the theory that cheap silver acts as a *bonus* on Indian exportation be accepted, and inquire how a revival of bimetallism would reverse the condition of trade thus alleged to exist. Bimetallism is to be adopted by all the principal commercial nations of the West: the silver-using regions of the East are not, we believe, to be included in the Convention. With the restoration of the system, it is expected that silver will rise in value in gold. £1 sterling (and we are now dealing with the Indian exchanges) is now the equivalent of 15 rs; it will, after the rise in value induced by the bimetallic system be equal say to $12\frac{1}{2}$ rs.; and we will suppose that the fixed ratio of the Convention corresponds with this equation of values. The price of corn in India, we will say, is *now* 15 rs. for 30 seers, and if the rupee price of corn remains unaltered, it will, after the fixation of the ratio, stand at 25 seers for $12\frac{1}{2}$ rs. for £1 sterling. Then the object of the revival of the system will have been accomplished, the £1 sterling will buy fewer rupees and less corn than is now the case. But this will only happen if silver prices remain unaltered. Prices in India can only remain unaltered, if (1) the bimetallic currencies take up all the fresh silver which the revival of the system calls forth for use as money, and (2) if that quantity is exactly as much as may produce a par of exchange represented by the equation £1 = $12\frac{1}{2}$ rs. If more than this quantity is offered for use, and if the bimetallic currencies leave any considerable part of the supply free to act on the exchanges through

* Appendix, F. R. No. iii. p. 88.

outside markets such as the Indian markets, then the ratio will be disturbed. But to go back to prices. If silver rises in value against gold, as the bimetallists expect that it will do, such a rise can only come from a demand for the metal for use as money, and this demand, in order to secure the rise in value, must exceed the supply. We will first suppose that the demand does outstrip the supply. In that case, the Indian silver currency will increase in volume rather more slowly than it does now (as part of the metal which would have gone to India will be intercepted for the bimetallic currencies) and prices will not rise, but will fall in India, the rupee will purchase more than it does now, nothing will have occurred to mitigate the appreciation of gold as respects Indian commodities, they will still be cheap compared with the commodities and the gold money of the West; and if the fall in prices in India and the rise in the purchasing power of the rupee were to correspond (as it might, although not necessarily would, correspond) exactly with the rise in the value of silver by the gold standard, then $12\frac{1}{2}$ rs. would buy as much corn as 15 rs. buy now, and the expectation that the rise in the value of silver will reduce the competition of India in the English market for corn will be disappointed. In the other case, if supply outstrips demand, the bimetallic currencies will only take up as much silver as will suffice to keep both gold and silver money in circulation at the fixed rate of exchange (£1 = $12\frac{1}{2}$ rs.). If more were taken up, the law of the fixed ratio would cease to act, and these currencies would become silver monometallic currencies. The revival of the system will no doubt stimulate the production of silver; and if its owners cannot circulate it along with gold in one quarter of the world, they will send it to the other and force a market for it in India. Prices will tend to rise from the volume of the currency increasing rather faster than the supply of merchandise in the markets, the purchasing power of silver may fall a little, 12½ rs. will buy a little less than 25 seers of corn, but there is no reason to suppose that the limits of the supply of fresh silver to the Indian currency will not be reached, long before the price in India touches the price in the market of importation, where, on the hypothesis of the bimetallists, it will have reached a permanently high level. In fact, the exportation will go on nearly as briskly as before. So long as the price of any exportable commodity is higher, say in England than in India, it will be exported, and the lower value prevailing in the Indian market will be determined by local causes connected with cheapness of production. An abundance of silver will, so far as it is taken up by India, cause prices to rise in that country; but prices can only rise slowly, as the extra supply of silver money will never exceed that quantity, which will bring prices up to the level at which all profit on the investment of imported silver in the trade of the country ceases, and that level, owing to the slow circulation of money in India and the rudimentary and tedious processes of production in that country, is very soon reached.

As the enactment of a ratio of exchange in a monetary law cannot regulate values, which depend for the relation which they hold to one another, solely on commercial considerations, so the competition of the cheap markets of India and Asia will not be destroyed, and will be but little affected merely by the revival of bimetallism, with its accompanying currency expedients. That object can only be arrived at by a great and necessarily gradual advance in the material prosperity of the inhabitants of that country, which will make the productions of their industry so valuable at home that it will become unprofitable to export them abroad.

To this we would add an argument rather differently stated, which leads to the same conclusion, extracted from one of the memoranda supplied to the Special Commission (Final Report, Appendix iii. pp. 89-91).

" As a fact, the prices of those commodities most generally used in India have, during fifteen years ending with 1884, shown a tendency to fall. The tables on pp. 379 *et seq*. of the Appendix B to the third report of the Trade Commission show this to be the case, and the following extract from p. 335 of the same appendix states the fall in the value of corn to be very marked. The rupee at the same time fell at much the same rate against gold. These are the elements of the situation. Do they prove or assist to prove that corn, having fallen 16 per cent. relatively to the silver money of India, and in another proportion to the gold standard in India, while the same article has fallen 29 per cent. against gold in England, is exportable with profit from India because silver has fallen 17 per cent. (from 1s. 11d. to 1s. 7d.) against gold?

" 'Taking the average prices of the markets of Cawnpore, Agra, Fyzabad, Amritsur, Multan, and Jubbulpore, it will be found that 1558 seers of wheat sold for 100 rs. in 1865-69. The same weight of wheat sold in the same markets at an average price of say 84 rs. in 1880–84, this being a close enough approximation in round figures to the percentage of fall of price, 84·34 on the average of fifteen years, 1865–84, as given at foot of column 19 of Statement B. But comparing 1865–69 with 1880–84 the fall in exchange with England was so great, say 15 per cent., that whilst the 100 rs. realized by 1558 seers of wheat in 1865–69 at the then average rate of 1s. 11·310d. produced in England £9 14s. 3d., the 84 rs. realized by the same weight of wheat in 1880–84 produced in remittance to England at the then average rate of exchange of 1s. 7·644d. only £6 17s. 6d., the difference of £2 16s. 9d. between the two results indicates a drop of 29 per cent. in the space of time under review.' These figures afford the following equation :—

Year.	Wheat in India.	Price in India.	Selling Price in London.
	Seers.	Rs.	£ s. d.
1869	1558	100	9 14 3
1884	1558	84	6 17 6
	Difference...	16 per cent.	29 per cent.

and show that Indian wheat fell by the gold valuation in the London market 29 per cent. in fourteen years, while it fell during the same period in the silver valuation of the Indian market 16 per cent.

"The exportation of corn from India to England must have been due to this fall in price, and whether the fall is described in terms of the rupee or of the £1 sterling is immaterial. The consideration which is material is this, that if in 1884, 1558 seers of wheat had cost in India £9 14s. 3d., or nearly that figure, as they cost in 1869, the corn would not have been exportable with profit.

"If corn had risen in price, the exportation would have been thereby prohibited, however cheap silver might have been in gold; and if the price had fallen, as it has fallen, then the exportation must be attributed to the fall in value of corn against gold, and not to the fall in silver by the same standard.

"If any condition of corn prices in the silver money of India, whether constant or rising or falling, cannot be connected with the fall of silver in gold, as effect is connected with cause, such a condition of prices must depend on the ordinary causes which determine the value of corn in gold, and those causes may operate wholly irrespective of the number of rupees obtainable for £100 in the exchange of the precious metals.

"That silver has a lower efficiency for the purchase of commodities in the East than in the West is an assumption somewhat hypothetical, since in Europe and the United States it is gold, not silver, which is principally used as money. Silver being only in circulation as a subsidiary coinage, its inherent or natural purchasing power can never be tested in the same way as it can be in India, where it is used as full-value money. But inasmuch as gold procures more of any commodity in the East than it can procure of the same description in the West, silver may be presumed to go further as money in India than it would if used on similar terms in

Europe. This circumstance, however, would be due to a low cost of production, and a prevailing cheapness in the East, and not to a low valuation of Indian silver money in gold.

"The theory that cheap silver, as such, stimulates the exportation of produce from India is contradicted by the fact that no coincidence is found to exist between a low valuation of silver in gold and an increase in the exportation of those commodities whose production would be most easily affected by such a stimulus. Furthermore, it is only by means of the currency of India that the stimulus of cheap silver could be applied in the manner assumed in the theory; and if it were so applied, the currency would increase in volume simultaneously with every point of decline in the value of silver in gold; but it does not. No such simultaneous increase has taken place, but, on the contrary, the largest additions to the Indian currency have not been made when silver has been cheapest; but in some periods of comparatively dear silver these additions have been larger than at other times when it was cheaper.

"The increased exportation of any article of Indian production, unless it can be shown to have resulted from the cheapness of silver in gold as such, *i.e.* from more rupees being obtainable for a sovereign than before, must be held to be owing to the article being of lower value in India than in England. Thus, if £100 will purchase such a weight of corn in India as will sell for £110 in London, that result must be due to the value of corn in gold in either place respectively, unless it can be clearly proved to be owing to the value of rupees in sovereigns in India by some stronger arguments than have yet been used for that purpose.

"There is another circumstance which goes to prove that it is not the cheapness of silver which bonuses Indian produce in the foreign trade of that country, but the appreciation of gold against commodities. It will be remembered that if the rate of exchange does not operate to fix prices in Indian silver money, or cause them to fall in the same valuation, then the assertion that cheap silver bonuses Indian exports falls to the ground, as it follows that their profitable exportation depends on other causes than the low value of silver in gold. If the conditions of the case were such as the assertion depends upon for acceptance as an economic theory, it would clearly be to the advantage of the owners of silver in Europe to transfer their silver to India, in order to purchase her produce cheap and sell it dear in Europe. But they do not do so, and the reason is as follows :—

"Commodities in international commerce are bought with commodities. However circuitous the course of trade may be, it is always exchanging commodities for commodities. Money and bullion are ordinarily only the equivalents in value used in exchanges in order to avoid resort to barter; when, however, the merchant sees no hope of profit in forwarding goods abroad to pay for imports by their sale at a higher value than he gave for them, he ships bullion as the least disadvantageous method of making his payment. Bullion, that is, treasure of the precious metals, becomes the commodity with which the debt is adjusted. In the same way, if for any reason such as is assumed to exist in the case under discussion, it were considered profitable to send silver bullion to the East, to be coined into money for the purchase of produce, the trader would seek to get the value of his bullion back in produce. He would have his pains for his profit, if it were returned to him in any other way, but whether he could import this produce and gain by its sale in Europe, would depend on the quantity of the commodity which he might have been able to procure on the conversion of his bullion into Indian money, and on the price at which he could sell it in the English market for gold. The amount of silver bullion exported would in the first instance be determined by the price of silver in gold in London; the trader would set off the gold thus spent in purchasing silver for export, against the gold price obtained on the sale of the produce when imported. These would be the two essential elements in the calculation. The amount of silver exported, or the number of rupees it might serve to coin, although they would be factors in the calculation, would not determine the profit or loss to be made on the transaction, that would exclusively depend on the amount of gold which the trader might put into his venture, and the amount which it might bring him back.

"It is evident that if, owing to the cheapness of silver in gold, vast stocks of the metal were transferred to India for coinage and use in the purchase of the produce of that country, one of two results would follow : either the commodities under purchase would rise in price from the quantity, remaining stationary, while money grew more abundant; or such a stimulus would be given to their production that on their import into Europe there would arise a glut in the market for them. In the one case their value would have risen in India to a point which would make their sale unprofitable in Europe; in the other case they would become so cheap in Europe, that the trader would get a smaller return for the gold spent on his exported silver bullion than if he had traded with it at home. No great value of silver could be used profitably in this manner, for whether silver owners send their metal to India to buy produce, or the Indians send their wares to Europe to be exchanged for treasure, a limit is placed on either class of transaction by the power of India to produce and export her commodities, and by the ability of the European consumer to take them off her hands at a profit to the producer and consumer alike. It is the actual, not the potential power of production which the people of India may possess, that in any given week limits the importation of silver bullion into India for coinage into money; and as in that country industry is almost entirely confined to manual labour, and cattle only are used where machinery and scientific expedients for cheapening and accelerating production would in Europe be employed, any increase in the exportations of India must be slow, however great the stimulus may be which an abundance of money supplies. Let the store of surplus silver in the West be ever so large, it will not be possible for India to extend her productive industries (except in the course of a very long time), to an extent which would enable her to mop it up and exhaust the supply. Any excessive exportation of silver to the East would therefore only result in loss to the exporter.

"It is a necessary conclusion from this argument that the exportation of silver bullion from West to East, not only cannot be dissociated from the influence of the gold standard, but is wholly dependent on the conditions which that standard may prescribe as to whether a profit or loss shall result. It cannot, therefore, be the case that silver thus exported, or silver previously exported, and already circulating as currency in India, shall fix those conditions likewise. Although the necessary intervention of the silver money of India in all business of this class appears to increase the profits obtainable from its pursuit, these profits are really determined not by the greater or less number of rupees which a sovereign will procure, but by the quantity of any merchandise which a given value in gold will command in the Indian market, and by the price at which the quantity will be resold in England. It is the efficiency of gold for the purchase of commodities on either side of the world which determines whether trade shall be carried on or not, and as long as from local causes Indian wheat can be grown, and brought down to the coast at such a low price as will allow of its profitable exportation and sale in London, the trade will flourish, whether the rupee exchanges for gold at 1s. 5d. or 1s. 10d. Were this not so, and were it the case that the trader looked rather to the number of rupees than to the quantity of merchandise which his gold would procure, trade would be conducted on the basis of two independent standards of value, the value of the article in gold at the time of sale, and the value of the gold employed in Indian rupees. As such a state of commerce neither exists nor is possible, it follows that both silver and commodities take their value from gold alike, and that it is the appreciation of gold, and not the depreciation of silver which gives the owners of gold any advantage they enjoy in trading with countries whose inhabitants exclusively use silver."

As an argument relevant to these observations, tending to prove the same point although stated in a different way, we may usefully extract the following passages from the final report of the Special Commission:—

"One of the difficulties of the question has always been to know why a large demand for silver in the East has not followed on its fall and cheapened cost in the West.

"When silver first began to fall, it was said that the East, whose mints and markets stood open to silver, would take the surplus silver as it did at the time of the gold discoveries, and that the gold price of silver would be thus kept at or near its former level.

"When it was found that this did not happen, the changes in the relative values of the two metals were attributed by many to the appreciation of gold. For this, it was said, would account for a fall in the gold price both of silver and of commodities, but would not necessarily cause any flow of silver from the West to the East; and it was consequently alleged by those who held this view, that this appreciation of gold was the cause both of the lower gold price of commodities and of the lower gold price of silver.

"But it is obvious, on consideration, that the same effect would be produced on the flow of silver to the East by a fall in the gold price of commodities and of silver, whether that fall was due on the one hand to the appreciation of gold, or on the other to causes which affected commodities and to similar causes which simultaneously affected silver.

"Let it be assumed that goods have fallen in gold price from causes affecting goods, and that silver has fallen in gold price in Europe from causes affecting silver. It is obvious that as regards articles imported into Europe from the East, the English importing merchant would make no new profit by exporting the cheapened silver and importing Eastern goods, if for the goods he imports he were to receive a gold price as much lowered as the gold price of silver had been lowered. And as regards articles of export to the East, there would be no greater profit in buying and exporting the cheapened silver than in buying and exporting other English articles, such as cotton goods and iron, which are fallen in gold price as much or more than silver.

"In examining the relation of commodities to gold, we have come to the conclusion that the greater part of the fall in the gold price of commodities in general, and among them, of the great articles of trade to the East, is due to causes touching the commodities rather than to an appreciation of gold.

"If, then, we are right in this conclusion, the fall in the gold price of commodities arising from these causes is itself the reason why the silver in Europe, though cheapened in its gold price from causes affecting silver, has not been exported to the East, and why such export has not maintained or restored the former gold value of silver.

"The calculations which were founded on a notion that a fall in the value of silver in the West must send silver to the East, and redress the divergence between gold and silver, have proved erroneous, not because silver has not fallen, but because other things have fallen as much or more than silver.

"It was assumed that other things would be equal, and they have not been equal" (Final Report, part ii., p. 75, § 60).

To these observations one of Commissioners objects: "With all deference to those who hold a different opinion, it appears to me that the explanation given in § 60 of part ii., why silver has not gone to the East, is unsound. Commodities, it is said, have fallen in gold price from causes affecting commodities; silver has fallen in gold price in Europe from the same cause. If the only change had been the fall of silver in gold price, the demand for the last would have absorbed large quantities of silver, because it would have been profitable to export the cheap silver to the East and purchase Eastern commodities and import them into Europe. But as commodities had fallen in gold price from causes affecting commodities, there was no such profit to be made by the export of silver, because the reduced gold price exactly balanced the extra profit that would have been derived from the lowered value of silver. Consequently, silver fell in value without any considerable quantity of it being exported to the East.

" However ingenious this explanation may at first sight appear, it contains a fatal flaw. The fall in prices from increased production, would have affected silver prices just as much as gold prices; and the lower gold price for which the imported Eastern commodities sold, would have been exactly balanced by the lower silver price for which they could have been purchased. If, under such circumstances, silver had also fallen relatively to gold, the profit to be made by exporting the cheaper silver would have been undiminished. The explanation, in fact, assumes (1) that the increased production of commodities would only affect gold prices and not silver prices; and (2) that silver prices were maintained 39 per cent. higher than they otherwise would have been by a not very great increase in the supply of silver which did not go to India" (Final Report, p. 141, § 36).

The objection to this argument is that it assumes a condition of prices which does not exist, it assumes that a gold price and a silver price are found in the same markets, and that one is independent of the other; while, as a matter of fact, in the West a gold price prevails and in the East a silver price. In no country are both metals used as money in unrestricted quantities, and in the absence of this condition there cannot be a gold and a silver price for the same commodity in the same market, and unless there is, the two prices will not necessarily go together. No market exists where such a condition of commerce is to be found. Failing this, the expedient is resorted to of finding a silver price by converting a gold price into silver by a calculation based on the market value of the metal in gold. This device is for economic purposes of very little use, because the silver which such calculations refer to, is to a great extent unsaleable, and because price is the expression of value in exchange in terms of the money used as the medium of exchange, and as no such exchanges can have taken place, as there have been no exchanges of goods through the agency of silver discarded from use, no silver price can exist, of the kind which the argument requires. Furthermore, silver prices and gold prices, where either prevail on different sides of the world, actually differ for the same article. We have given an instance of this in the prices of cotton goods in India and in England in 1887. In that year, grey shirtings were priced in silver in Bombay at 79 to 100, taken as a datum price for 1873, while the average gold price for the same article in London in 1887 was 60 as compared with 100 for 1873. Thus Manchester goods cost 19 per cent. more in India than in England at the same time; and, in face of these figures, it cannot be asserted that "the fall in prices from increased production would have affected silver prices just as much as gold prices; and the lower gold price for which the imported Eastern commodities sold, would have been exactly balanced by the lower silver price for which they could have been purchased." In this case increased production did not affect gold and silver prices alike, and the calicoes manufactured in Bombay mills (the counterpart of Manchester-made cottons) could not have been purchased in Bombay for a lower silver price which would have exactly balanced their low gold price in London, because the Bombay silver price of the article was to the London gold price as 79 is to 60. When the theory embodied in this argument is tested in the only way in which it can be tested, it is found to be contradicted by facts.

In the West, the effect of increased production on prices is clearly traceable in the enhanced purchasing power of gold money, as its use is neither hindered by legislation nor other circumstances. But if we look to India for the effect which large stocks of silver available for money and an increased production of commodities might be expected to have on prices, we find the action of these two causes not quite free to produce its natural effect, because the supply of gold for coinage is cut off by the monetary law, and the supply of silver diminished by local circumstances. India has imported during seventeen out of the last twenty-two years between 20 and 50 millions of rupees' worth of gold annually, which has not been converted into money, or exchanged for silver for coinage. The potential volume of the stock of money has in this way been decreased, because the gold thus imported cannot be used as money. At the same time the silver bullion, from which alone money can be fabricated, has been imported in a smaller amount than it would have been if the gold imported had been left in the West, and silver taken to India as the price of that part of her exportations with which the gold has been purchased in its stead. The value of the merchandise imported during the last twenty years and more has been from five to ten times greater than the silver metal imported. The one constitutes the annual additions made by the foreign trade of the country to the commodities under exchange in her markets, and the latter the supply of money-metal from which the currency of the country can obtain its annual increment. In addition, the currency has to do the work of exchanging an enormous increase in the commodities produced for internal consumption, the magnitude of which can be inferred from the expansion of the foreign trade and from many other signs of the advance of the country in material prosperity. Besides this, a considerable portion of the metallic currency of India serves to fill a void by substituting money transactions for exchanges in kind, and thus reducing the amount of business done by barter. For these reasons it is evident that the currency of India is inadequate to the requirements of its commerce. India is a more backward country than either the United Kingdom or than France, and presumably requires more coin per head of the population than those countries. If India were equipped with currency of all kinds on the scale of the United Kingdom she would have four times as much as she has, and, judged by the standard of France, eight times as much. If it is the case that in gold-using countries over-production of commodities, or a disproportion between commodities and money has depressed prices, in India a rise of prices has been prevented, not by want of the money-metals, but by the custom of selling goods abroad for gold instead of silver, and by a legislative prohibition on the use of gold as legal-tender money, against which as a set-off is the prevalence of a local custom of exchanging goods in kind without the intervention of money.

We thus find in the two typical gold and silver-using countries, England and India, that prices are affected in different ways by the influence of production on the standard of value, and there is no "fatal flaw" in the reasoning conveyed in the foregoing extracts from the Report and its Appendix, which satisfactorily explain why silver has not gone to the East in unlimited quantities, and incidentally disprove the theory that cheap silver *bonuses* Indian exportations. Cheap silver can only go to India in just such quantities as her people can afford to purchase it with their own productions. Part of these productions they exchange for merchandise, always a more profitable exchange than that of goods for bullion, part they exchange for gold, and part for silver; and they have no more commodities to give for more silver. If it were the case that cheap silver acted as an inducement to exportation, and speculators had sent out increasing supplies of silver to India for the purchase of goods for exportation, the stock of money would have increased faster than the stock of commodities, and prices would have risen to a figure which would have made it unprofitable to buy them for resale in Europe, where prices are fixed by the standard of gold, and do not follow the alternations in the silver prices of the same goods in the Indian markets. It follows from this, that although silver has become cheaper in gold than it was, the profit to be made by exporting silver to India for the purchase of produce has not increased, *pari passu*, with the fall in the gold price of silver, and so far from the capacity of India to absorb silver being illimitable, which in the event of a great fall in the gold price of silver was calculated upon as a matter of certainty, it is strictly limited by the conditions above described.

CHAPTER IV.

COMMERCE AND THE BIMETALLIC PAR.

Bimetallism does not ensure an unlimited circulation of both kinds of coin—The bimetallic par commercial, not legal—A premium on gold under fixed-ratio system amounts to collapse of the system—Illustration of commercial theory from Indian trade and exchanges—Ratio for gold and silver depends on their ratio of value to commodities—Dilemma involved in the bimetallist theory of the exchanges—Defect in the theory of the effect of fixed ratio on value of silver in the East illustrated—Proving the supremacy of the commercial over the legal valuation.

THE end and object of a bimetallic system is to circulate gold and silver money for the purchase of commodities in such quantities that no one can perceive there to be a want of either kind of coin for business purposes. It is nothing to the purpose to say that such a system is in working order so long as any one can *coin* gold and silver money into the currency at the prescribed ratio of value. If we are to adopt the bimetallism of the Latin Union as the currency system of the British Empire, we must first be satisfied that it will provide us with any amount of either kind of money which commerce may require at all times and under all circumstances. When a fixed-ratio system fails to secure this, it ceases to be in working order, for the maintenance of a fixed rate of exchange is only nominal when it is secured by practically discarding one of the two metals from use, or only permits its use at a premium. A system which involves the use of an alternating standard, which often becomes monometallic, and can never be relied on for any length of time to continue bimetallic, and which, therefore, neither creates nor fixes nor even maintains an equilibrium of value between any given quantities of gold and silver money, is in no way preferable to a monometallic system with a fixed standard, and provides no remedy for the particular evils and inconveniences which commerce and industry suffer from fluctuations in the price of the precious metals in one another.

The following evidence throws some light on this part of the question, and leads to the conclusion that it is not the monetary law under a bimetallic system, but the commercial law of values which regulates the rate of exchange between gold and silver money when both are coined, and can be (if it is profitable to do so) put into circulation together in unlimited quantities.

In describing the principle upon which an association like the Latin Union acts, in preserving a fixed ratio between gold and silver in countries which do not belong to the Union, the effect, that is to say, of the existence of the Latin Union upon England as respects silver, Mr. H. H. Gibbs says, that it is not a fixed ratio or a fixed price which is produced, but a par of exchange. If, for instance, only 59*d.* per ounce is offered for silver in the London market, and the bimetallic currency will take it in on terms based on a price of 60*d.*, then that becomes the price in London as well as in Paris, because the fact that silver can be sold at that price in Paris is a sufficient answer to any one offering less in London (Q. 3551). And that if an enormous quantity of silver were being continuously sent into France, the supply would constitute a forced import into France, with the result that these imports would materially alter the exchange between France and England, and continuously alter it, until it rose to that point at which the value of the silver in England would be much less than 60d.; that if it were a question only of exchange as matters then stood (March, 1887), the exchange would have to be 37 francs to the £1 sterling, to bring the price of silver down to what it was (Q. 3555).

When asked, if through a depreciation of silver in monometallic countries, the whole of the gold is driven out of a bimetallic country, that country loses all efficacy as a compensating machine? Mr. Gibbs answered, " No. That has been said over and over again, but nobody has ever attempted to give me any real proof of the fact, or rather disproof of what I say, that whatever was the case, if there was not a gold snuff-box left in France, yet if I sent a bar of silver to the French mint, I could draw upon the number of francs that came to my credit accordingly, and unless the amount of my shipments to Paris, and other people's shipments, had so turned the balance of trade against France that the exchange had risen, I should say beyond its normal point, I should always get my 60d. here in England, my $\frac{?}{?}$ of £1 " (Q. 3556).

Now it is evident that if the gold available for use in a bimetallic country were reduced to a single snuff-box, two kinds of money would not be in circulation, but only one kind for the purchase of commodities, and it proves nothing for the system as one calculated to secure the exchange of both kinds of money at a fixed rate that a bill for gold on England could be bought with francs in France at a premium on the par fixed by the legal ratio, but quite the contrary, for in that case the real value of gold and silver in one another would differ from the legal valuation; that is to say, that the law would be unable to maintain the value even within the limits of its territorial range. This becomes clearer if we take the case of a trader sending silver to Paris, coining it into 5-franc pieces, and electing not to draw a bill on England, but to buy napoleons in order to export them. If his silver bullion amount to a million of francs, he should, at the legal rate of exchange, get 50,000 napoleons or thereabouts, but Paris being nearly denuded of gold, he is only able to buy say 40,000 napoleons. This result is, in the opinion of the witness, attributable to a fluctuation in exchange, which is indeed true, but it is nevertheless a collapse of the system of the fixed ratio. When a purchaser cannot buy napoleons at the fixed rate, the system has ceased to work, and a currency system which is set up in order to circulate two kinds of money, and only circulates one, is a complete failure.

Being asked how a country, when she had ceased to hold both metals, and had no more gold to pay, could be considered as a regulator of their relative values, Mr. Gibbs admitted the difficulty of explaining how a merely nominal bimetallic law could regulate in any way the price; and added, "I cannot help suspecting that there must be some flaw in my argument. I do not see it yet, nor has anybody attempted to show me how the absence of gold can prevent your sending silver to Paris and drawing on it, and selling your draft at the exchange of the day" (Q. 3571). The flaw in the argument consists in the discussion being shifted from the issue on which it really rests, viz., whether under the system of the fixed ratio gold and silver would always exchange for one another at the prescribed rate, on to a very different issue, viz., whether a trader in a bimetallic country could or could not always get gold at some price or another. The first issue is disputable, about the second there is no dispute at all. The line of argument which Mr. Gibbs has adopted proves that the commercial value of gold and silver in one another ultimately governs the exchange and determines the occasions when $15\frac{1}{2}$ to 1 shall rule, and when some other rate shall rule; when 20 francs shall always exchange for a napoleon, and when not a single napoleon shall be procurable except at higher price.

There may be some among our readers who during the decline in the value of silver have endeavoured, in making remittances from India, to get round the exchange by buying produce with rupees and selling it for sovereigns in England. On making their calculations, however, it has invariably turned out that the estimated return to such an experiment would be no greater than that obtained by purchasing a bill of exchange; and there would be in addition the risk of loss from a fall in the price of the article in the market of sale. How can this coincidence, between the silver and the gold price of merchandise on either side of the world and the rupee price in India of sovereigns in England, arise, except for the reason that the latter depends on the former?

The weakness of the logical argument for bimetallism consists in this, that it refuses to recognize the fact that a given sum in silver is equal to another given sum in gold, because each of them is equal to a given quantity of tea or saltpetre or indigo on either side of the globe; and that as these two sums of silver and gold alter in their equivalence of value towards commodities, so the ratio of exchange alters for gold and silver in one another.

If at the same time a bimetallist were to admit that the relative values of the precious metals are determined in this way, then he is driven to the conclusion that the ratio must alter with every variation in the relative values of commodities, as expressed in gold prices and silver prices respectively,— which indeed it does; or that the fixation of the ratio which he claims for his bimetallism is obtained by the system possessing a power to regulate the values of commodities in the money of the countries where they are produced as well as in that of the countries where they are sold—which is not possible.

It is the weak point in the economic argument for bimetallism that its advocates assert the power of its monetary law under certain circumstances to supersede and regulate the natural law of values, so far as it affects gold and silver money, while they fail to perceive that it cannot do this unless it can first control the relative values of the commodities themselves when expressed in terms of the two metals. The economic basis of their theory is really (although perhaps not ostensibly) an assumption that a monetary law regulating the coinage of gold and silver money for five European nations prescribes the price of Chinese silk and tea, Indian wheat and indigo, and similar produce, in silver in those countries, and their price in gold in England also.

Their economies do not go to the depth of discovering that the silver price of commodities depends on conditions affecting their production, and the supply and demand for silver money in the markets of the producing country, and their gold price depends on conditions affecting the cost at which they can be laid down in countries where they are sold for gold compared with the supply and demand for gold money in those places. Bimetallists are unwilling to acknowledge that if a piece of silk and a chest of indigo are worth 120 dols. and 240 rs. respectively (a dollar and two rupees being of the same value), and each article of merchandise is worth £20 at a time when 120 dols. and 240 rs. should by the bimetallic standard be worth £24; then a new ratio of value is evolved differing from that of $15\frac{1}{2}$: 1, and that the equivalence of gold and silver by the standard of silk and indigo would stand at $15\frac{1}{2}$ ozs. of silver = $1\frac{1}{2}$ ozs. of gold. This is natural enough, because this circumstance proves that their monetary law does not supersede or regulate the commercial law of values. They therefore take refuge in the assertion that because bimetallic mints are open to the coinage of both gold and silver at $15\frac{1}{2}$: 1, on an occasion when gold has disappeared from circulation at that rate in consequence of its undervaluation, there has been no collapse of the fixed-ratio system, only a variation in exchange. But in point of fact this relation of value between silk and indigo on the one hand, and gold and silver on the other, proves that a force is at work more powerful than that of the bimetallic tie which has produced a rate of $15\frac{1}{2} : \frac{1}{2}$, in suppression of the fixed ratio of $15\frac{1}{2} : 1$, and this force is the natural law of commerce, which they contend is subordinate to the bimetallic law of value.

When therefore bimetallists argue that their system does not pretend to fix the commercial value of gold and silver, but that by the operation of the mint regulation for the coinage of francs and napoleons and of the decree which rules that a fixed weight of one metal (in coins) shall be legal acquittance of a debt due in a fixed weight of the other, a coincidence is created between the commercial and the legal valuation; they, in words, concede the supremacy of the commercial law, while, in substance, they assert the predominance of the monetary law.

Thus, although the system may be said not to fix a ratio, but to produce a par of exchange; the par of exchange which it produces is that determined by the action of commerce on the exchanges; and the coincidence of the legal with the commercial par (when they do coincide) is owing not to the regulating influence of the monetary law, but to the superior force of the natural law of values; that is to say, that under the bimetallic system it is the international and not the domestic rate of exchange which fixes the value of one metal in the other. How then does this foreign rate of exchange act on the silver and gold of France except through trade? What is that force under stress of which it was often impossible to get a bill in London for £100 at 25 francs, and a fraction to the £1 sterling, but the commercial value of silver and gold in one another? Mr. Gibbs explains such an argument as this away in the following words : "I must repeat that one of the three essential points of that law (the French monetary law) is that the debtor has the liberty of paying in which metal he will. . . . But where for his own convenience the creditor voluntarily pays the debtor so many centimes to induce him to forego a right which still exists, and on which he, *ipso facto*, insists, the law is *not* broken; nor can it be said that the ratio fixed by the law is in any way disturbed by a separate bargain which recognizes its existence" (Q. 3608). This explanation, however, fails to meet the case, which is that the monetary law is unable to induce such a condition of values that the parity of exchange shall always be that which it prescribes. When more than 20 francs are given for a napoleon, there is no question of favour or concession on either side; the exchange is made at say 20·20, because that is for the moment the commercial value of a napoleon, and neither party to the transaction gains any advantage over the other, or is better or worse off than he would have been if the exchange had been made at 20 francs on another occasion, when that rate ruled in the market.

Bearing on the commercial as contrasted with the currency regulation of the values of the precious metals, we find it claimed for the French system, that it "produced a par of exchange" as distinct from a fixed ratio or a fixed price (Q. 3551); while in Q. 3607 and its answer the following argument occurs. It is said that "France coins her silver at a certain ratio to gold," and English and French gold being of course the same, to a definite proportion of English gold, thus "a definite par of exchange is created between French silver and English gold." "India coins her silver into pieces bearing no legal relation at all to gold, there is therefore no par of exchange between Indian silver and English gold. But so long as there is a par between French silver and English gold, Indian silver and French silver being the same, the same par must necessarily exist for both. Therefore, while France is bimetallic, the price of silver in London will be at least that which corresponds to the Paris exchange, whatever may be the balance of indebtedness between England and India. But if the bimetallic law no longer exists in France to hold the balance, the price of silver will be governed by the balance of indebtedness between England and India or other silver-using countries."

Here, then, we have it distinctly stated that because France, in obedience to her domestic monetary law, coins silver and gold at a definite ratio of $15\frac{1}{2}$ to 1, and because India does not do so or coin gold as legal-tender money at all, Indian silver and French silver hold one and the same relation to French gold; but Indian silver holds no par of exchange to English gold. It follows from this argument as a necessary conclusion that if India, up to 1873, had followed the example of France, and coined her silver into pieces bearing a definite legal relation to gold legal-tender money, then there would have been a par of exchange between Indian silver and English gold. But this is precisely what the East Indian Company did at the end of the last and at the beginning of this century. The gold mohur and the rupee were both of definite constitution, and alike legal tender at a fixed rate of exchange, but the law was frequently unable to keep both kinds of coin in circulation at the legal rate—the legal and commercial rate did not always go together—and as, latterly, gold became undervalued at the exchange fixed by law, in about 1827 the gold mohur was practically out of circulation in India, and India became silver monometallic, with a legal-tender gold coin nominally current, as France for a similar reason has been at different times. The rupee at that time held the same kind of parity to the £1 sterling that the franc held to the napoleon in the French currency, but in each case it was a varying not a fixed parity of value. The greater abundance and more active circulation of coined money in Europe than in India possibly reduced the range of variation between gold and silver money in France to narrower limits than less favourable conditions prescribed in India, but the conditions of the variation were essentially the same. The French system met them by throwing a greater or less quantity of the dearer metal out of circulation. The Indian system met them by throwing gold out of circulation altogether.

As a matter of fact, the influence of the French coinage law in creating a definite par of exchange has no existence. Parities of value are of two kinds—metallic and commercial. The first is that which subsists in coins made of the same metal. Nature has made metal—gold, for instance—homogeneous, and in consequence equal weights have equal values. A napoleon and a ten-mark piece are to the £1 sterling as 0·7930 and 0·4894 to 1 respectively, because the fine gold in each holds that proportion to the fine gold in the English coin. But this is not the parity which the witness, whose opinion is above quoted, refers to. Silver francs and silver rupees have with gold coins no metallic basis of value common to both. The parity of value in the witness's mind must have been the commercial parity. We have shown that this cannot be created by the action of the French coinage law, for the argument in favour of that theory is in conflict both with facts and with reason. It is defective also in another respect. It runs as follows: "India coins her silver into pieces bearing no legal relation at all to the gold; there is therefore no par of exchange between Indian silver and English gold." But, as a matter of fact, India coins her silver with just as definite a relation to gold as France coins hers. When silver is at $60\frac{3}{8}d.$, the rupee is worth $1s.$ $10\frac{1}{2}d.$, and the franc is worth $8\frac{3}{4}d.$, and these values stand to one another in the same proportions when silver is at $50d.$ and $52d.$, or at any other price in gold. Therefore, as far as the coinage of Indian silver at a proportionate value to the £1 sterling is concerned, that circumstance should procure for it any advantage which, it is asserted, the same conditions of French coinage bestow on French silver. But the argument above quoted goes on to say that as there is no law in India by which gold and silver money are coined in pieces bearing a legal relation to one another, Indian silver money does not enjoy this advantage. It is, therefore, *law* which makes all the difference. There is, nevertheless, a law in India (the Indian Coinage Act, 1870) under which a gold coin—the gold mohur—is coined, which contains exactly as many grains of fine gold as the rupee contains of fine silver. It was estimated, in 1870, to be fifteen times as valuable as the rupee, and it was so then, and it holds to the £1 sterling the metallic par of 1·4603 to 1. Why, then, should not the silver and gold coins of India be on exactly the same footing towards one another as those of France are? They actually are. It is true that the gold mohur is not a legal-tender coin, while the napoleon is; but this does not affect its exchange value with rupees at the market price of gold in silver, while for international purposes its exchange value with sovereigns would on this account be slightly lower than its metallic value in the same coins. The parity of value between francs and napoleons, and between rupees and gold mohurs, is determined in exactly the same way, that is to say, by commercial, not by legal, considerations. When the gold mohur exchanged for 15 rupees, the napoleon exchanged for 20 francs; when it exchanges for 20 rupees, the napoleon costs a third more in francs also, or rather would cost, but for the peculiarity of the bimetallic law which then comes into action, and drives gold out of circulation altogether. Matters, as we know, never went to this extremity; the system collapsed before the napoleon rose to 26·66 francs.

The gold mohur not being legal tender, but at the same time being of a definite constitution, and having no artificial value placed on it, is a perfect measure of commercial values in respect of gold and silver money, and serves to prove that the fluctuations in the relative values of the two kinds of money in India are the result of commercial causes, although they are coined in pieces having towards one another a similar legal relation to that which exists in the case of the gold and silver money of France, except, of course, that the gold money of India is not legal tender. The latter circumstance does not affect the argument, for it is not asserted that it is the quality of legal tender in the French money which primarily secured to it its fixation of exchange value, but that the bimetallic tie, the monetary law, by investing both kinds of money with the legal-tender quality, created a fixed parity of value between them. If under the system of the Latin Union free scope had been given to the action of commercial causes, they would have produced the same results, and the fixed-ratio mintage law would have proved unequal to maintain any other parity of value between Indian silver and English gold, or between French silver and French gold, than that which at the same time subsisted between rupees and gold mohurs. To use the language of the argument, "the same par must necessarily exist for both;" but it would be the par of commerce, not the par of law. Clearly it is not the monetary law which regulates the value of gold and silver in one another, but the commercial law only; and on the occasions when the monetary law appears to regulate values, that appearance is produced by an accidental coincidence between the legal and the commercial valuation.

Mr. Gibbs is quite justified in speaking of the bimetallic law as "holding the balance." But to hold the balance is a very different thing from fixing the contents of the scales. The balance certifies the quantity of each article which equals the other in weight, but the quantities themselves are determined by natural causes which act independently of the beam and the scales. The French currency system certified that at one time a larger, at another time a smaller weight, of silver coins equalled in value one gold coin, each class of coin being fabricated in definite proportions of metal; but what the number and weight of the coins might be, *that* was in each case fixed by the action of the commercial law of values. Its function was, to use the late Mr. Bagehot's description, "to act as an equalizing machine, it took the metal which fell, and sold the metal which rose." It secured to the currencies of the Union only just as much or just as little gold as could be used, on the conditions prescribed by law for its exchange with silver, without loss to those employing it as money; but what that quantity might be, how much gold should be taken into and how much thrown out of the system (and the same with the quantity of silver), was settled by the market, by the exigencies and conditions of international trade. It was commerce, not the French monetary law of 1803, which dictated the price at which gold should be sold for silver, and silver for gold; and when the law interfered to prevent the market price being given, commerce withdrew one metal or the other from its influence, and only replaced it when its own valuation again came into harmony with the legal rate of exchange. The system did little or nothing towards creating or determining the varying parity of value between the two metals; that was done by numberless exchanges going forward in every part of the commercial world. When the balance of trade had so turned against a bimetallic country that the exchange had risen beyond its normal point, the system was powerless to keep the value of gold and silver constant at the point where the law had put it; much less then could it avail to create that equivalence of value upon which the point of exchange for the precious metals in one another depends.

It is really the commercial value of the precious metals in one another, a value independent of law, and which is regulated by that amount of the same commodity which will exchange for any given sums of gold and silver at the same time, and in the same market, which fixes their rate of exchange; and except the bimetallic system can first create this commercial value, it must necessarily, when it fails to do so, fail also to ensure the exchange of both kinds of money at the rate it prescribes.

If under the bimetallic system the mass of gold and silver money in use in France had never varied, and at the same time the two kinds of coin had invariably exchanged at the legal ratio, there would have been some reason in asserting that it had fixed their relative values; but, on the contrary, the chief merit of the system consisted in this, that it secured the greatest possible variation in the mass of either kind of coin in circulation in the country, and these variations, measured as they were by the quantity of the cheaper metal taken into, and by the quantity of the dearer metal thrown out from the circulation, arose almost exclusively from variations in the commercial value of one kind of coin in the other. To the free play of these variations the system, within certain limits, gave free scope; to some extent, doubtless, it restrained them, and gave a slightly enhanced purchasing power to either kind of money alternately;

but the time came when these fluctuations in the natural values of gold and silver threatened to roll wide of their ordinary limits, and to pass beyond the control of the system. Its continued maintenance was foreseen to involve the loss of the dual standard, and the substitution of a monometallism of the cheaper metal. Bimetallism was in consequence speedily abandoned by the countries associated in the Latin Union.

When the action of bimetallism is reduced to dependence on the exchanges, and the price of gold bills on London in silver francs varies from the legal rate of $15\frac{1}{2}$ to 1, at times when the price of French gold in French silver money varies from that rate also, what becomes of the contention that: " it is sufficient for a government to say that debts shall be paid indifferently in either of two metals at a certain ratio, for that ratio to be the one for which those metals will always exchange?" (Q. 3493). The facts of the case are the very reverse of the contention. Something besides law must exist in order to enforce such a ratio. It is necessary that a commercial as well as a legal equilibrium should be established between the value of any given quantities of both kinds of money; and as on occasions when the exchanges and the legal ratio are in conflict, the commercial parity supersedes the legal parity of value, the unsoundness of the theory which this part of the evidence was directed to support becomes evident.

CHAPTER V.

MONEY AND PRICES.

Origin of the connection between money and prices—Definition of price—Action of money on industry illustrated—How abundance and scarcity of money act on trade—Views of Commissioners on the effect of money on prices—Statistics of the decline of prices and increase of trade—Statistics of the use for, and the supply of, gold—Opinion of the Commissioners on influence of the fixed-ratio system on gold and silver values controverted—Accepted theory of prices questioned—Professor Marshall's opinion—Definition of money—Mr. Macleod's opinion—Mr. Fowler's opinion—Credit and money, their influence on prices—Reasons why they affect prices differently—Wealth of a nation depends on increase of production, not on increase in credits—Mr. Macleod's view of the rise of prices in the last 200 years disputable—Influence of the use of money in initial and final processes of industry on prices—Reasons why abundance and scarcity of money raise and lower prices—How credits and money affect the volume of the loan fund—Theory that the supply of money depends on prices examined—Causes which constitute money the regulator of price—If money depends on prices, what do prices depend on?—Another view of the quantitative theory of money—Abundance of money a real stimulus to production—Conclusion in favour of the necessity of an expanding currency.

THE industrial competition of Asia being, then, a question, not of currency, but of production, a question of cheapness, not of the exchanges, we have to consider how far prices are affected by an abundance or a scarcity of money, and to what extent the system of the Latin Union acts on prices by securing a sufficient supply of capital to industry; an inquiry which is directly pertinent to a plan calculated to secure the expansion of the currency, in correspondence with that of the commerce, of India.

The intrinsic value of all commodities, and, therefore, their value in exchange with one another, depends partly on the cost of their production, and partly on the demand for them contrasted with the supply forthcoming to meet the demand. It is needless to inquire in what proportion the value of anything is attributable to either of these causes, because so long as the precious metals and merchandise derive their intrinsic value from the same causes, it follows that their relative values are also subject to the same influences. No one, we presume, will deny that the values of gold and silver in every kind of exchange are regulated partly by the cost of production and partly by the action of demand and supply. It is, however, certain that the latter consideration is of more importance in the case of gold and silver money than in the case of merchandise,* because the special use, and, therefore, the immediate cause of the value of metallic money is limited by the proportion which the money coined from any given weight of gold or silver metal bears to the whole stock of money of that kind in use among nations trading together at any given time. Furthermore, as the employment of the precious metals as money is for use and not for consumption, the

* The use of the precious metals in the arts may, as irrelevant to this part of the argument, be put aside.

additions yearly made to coined money are made to a stock constantly increasing in volume; whereas, ordinarily, the additions made annually to the stock of merchandise in commerce is made to a stock which is decreasing or stationary, and never for any length of time increasing in amount by accumulation. This characteristic of money becomes of great importance in connection with the influence of prices on industry.

Price is the expression of the value of any two commodities in one another in terms of metallic money, and while it is necessary to keep the idea of value distinct from the idea of price in one's mind, value is by no means excluded from the idea of price; but, on the contrary, while price may alter and values remain the same, price rests for its foundation on value; thus, 100 tons of coal at 20s. may be of the same value as 50 quarters of wheat at 40s., and each be worth £100 at one time, and at another the same quantities of both may sell for £80, in which case their price will have fallen while their value has remained the same, and the value of the third factor in the equation, money, will have risen from the same causes which have kept the values of the two commodities constant. Lord Liverpool has defined good money as that which is at once a standard of value and an equivalent in exchange; and were it not the fact that gold and silver money are equivalents in exchange, money would not have the effect which it actually does produce, on prices. It is its intrinsic value which gives to money its purchasing power, and that value depends on the same conditions as the values of commodities.

Money and merchandise are interchangeable because they are alike produced by labour—which term includes all kinds of expenditure incurred to bring them to market—and are alike amenable to the law of demand and supply. But it is, at the same time, no misuse of language to speak of money as a commodity, because it possesses a quality which commodities ordinarily have not. Such an expression, however, is incomplete as a definition, and leads to a confusion between two things which in one essential respect are different, although in other respects they are similar.

The quality which differentiates metallic money as a commodity from merchandise is its capacity for employment in use, and its incapacity for employment in consumption. Metallic money can be used both for exchanging two commodities, for any given quantity of which (that may at the moment be under exchange) it is the equivalent in value, and also for loan and re-investment at a profit. Both these kinds of employment are not possible in the case of ordinary merchandise. A farmer may raise 100 quarters of wheat, he may exchange them away for clothes, coals, or anything else, but he can only re-invest a few bushels of the corn by sowing it on his land, and he can lend none of it for profit. In the same way, coal, iron, hides, indigo, etc., when produced, are consumed; they can be sold and so exchanged, but no part of them can be re-invested or lent at a profit. The producer who sells his produce for coin, in obtaining money, not only gets its full equivalent in value, which he can either exchange by purchase for something else, or hold in reserve with the prospect that it will rise rather than fall in value, but he has an alternative use to which he can put it, that of reinvestment as commercial capital, or putting it out in loan at interest, by either of which methods its quantity increases year by year at a calculable rate of progression.

It is in this double use of money that the stimulus resides which high prices afford to industry. It is true that a high price may bring in no larger a return of any commodity in the exchanges of trade than a low price; low prices, of course, offer the same advantages as high prices, but in a different degree. The more money a producer can obtain by increasing the out-turn of his industry, the greater the rate at which his wealth will increase; and as high prices can only rule when money is abundant, an abundance of money implies increased opportunities of profitable trade and a quicker rate of accumulation as the necessary accompaniment of increasing profits, and acts as an incentive to industry; while a scarcity of money and low prices are the principal causes of a depression of trade. Furthermore, at times when a low level of prices prevails, the returns to investments and loans are not only less, but are more uncertain than at a time of high prices; capital is less sought after for commercial purposes, and the rate of interest is often lower, and as the margin of price within which a profit must range is narrowed, the success of trade ventures is less assured. In treating of the relation of metallic money to prices, it must not be forgotten that it is the money in use, whether in circulation as coin or in the form of paper money (to the extent to which the latter may be supported by bullion reserved for that purpose), to which this argument applies. Paper or documentary money unsupported by such reserves, and bullion or hoarded coin, however much of it there may be scattered about the world, have no permanent effect on prices. It is the stock of money in use, not the stock of money-metal or of coin which may be available for use but which for various reasons is withdrawn from use, that as money influences prices. High prices, then, the result of an abundance of money, are always accompanied by, because they induce, a prosperous state of trade; they impart activity to industrial enterprise and stimulate production. These results in their turn excite a demand for further supplies of money, and thus an abundance of money and commercial activity act and react on one another to the great increase of both. If monetary laws lay no prohibition on the coinage of the precious metals and their free circulation as full legal-tender money, the trade of a country may secure a development indefinitely great; and the material prosperity of the people, from a growing capacity to create commodities for exchange, and from the rising value of the proceeds of its industry when they come to be measured in the productions of other countries, assumes a condition of continuous and uninterrupted progress.

That part of the work of the Commissioners which related to the cause of the fall in prices and its remedy was not, therefore, least in importance or interest among the subjects of their inquiry. At first sight this decline would appear to have arisen from a scarcity of money, and this scarcity, from one point of view, would be owing to the demand for silver having diminished as a consequence of the collapse of the system of the Latin Union. The rupture of the bimetallic tie is held by some to have arrested the demand for silver, and rendered useless a portion of the existing stock of the metal by limiting its employment to that lesser quantity which could be taken up into monometallic currencies, where it would be used only as token, instead of as full-value money. This aspect of the question, however, only covers a part of the field over which the causes that have brought about a fall in the money values of commodities have been at work.

It would hardly be possible to abbreviate the statements of fact and the arguments to be found in §§ 46 to 63, part i. of the Final Report of the Commission, which deal with the appreciation of gold in relation to the fall in prices which has occurred since 1873, without destroying their force; but their result is to leave no room for doubt that the decline in prices is owing partly to considerations affecting commodities, and partly to the world's supply of gold being inadequate to the work of exchanging, which a greatly increased volume of industrial productions has thrown upon it. And of these two sets of causes, the monometallist party in the Commission consider that those touching commodities rather than an appreciation of the standard are accountable for the fall (Final Report, p. 72, § 47). In the case of our own country, with which we are most concerned, Sir Louis Malet quotes figures from the Board of Trade returns, to show that the declared value of our foreign trade is on an average, taken over four years, 1884–87 inclusive, less by

240½ millions per annum, or 29 per cent. than it would have been if it were estimated at the prices prevailing in 1873 (note by Sir L. Malet, Final Report, p. 113). The total value of the trade declined from 626 millions sterling in 1873, to 583½ millions sterling in 1887; while the total tonnage employed in carrying it advanced from nearly 38 millions in 1873 to a little over 56 millions in 1887. These figures prove as conclusively as any to be found in this report, that in recent years prices have declined while the volume of trade has increased; and as low prices do not produce an expansion of trade, they prove that the production of commodities increased more quickly than the supply of money with which they were exchanged for one another, that is to say, the decline in prices was largely due to over-production. Not only is there evidence in detail that the production of many of the principal staples of commerce has increased, but when the quantities and values of imports and exports are compared with the entries and clearances of shipping in the same trade, the accounts for France, Germany, the United States of America, and Italy, as well as those for our own country, place beyond doubt the fact of a marked decline in the gold prices of merchandise. There has, at the same time, been an unusual intensity of trade competition. An immense increase in the quantity of commodities produced, accompanied by a reduction in the cost of transport and growing facilities of communication, and improvements in the organization of credit, directing the flow of capital towards commercial enterprise, characterize the industrial history of this period. These are circumstances affecting commodities.

The circumstances which touch the appreciation of the standard are, that there has arisen a greatly increased demand for gold in the United States, while the out-turn of the metal from the mines in that country has actually fallen off (§ 62 n.); that a new demand for gold on the part of Germany, the Scandinavian kingdoms, Italy and Holland, set in, which was supplied from abroad, and at the same time the annual drain of gold into India (taking into account the net imports only) was only less on the average by about half a million sterling a year between 1876 and 1888, than it was in the ten years ending with 1875. This current of gold constantly setting towards India and never flowing back again, which carries away, on an average, $2\frac{1}{2}$ millions sterling a year, has seriously diminished the supply available for other countries, where it might have been used as money. In India it has been wholly lost to commerce. The abstraction of such a mass of gold metal, which exceeds 130 millions sterling in value during the last fifty-four years, is calculated to enhance the appreciation of gold elsewhere, and to aggravate its injurious effects on trade and industry in a very material degree. The reduction in the annual supply of gold available for countries outside the United States amounts in recent years to 15 millions a year, while the supply of silver to the same countries has only increased to the value of $4\frac{1}{4}$ millions (Final Report, p. 25, § 66). During the ten years, 1876–85, the supply of gold available for money, after deducting that absorbed by the United States and India, was $124\frac{1}{2}$ millions less than in the ten years preceding (Final Report, p. 11, § 37).

The Commissioners reject the theory that the

maintenance of the bimetallic system while it lasted is accounted for by the commercial conditions under which it worked being favourable to the legal ratio. They admit that it may be true that those conditions helped to make the system operative; but unless the system itself is taken into account, they hold this theory to be an inadequate solution of the problem. Why, they ask in effect, with similar circumstances and conditions of a like nature more or less operative both before and since 1873, has the effect on the relative values of the two metals been very different? But the state of affairs since 1873 has been marked by a peculiarity of its own. Since that year, upon gold has been thrown a much larger share of the work of commerce than it had previously undertaken in gold-using countries. The amount of silver money used either as coin or as a reserve for the support of paper money has, at the same time, been much diminished. During the time that gold has been put to double tasks, the supply has been growing less. In addition, the resumption of specie payments in the United States and in France, instead of being met by both metals mainly fell upon gold, and caused a contraction of the currencies which would not have been so severely felt had not silver been partly demonetized in 1874–78. We venture to say that neither this condition of things nor anything approaching to it, and calculated in the same degree to affect the commercial values of the precious metals in one another or in their relation to the value of commodities, occurred previous to 1873. Up to that time, whatever the variations in the productiveness of the mines may have been, the legal regulations which directed the supply of gold and silver to the world's currencies had been, with the exception of the suspension of cash payments during the American civil war, in force with no material alteration for many years; but after 1873, every alteration which it was possible to make in the currencies of many of the principal commercial nations, was made, and the free action of commerce on the values of the precious metals was more seriously interrupted than it had ever been before, not only by these changes, but by a general resort on the part of those nations to protective customs tariffs. Such a fiscal system exerts a most disturbing influence on the determination of values, as the result of, and as they would be determined under, the operation of natural laws; and this, in connection with the causes enumerated above, wholly destroys the analogy which the Commissioners seek to draw between the situation preceding and subsequent to 1873, when they call in question and underrate the extent to which commercial considerations assisted in the maintenance of the system of the fixed ratio during the period of its existence. These circumstances point to the conclusion that the fall in prices is due both to an appreciation of gold arising from an inadequate supply, and to causes affecting commodities which may be described as over-production. How far the partial disuse of silver as money, and its consequent decline in the gold valuation has affected prices, will be considered in connection with the inquiry into the influence of the bimetallic system on the regulation of commercial values.

At the threshold, however, of the inquiry into the connection between an inadequate supply of metallic money and a fall in prices, the Commissioners notice a preliminary objection which traverses the assumption that there is any necessary connection between these two elements of the subject-matter of their inquiry, which they state in the following terms (Final Report, p. 20, §§ 58, 59) :—

"Much controversy has taken place both with regard to the fact above alleged of a general fall in prices, and with regard to the cause to which it is ascribed.

"Before dealing with these questions, however, we must notice a preliminary objection which traverses the assumption that there is any necessary relation between the general level of prices and the scarcity or abundance of gold. Because the prices of commodities are expressed in terms of gold, it has been assumed that a transaction of sale or purchase is in substance what it purports to be in form, namely, an exchange of commodities against gold; and this assumption, it is said, necessarily underlies all the arguments with regard to the supply of gold which are drawn from considerations affecting the prices of commodities.

"But it is pointed out—

"1. That in any one area the nominal value of the transactions is always enormously greater than the quantity of gold available; and that, therefore, it would be impossible for all the transactions pending at any one moment to be actually carried out in the terms in which they are expressed;

"2. That, as a matter of fact, gold actually passes in only an infinitesimal number of transactions;

"3. That in all other transactions the consideration which passes from the purchaser to the seller is really not gold, but a promise to pay gold;

"4. That the prices will consequently be regulated, not by the quantity of gold, but by the quantity of such promises, which will be received in the discharge of debt as equivalent to gold;

"5. That the quantity of such promises to pay, or in other words the volume of credit, has, no doubt, some connection with the quantity of gold; but that the relations between the two are very complex and obscure, vary in different countries and different states of society, and cannot be reduced to any definite rule;

"6. That the connection between the supply of gold and the prices of commodities is consequently not direct, but indirect, acting through the medium of credit, and that a rise or fall in the general level of prices may therefore prove nothing as regards a supply of gold, since it may be due to a diminution or expansion of the volume of credit without any corresponding alteration in the amount of gold."

To these arguments it is replied—

"1. That a distinction must be drawn between that portion of the supply of gold which is actually circulating as coin, and is used in the smaller transactions of commerce, and that portion of the supply which is held in reserve by banks and similar institutions as a basis for the credit which they create;

"2. That between gold in the latter form and the quantity of credit there is a direct arithmetical relation, which may vary in different countries and in different states of society, but which in any one country or any one state of society will be tolerably uniform;

"3. That whatever proportion the volume of

credit may bear to the quantity of gold on which it is based, the value of the former must, in the long run, conform to the value of the latter;

"4. That the supply of gold also operates directly upon the prices of commodities by its effect upon the rate of discount;

"5. That in face of the fact of an alteration of 30 per cent. in the relative value of gold and silver in recent years, and the corresponding relative alteration in the gold and silver prices of the commodities interchanged between the gold-using and the silver-using countries, it is impossible to deny that the standard of value is intimately connected with prices."

These passages refer to the evidence of Messrs. H. D. Macleod and W. Fowler, and that given by Professors Nicholson and Marshall; and discussing the arguments raised in them, the Comissioners express an opinion that the causes which contribute to affect prices are so subtle, and the information which they possess so uncertain, that it is impossible to arrive at any certain conclusion or do more than hazard a statement approximately correct (Final Report, § 46, p. 72).

While Professor Marshall accepts the common doctrine that prices generally rise, other things being equal, in proportion to the volume of the metals which are used as currency; he points out that it is not possible to trace any statistical connection between the amount of currency and the general level of prices, because the volume of currency may remain the same while the mass of commodities offered for exchange may alter, and because the number of times that either commodities or the coins in circulation change hands cannot be calculated, nor can the proportion which purchases with coin bears to purchases made without coin be in any way known. This is very true; and because political economy is not an exact science, and because the circumstances with which it has to deal, do not arise in the operation of immutable physical laws, but depend almost entirely on human volition, directed by a more or less intelligent self-interest, it is not possible to formulate them in any such order as would yield a certain and calculable result in every given case, or even in any great number of cases. It is, however, open to those engaged on this field of research to take advantage of a few broad lines marked out by the experience of mankind, which serve to direct us towards some general conclusions; and having ascertained the facts bearing on any particular matter under inquiry, by arguing on them under the guidance of the ordinary processes of reasoning, to arrive at conclusions which, as far as they go, will prove to be sound.

Money is a term used in different senses according to the context in which it is found; it should therefore be stated that for the purposes of the issue raised in this particular place our own currency must be taken as the limit of the field of discussion, and the term *money* to mean full-value metallic money such as sovereigns, and also Bank of England notes; and credits to mean all other forms of fiduciary money such as bills of exchange, cheques, entries in bankers' books, etc.

While Mr. W. Fowler does not go so far as

Mr. Macleod, who is of opinion that the "quantity of money in any country bears no necessary relation to the quantity of other goods in it, nor to their prices" (Q. 7224); he considers that in connection with prices, "people talk a great deal more about the amount of money in the country, that is to say, bullion or coin, than they ought to do."

Both these witnesses, however, seem to overlook the fact that as the extension and contraction of credit depend on the supply of metallic money, which is the commodity with which trade balances are adjusted, and is therefore the ultimate resource effecting exchanges, it must, *ex vi termini*, be the regulator of price; that is to say, it must fix the terms in which the value of one commodity as compared with another is expressed.

This view is not in conflict with that which Mr. Fowler expresses when he says, "prices depend on facts as to goods more than on facts as to money." We should be inclined to put the word "values" in the place of the word "prices" in this sentence, because (as we show elsewhere), values are determined by the quantities of any two kinds of goods surrendered by their owners in exchange for one another, whereas prices are fixed by the quantity of goods which are surrendered for a given sum of money. Values depend essentially (but not exclusively) on the facts as to goods, and can be ascertained without the help of money at all; but prices depend on the use of money in exchanges, for without money there could be no price; price being the expression of the value of commodities in one another in terms of money. Money at the same time largely affects values, as distinguished from prices, since without metallic money production could hardly go on, nor retail sales be effected, and these are the first and last stages in the processes of commerce.

The Commissioners ask (Final Report, § 41, p. 70), " How then does an expansion or contraction of the metallic currency affect prices?" Where does the volume of the currency come into contact with and exert its influence upon prices?" It is true that a merchant when fixing a price asks no questions about the volume of the currency; that information is ready for him in the high or low price which rules in the market for his merchandise. But the volume of currency exerts an influence on prices in this way: when it increases from an abundance in the available supply, a considerable part of the increase is provided by those owning money forcing a market for it. To put the matter in the simplest way. A capitalist, let us suppose, has £100,000 which he is holding until he can invest the money well, as he depends upon the interest of this money for his income. He requires money for his weekly bills, and invests it in some manner which is not quite as lucrative as he would wish, he in fact forces a market for it. A thousand others are doing the same thing at the same time, as money has been, *ex hypothesi*, accumulating with a view to profitable investment faster than the opportunities of so disposing of it have occurred. They pay more for stocks, merchandise, materials for manufacture, and everything else which they spend their money on than they otherwise would, and the volume of the currency is increased by these accumulations of capital being thus employed, and prices in consequence rise. Another class of capitalists have money to put into trade, and high prices prevailing, their margin of profit is wider than it would otherwise be; they no longer lock up their capital, but embark it in mercantile ventures. Another million thus goes into circulation, and stimulates the activity of those industries which are connected with these enterprises. These activities increase the demand for more capital for use in other trades which are fostered by the expenditure of those into whose hands the increase in the circulation first falls. Prices rise, and as long as the supplies of money are replenished by the prevailing abundance of money, the rise in prices is maintained, the expected profits are realized over and over again, and trade continues to prosper. In this way a plentiful supply of money increases the volume of the currency, comes into contact with and exerts an influence on prices. In these and similar cases the origin of the upward movement of prices is an increase in the stock of metallic money, and when a scarcity of money prevails, these processes are reversed and prices fall. It is impossible for prices to get away from the influence of metallic money. All the results which discounts, credits, bank-rates, and exchanges are supposed to produce on prices, if traced to their origin, are found to arise in an expansion or contraction of the volume of metallic money in circulation. But this is not the view of the matter which Mr. Macleod has set forth in his evidence before the Special Commission, although it is in accordance with that which has always been accepted by economists; viz. "that the mass of the measure of value, as compared with the mass of commodities, is that which in the long run and as a whole is price; that it not only regulates price, but is price" (Q. 4684).

Mr. Macleod, in his evidence (Q. 7224), contended that the quantity of money in any country bears no necessary relation to the quantity of other goods in it, nor to their prices, and this opinion is derived from the important part which he considers that credit, as contrasted with money, plays in modern commerce. Mr. Macleod is of opinion (Q. 7177) that credit in all its forms has exactly the same influence on prices and on production as an equal amount of bullion; that (Q. 7206) if a man buys with credit it produces exactly the same effect on prices as if he buys with gold; that (Q. 7312) if you want to buy a thing you must either buy it by money or credit, and that credit has the same effect on prices as money has.

Tooke's opinion is rather different from this. "There is no doubt that a use of credit, whether by Government or by individuals, is virtually, *while in operation*, equivalent in its effect on prices to money" ("Tooke on Prices," vol. i. p. 94, note). The italics are ours. Mr. Macleod's theory of the efficiency of credit as money contains no such limitation as these words imply.

For the purposes of this part of the inquiry, it was taken that the coin in circulation in the country amounts to 100 or 120 millions, and that the amount of credit is 6000 millions (Q. 7193), or from fifty to sixty times the currency. The examination of Mr. Macleod's theory soon made it apparent that many kinds of credit which go to make up this 6000 millions, either serve only to move money from one industry to another, and are therefore not effective additions to the circulating medium, or are not employed to effect exchanges of commodities at all, and cannot therefore assist in determining market prices. The witness therefore qualified his previously expressed opinion by saying (Q. 7366), " I only consider those things have an effect on prices which come into commerce." Even with this limitation on the meaning of the term "credits," credit and coin have not pound for pound the same effect on prices, for it was shown (Qs. 7194–99) that while the withdrawal of 120 millions of coin from circulation would cause a collapse of our whole system of commerce, the withdrawal of the same amount of credit would have very little effect on prices.

Credit and coin can only take an equal share in fixing prices, if the nature of the two methods of commerce—that is, the exchange of goods for coin and exchange of commodities against one another, under that which has properly been called a highly organized system of barter, and to which the Clearing House gives its name—were identical, which they are not. Shiploads of corn, wool, and hides, and tons of iron, copper, and coal are exchanged for one another by the banks giving their owners credit corresponding to the money value of the merchandise. The credit opened, say on the basis of £10,000 worth of corn on board a ship at sea, allows the owner to draw cheques with which he pays for £10,000 worth of copper still in the smelting house, and by the sale of this, when it comes into the market, his credit for

I

that transaction is extinguished, and ceases to work, and the effect on prices of this credit begins and ends with this particular piece of business. But in the case of coin, if instead of obtaining a credit for £10,000 the trader were to coin bullion to that value and pay down that amount of money, the money would go on working, and not only exchange the corn for the copper, but wool, iron, and hides for coal, tin, etc., to that value in each case, and so on through innumerable exchanges of other commodities. The 6000 millions is the sum of all mercantile credits, the effect of each of which on prices is single and determinate. Not so with coin, which continues to influence prices as long as it is in use.

In order to compare this volume of credit with 100 or 120 millions of metallic currency, it must be assumed that each coin is withdrawn from circulation as soon as it has made a purchase, in the same way that a credit is exhausted and extinguished as soon as it has done its work. The coin can be used ten thousand times, the credit cannot be used again; another credit has to be created for each fresh transaction, while additional sovereigns need not be coined for the purpose of further exchanges. A bill of exchange for £100 may be endorsed twelve times and be still the same bill of exchange, though it is not the same in the sense that 100 sovereigns changing hands twelve times are the same coins; the twelve endorsements constitute twelve transactions, and as none of the endorsements have been placed on the bill without consideration passing to the endorser, it is supported in its course through business by twelve separate credits, and does the work not of £100 used over and over again an indefinite number of times, but the work of £1200 used once and then withdrawn from circulation (Qs. 7331–36). The sum of the credits—6000 millions, or whatever it may amount to—must not be contrasted with 120 millions of coin in circulation, but with that figure multiplied by the number of exchanges which the currency serves to effect, i.e. by many hundreds of millions.

Understood as the expression of a force in commerce, it may be conceded that the extension of credit contrivances has its effect on prices; but the force itself to which the high level of prices in England, compared with that prevailing in more backward countries is owing, is the continued and increasing productiveness of British industry all the world over. Credit only adds to the wealth of a country so far as it is backed up by commodities. If mercantile credits increase, they increase in correspondence with an increase in industrial productions, and with the purchase and sale of increasing quantities of goods, and the country is richer, not by the increase in credits, but by the increase in commodities. When a shipload of corn is exchanged against a given value of iron by the employment of credit instead of money, one or the other of them plays the part which coin would take were the exchange made with money. If the value of the corn is £10,000, then £10,000 is added for the moment to the circulation, and if in one day a thousand such transactions are carried through, then the effect on prices is the same as if ten millions were added to the circulation, and withdrawn and wiped out of existence after being once used. It follows that credit, or to speak more exactly, the value of the commodities upon which credit rests, has an effect on prices; but it is not a continuing effect, and it is very much less, almost indefinitely less, than that which would be produced by a permanent addition to the currency, in any given space of time, of a mass of coin equal in value to the nominal value of the credits created during the same period.

In his answer to Q. 7231, Mr. Macleod attributes the rise of prices which has taken place in England since the Conquest, and the decline in the rate of interest since the time of King Charles II., to the development of "credit," because "credit has exactly the same effect on prices as money." His argument seems to be that credit has made as effective additions to the circulation, as if coin to the nominal value of the credits had been added to the currency; and that the rate of interest has declined because instead of money being advanced on bills of exchange, credits are opened which compete with one another, and bring down the rate of interest. This view of the matter, however, takes no note of the production of commodities, and ignores the fact that credit in sound banking is only extended to those who are known to have means at command wherewith to meet their obligations. "If credit is as good as money, and anybody can create credit," says Mr. Macleod, "I do not see any limit to prices." This conclusion proves nothing, and the fallacy which vitiates is to be found in the assumptions upon which it rests being in disagreement with actual facts; and these are, that "credit is as good as money," and that "anybody can create credit." The limit to prices, that is to say, to a rise in prices, is set by nature, in the difficulties which she places in the way of the profitable excavation from the earth of the money metals; and credit is limited by the capacity of the producing classes to create commodities which have a sufficient commercial value to serve as a basis for credit. Credit, as we have shown, is not as good as money, and so far from being unlimited, it is strictly limited both by the value of the commodities which it is employed to exchange, and by the amount of the loan fund, which is the ultimate guarantee for the settlement of the balances arising out of these exchanges. Nor is it every one who can create credit, for mercantile purposes those only can do so who own merchandise or wealth in one of its numerous forms, and then not beyond the limit of its value.

There is, moreover, an influence which money (using the term in the sense above defined) exerts on prices, which these arguments do not touch, and its character being more international than local, it tends to diminish the influence of credit and to increase its own, on prices, universally. The more civilized a country is, the larger is its expenditure of money in the initial stages of production. In some backward countries, payments in kind, or in grants of land, or labour rents, are often substituted for money. There is, for example, more money spent in bringing the same weight of corn to market in western Europe than in the plains of India. Such arrangements lessen the use and demand for coin. Similarly in the final stages of commerce, *i.e.* the ultimate consumption of commodities, the custom of cash payments is in progressive communities largely and increasingly prevalent. On the other hand, in semi-civilized countries, book-debts and barter to a great extent take the place of cash dealings; but even in these countries, as people become familiarized with the use of metallic money, the demand for the precious metals is incessantly growing. It is chiefly, though not entirely, in the intermediate stage in which commodities change hands in the wholesale trade that coin is dispensed with; but even in these exchanges the amount of coin available for the expenditure which production involves on the one hand, and for retail purchasers on the other, is the principal factor in the fixation of price. If a shipload of corn from India and a shipload of wool from Australia change hands by the balancing against one another of cheques for so many thousand pounds, that which the valuation rests upon, which determines what the figures shall be which are entered on the cheques, is the amount of coin spent in bringing the merchandise to market compared with the amount of coin which, by the trader's estimate, will be realized when the corn reaches the baker and the wool reaches the clothier; and these estimates in their turn are based on the prices which these tradesmen calculate that they will obtain by the sale of loaves of bread and bales of cloth across the counter.

Prices, therefore, so far from being independent of the stock of coin in the country or in the world, are directly due to the relations which capital holds to commodities in commerce. They would no doubt be very different from what they are, if credit did not exist, and if commodities were at the same time produced in undiminished quantities, and could only be exchanged for one another by the passing of coin. But as trade is conducted amongst us, that which fixes the price of commodities is their value in one another, and that value depends upon what they cost to produce and what they sell for; the measure of that value is the relation which the volume of merchandise bears to the stock of money in use for the purchase of goods. If the stock is large, that measure may be extended and prices be high; if the stock is small, the measure will be contracted, and prices will be low, although on each occasion the relative value of the commodities may remain unaltered. Price is the expression of that value, and it speaks in varying tones as the stock of money available for the initial production and ultimate purchase of commodities has greater or less demands made upon it for those purposes. So far as credit is concerned, its influence on prices is apparent rather than real. The actual influence is exercised by the various kinds of merchandise which credit serves to exchange, and by the relation which their volume holds to the coin in circulation in the country. If, therefore, a currency system has a tendency to enlarge the volume of money in circulation throughout the world, it operates to raise prices in two ways; more money is given than before for the same article, because there is more to give, and "credits" at the same time increase with the increase in the fund which is available for loans and for the ultimate settlement of credit balances; and all the results on prices which can fairly be ascribed to the operation of credit under the conditions imposed by sound banking and honest trade, have their origin in the expansion of the volume of metallic money, actually or potentially (as in the case of bank-notes), in circulation.

"There are," as Mr. Macleod very truly says (Q. 7231), "two great branches of commerce. There is, first of all, the commerce in commodities, and in the next place, there are commercial and mercantile loans and bills. Now, one part of money goes to exchange with commodities, and another part goes to buy and sell debts. One part of the money goes to affect prices, and the other affects the rate of interest."

We have seen the effect on prices exercised by that part of money which goes to exchange with commodities. The way in which the other, which goes to buy and sell debts, affects the price of money, that is to say, the rate of interest, is as follows.

The proportion of the two parts must obviously vary with the increase or decrease of the metallic circulation. A sudden and large increment to the circulation will—unless there is at the same moment a correspondingly large and sudden increase of commodities offered for sale for money, which can scarcely ever happen—permit both an enlargement of the loan fund, and cause the rate of interest to fall. On the other hand, if new openings for profitable commerce occur without any addition being made to the supply of money, the rate of interest will rise. And as it is the mass of commodities exchanging with one another which lays down the limits within which credit is obtainable, the effect of credit on the price of money is determined by the number of transactions dependent on the loan fund; or in other words, by the number of credits for the ultimate settlement of which the loan fund is the guarantee. It therefore follows that an expansion of credit, so far from diminishing the demand for metallic money, must necessarily be accompanied by an increase in the supply, as such an expansion is only possible if the guarantee for the ultimate settlement of the increased volume of credits, that is, the loan fund, is itself increased. That this is the case is proved by the circumstance that the country which has absorbed most gold in recent years is the United States of America, and there is no country in which a greater development of credit and banking has taken place than in the States. But this increase in the loan fund, upon which the expansion of "credits" depends, is derived from an increase in the metallic circulation, of which, as has already been said, a proportion goes to exchange commodities, and as this proportion is enlarged, prices necessarily rise. Whether, therefore, we look to the prices of commodities or to the price of money, metallic money must be held to exert an influence on prices, not less, but greater than that of credit or documentary money to the same value circulating in the market at the same time. It is, therefore, an economic error to assert that (Q. 7224) "the quantity of money in any country bears no necessary relation to the quantity of other goods in it, nor to their prices." An increase in the supply of money involves an increase to the capital fund of the country on which the vitality of its commerce depends. Productive industry expands because its natural aliment, capital, is obtainable in larger quantities, and although the proportion supplied in coin is very small in comparison with the nominal value of the "credits" which commerce creates, yet the scarcity or abundance of metallic money exercises a paramount influence on the extent of these credits, and therefore on the contraction or expansion of industrial enterprise. Money, to credit, is like seed corn to the harvest: the less sown on the land, the smaller the returns into the farmers' barns; and the less metallic money there is in circulation, the less capital will there be at the traders' command, and the smaller will be the bulk of merchandise in commerce, and the lower will be the level of prices.

The difference between a rich and a poor, an advanced and a backward country, between, for instance, England and Hindustan, consists in their respective powers of production. The power of producing commodities in demand among mankind is wealth. The machinery of production is kept at work by money, credit, and barter. Of barter as a means of exchange in use among primitive people, we need not here speak. Credit, we have seen, rests on money as its ultimate basis, and the exchanges of commerce which credit is capable of effecting are assisted or hindered, and their amount, and therefore their aggregate value, affected for better or for worse by the supply of money; and as industrial production cannot go on except by exchanges and therefore by the use, greater or less, of money, and as also production is impossible as the first step to trade without the expenditure of coin, it ought always to be the main object of currency legislation to afford facilities to the people to add to the stock of money in circulation among them. So far as legislation fails to effect this object it restricts the flow of the precious metals into the currency of the country, and interferes with the natural expansion of commerce; it incidentally depresses the level of prices and diminishes the stimulus to industry which high prices afford, and in limiting the operation of credit checks industrial enterprise, and under some circumstances compels resort to barter. Of the injurious effects of the custom of barter on the prosperity of the people, as the result of defective monetary arrangements, the internal trade and the currency law of India afford conspicuous examples.

It is of importance to settle this question, whether the abundance or scarcity of money in connection with merchandise regulates price, because if Mr. Macleod's view of the matter is the correct one, it becomes of no importance whether there is much or little money in circulation, and the bimetallic system can afford no relief to the depression of trade and industry by exercising the power which it claims to possess of supplying to commerce any amount of either kind of money which it may require; nor will an increase in the currency of India commensurate with the growth of its commerce be of any advantage to the people of that country.

Another theory has been started, opposed to the quantitative theory of the action of money on prices, which, while it admits that there is a relation between the supply of money and prices, aims at proving that prices assist in determining the quantity of the precious metals to be used as money, rather than that prices are themselves determined by that quantity.* The groundwork of this theory is that the general economic circumstances of a community of which the range of the prices of staple articles is an important part, and that in a greater degree the

* *The Nineteenth Century*, November, 1889: Article, "A Problem in Money," by R. Giffen.

range of incomes (and incomes are a part of prices), determine in ordinary circumstances the quantity of the precious metals used as money in circulation in that form. Further, that the amounts of the precious metals so used as money do not vary proportionately with small or ordinary fluctuations of prices, although they are liable to great changes corresponding with great changes in the range of incomes and the range of the prices of staple commodities.

Token money may be put out of consideration in this case, as its supply is arbitrarily limited; full-value money, supplied in quantities only limited by the volition of the people, is of these two kinds of money that which exerts any material influence on prices. It is true that the amount of this kind of money would not vary proportionately with small or ordinary fluctuations in prices; these fluctuations depend on the quantity of goods in commerce in relation to the quantity of money at hand to effect their exchanges with one another. If these goods increase faster than the supply of money, a variation in price will occur, prices will fall, the quantity of money will not have varied, and this stationary condition of supply, coupled with an alteration in the demand for money arising out of an increased presentation of goods in the market, will create the fluctuation. The quantity of money in this case, clearly, affects prices.

The author of this theory goes on to describe our full-value gold money, although unlimited legal tender, as a kind of small change only, because the banking system of this country reduces the gold coin in circulation to the lowest possible quantity, and argues that the amount of such small change is strictly regulated by the habits of the people, and not liable to change—or to change greatly—with ordinary fluctuations in prices. The bank reserves, he considers, are of great importance in this connection, as by them wholesale payments are made; but that the demand for the precious metals as reserves, is also a demand for a fixed quantity, or nearly so, dependent on the habits and customs of a commercial community in given economic circumstances, among which the range of prices is only one of the factors, and that it is not a demand which varies materially with ordinary fluctuations of prices. Also that this theory holds good of that part of the reserves which is used as a guarantee of wholesale payments, which is remitted to and fro, and is at one time part of the reserve in England, at another time in France; that the whole reserves and precious metals in course of remittance in the civilized world may be considered a single fund, which varies even less as a whole than the particular part of it in individual countries.

There is, however, no evidence that the demand either in respect of the money in the pockets of the people or in the bank reserves, is a "*fixed* demand;" on the contrary, the fluctuations in price which arise from the supply being in excess of, or inadequate to, the demand for money, proves that the "demand" is *not* fixed, although the supply may be stationary; were the demand fixed, no fluctuations would occur. The same supply of money has to do more or less work according as commodities in exchange increase or decrease; in the one case there is an increase and in the other a decrease in the demand for money, with a corresponding fall or rise in prices. The circumstance that the amount of money in the reserves does not oscillate with any special reference to the usual fluctuations in prices, is that which constitutes money the regulator of price. Price is the proportion subsisting between money and the work which money has to do; price is (as has been said before) the expression of the value of commodities in one another in terms of money. Money very truly is, as the writer in the *Nineteenth Century* argues, in any view of the case, merchandise, and the demand for money a demand for merchandise, and it is this which makes it so sure a denominator of values; it varies in its own value relatively to all merchandise less than the value of any single kind of merchandise varies against that of any other kind, it has therefore more stability of value than any other commodity under exchange in the market. The incident in the use of money which this writer mentions (above quoted), that the whole reserves in the civilized world may be considered as a single fund, which varies even less as a whole than the particular parts of it in individual countries, is an element of this stability of value, and contributes to the efficiency of money as a regulator of price. One supporter of this theory argues as follows: "What is the quantity of money in use but the number of the batches of commodities in the market multiplied by the price of each batch? It is impossible to bring money into currency without simultaneously creating a demand for commodities. A supply of money in circulation and a demand for commodities are inseparable, like the convexity and concavity of a circle. They are not two facts, but two sides of the same fact. Of course, if a sudden increase in the demand of commodities is not met by a corresponding increase in production, there will be a temporary rise in prices, but when production overtakes the additional demand prices may again subside, although the volume of money in circulation has permanently expanded." *

This line of reasoning is partly beside the mark, and partly serves to prove the contrary of its contention. If prices determine the quantity of money, it is a mere *petitio principii* to talk about batches of commodities multiplied by the price of each, until it is ascertained what price is? what it is composed of? how it is evolved out of the elements of its composition? To say that "it is impossible to bring money into currency without simultaneously creating a demand for commodities," implies that high prices stimulate the production of commodities; in other words, price being the quantitative relation between money and commodities, the higher the price the greater the supply of commodities—not of money. As regards money rather the contrary. High prices offer less inducement, *per se*, to the circulation of money than low prices, because in the former case a given quantity of money commands less value in commodities than in the latter case, and, *e converso*, high prices allow of a given batch of goods being sold for more money than low prices allow. This view of the relation of money to prices is put forward in connection with the *merchandise* theory of money, and if that theory is sound, as no doubt in the long run it is, then it follows that in a free currency, money is of value in inverse ratio to its quantity, just as any other merchandise is in commerce.

"A supply of money in circulation, and a demand

* *Times* (Correspondence), January 11, 1890.

for commodities," are truly described as "inseparable;" but whether the demand for commodities will produce the supply desired is quite another matter, and until the demand does effect this object, the quantity of money being slightly in excess of the quantity of goods under exchange, prices remain high. And it is equally true that "when production overtakes the additional demand, prices may again subside, although the volume of money in circulation has permanently expanded." This argument does not touch the point at issue, which is, that although prices may have subsided without a contraction of the circulation, they are fixed by the relative quantities of money and commodities, whatever those quantities may be. Because these quantities have assumed a different relation to one another from that which they held before, that is to say, because prices have altered, not an iota is added to the proof that the resulting alteration of price has altered the supply of money; on the contrary, the increase in the circulation of the money is shown to have been an antecedent condition to the rise and to the permanent alteration of the price. The theory clearly involves an inversion of cause and effect, and shows how impossible it is to get away from the influence of money on price. If it were possible to do so, if it were the case that money did not determine prices, but that prices determined the quantity of money in use, it would then become necessary to show what it is which creates prices in the first instance. The plea that "the general economic circumstances of a community . . . determine the quantity of the precious metals used as money in circulation," is wanting in particularity, and is too indefinite for the purpose of practical investigation into the causes of which price is the effect, and therefore fails to overthrow the foundations upon which the hitherto accepted definition of price rests, viz. that price is the relation existing between the mass of the measure of value and the mass of commodities in commerce.

There is another view of the quantitative theory of money which regards its increase for commercial purposes as superfluous. It states that to double or to halve all the money in England at a stroke would make no one richer or poorer; that it is a mistake to suppose that currency makes trade; that if we had more circulating medium we should be no better off. This is not without truth; but the generalization is too wide, and covers more ground than it can hold. Whether an increase or decrease of the currency in circulation is beneficial, or the money useless, depends on its correspondence with the supply of commodities under exchange in the markets. If the supply is stationary, and circumstances do not permit the use of expedients in substitution of money, while the work thrown on the currency is increasing, the country is decidedly the worse off.

The late Mr. Bonamy Price used to employ the metaphor of a cart to illustrate the function of money as a vehicle for transferring property from one man to another. If there are many carts, the transfers are quick and numerous; if few, the contrary. If, for instance, one district produces coal and no corn, and another corn and no coal, the one cannot supply the wants of the other with sufficient completeness unless the means of transport are commensurate with the loads of corn and coal which are ready for despatch from either place. It may be said that as money decreases in quantity each unit serves to transfer more property; while, in the illustration, the carrying capacity of the carts does not increase with their deficiency in numbers. This is of course true, and it is proved by the circumstance that the more wealthy a community becomes, its monetary system becomes more complete; and although its requirement for money increases, it does not increase in the same ratio as its wealth. But that the expansion of industrial production does involve an expanding demand for money is proved by the issue of the event, by the fact that great producing countries hold and use, *per capita*, more money than those which are behind them in the scale of material prosperity; and this element in the case the theory in question overlooks. In such countries the custom of barter generally prevails, indicating a condition of industrial stagnation from which extrication is impossible as long as the people are prevented by legislative interference from supplying themselves with the material for money as fast as they may require it.

Mr. Price's analogy of the cart is much to the point, although it may not go on all fours with the relation of money to trade. Gold may, under pressure, carry a double load which a cart could not do; but this advantage is individual, not general. Where the supply of money is restricted, it is in a few hands; it is less diffused among the public generally than when it is plentiful, and, like the carts, can only do duty for those who hold it. To this it will be answered, that if it were increased, similar inequalities of distribution would occur, a large part of the supply would be concentrated in a few hands, a small part be found among the remainder of the population. But this is not altogether the case, such an abundance is the result and sum of a vast amount of individual effort, of industrial activity moving from a thousand new centres on to fresh fields of production. An abundance of currency assists enterprise in a manner that nothing else can; a scarcity of money (since money is the mechanism of industry) prevents this movement by withholding the apparatus of motion. Men create less wealth because at every turn they meet with difficulties in detail in carrying out their plans, obstacles to ready payment for services, to co-operative union, to quick returns of profit, and so forth; which, as the volume of the currency increases, disappear. Double the money in circulation, or double the carriage used for exchanging the produce of the two districts, and you double or quadruple the returns to the industry of the whole people by providing an indefinitely greater number of men with the mechanism of exchange; and in doing so you extend to incalculable limits the range of production, and the potentiality of wealth. True, it may be, that a *sudden* access of money does a nation more harm than good: this is because the increase is not the result of sustained effort, of the creation of commodities by honest industry, and therefore openings for applying it at once to a further development of industry have not been already provided and are not at hand; but at the same time an artificial restriction on the supply, such as the general disuse of a large portion of one of the precious metals as money involves, is calculated to repress industrial energy, and choke the springs of enterprise at their source; while to allow a people full liberty to use as much money of each metal as they may require, secures a gradual increment to the currency which is an unmixed benefit to the community.

The conclusion which these considerations lead up to is, that the bimetallists are right in insisting on the importance of an enlargement of the measure of value, or, which is the same thing, of the volume of the metallic circulation, corresponding with a progressive expansion of industrial production, as a means towards keeping prices steady; but whether their system is capable of bringing this enlargement about is quite another matter, and into this part of the question we proceed to inquire.

CHAPTER VI.

BIMETALLISM AND THE SUPPLY OF MONEY.

Claim of bimetallism to increase volume of currency and raise prices examined—Alleged universal influence of bimetallic valuation of gold and silver money disposed of by the facts of 1873—Influence of the system confined to use of one, not of both kinds of money—Causes and occasions of replenishment of a bimetallic currency—Opinions about the action of the bimetallic tie on the exchanges—Had the system been maintained, silver monometallism would have resulted—Supply of gold to bimetallic countries could not have been secured—View of the action of the monetary law in the "Theory of Bimetallism" examined—Relative value not dependent on relative production—Effect of annual production on relative value of precious metals—Which has but little effect on their value in commodities, and therefore on their exchange value—Manner in which the system fails to secure sufficient supply of money—Restricts supply in correspondence with the supply of the dearer metal—Real rise of values only accompanies rise of prices in terms of the dearer metal—When both kinds of money are supplied at commercial rates of exchange no such limitation exists—Conclusion, that the alleged universal influence of the fixed-ratio system over the values of gold and silver cannot be proved—The strength of the bimetallic tie depended on the quality of legal tender it gave to money, not on the fixation of the ratio.

ONE of the Commissioners describes the bimetallists as holding generally "that the present depression of prices is mainly the consequence of a scarcity and appreciation of gold; that gold is now appreciated owing to its supply being inadequate for its purposes; that to create a new standard of value, combining gold and silver in a permanently fixed ratio to one another, would enlarge the mass of the measure of value and relieve prices from the disturbing influences to which they are now subject" (Qs. 7222, 23).

This description may be amplified from the evidence of two eminent bimetallists, who are of opinion that the operation of the system will be: to act upon prices by restoring the *status quo ante* on the presumption that the existing state of things has been the cause of a general fall of prices; that bimetallism would increase the amount of silver which would come within the privilege of being legal-tender and thereby increase the volume of currency in gold-using countries (Qs. 4458, 59); that the appreciation of gold would be neutralized to some extent through the greater abundance of the standard money; that this increase of the standard money would act in the same way as if gold discoveries were made; that the system would act beneficially by increasing the quantity of money and stimulating trade; that a great expansion of trade and commerce would result from both metals being freely minted without any very great disturbance or very great inflation of prices; that a tendency would be exhibited towards a rise in price, and that this tendency would stimulate trade (Qs. 4073–76).

The investigations of the Special Commission into the origin of changes in the relative values of the precious metals affords very good reasons for questioning the ability of the system of the Latin Union to obtain these results. It comes out very clearly that one feature of the French system has been that since 1803, France has sometimes had a currency approaching to monometallism, if not actually monometallic; and it has happened that whenever the compensatory action of the law of the fixed ratio has been called into play, its result was to confine the currency almost entirely to that metal which was the cheapest for the time being. Thus from 1816 to 1820, gold was practically the standard, and from 1821 to 1850, silver, and from 1820 to 1847, there ruled a premium on gold varying from a little below 1 to 2 per cent.

This being the case, and the bimetallic system having thus for long periods of time bestowed a monometallic currency on France, it follows that whatever advantage trade might derive from that enlargement of the measure of value which is supposed to be secured by the use of both gold and silver money in unrestricted quantities at a fixed rate of exchange, was not obtained on those occasions. The Commissioners, nevertheless, state their opinion to be as follows: "The view that it (the bimetallic system) could only affect the market price to the extent to which there was a demand for it (silver) for currency purposes in the Latin Union, or to which it was actually taken to the mints of those countries is, we think, fallacious. The fact that the owner of silver could in the last resort take it to those mints and have it converted into coin which would purchase commodities at the ratio of $15\frac{1}{2}$ of silver to 1 of gold, would, in our opinion, be likely to affect the price of silver in the market generally, whoever the purchaser and for whatever country it was destined. It would enable the seller to stand out for a price approximating to the legal ratio, and would tend to keep the market steady at about that point" (part i. §§ 192-196).*

The question here obviously arises; why, if the French system could affect the market price of silver and gold, beyond the extent to which there was a demand for it for currency purposes in the Latin Union or to which it might be taken to the mints of those countries, did not the Union accept the discarded silver of Germany in 1873, and trust to the power, which it claims, of attracting as much money-metal as commerce requires into its system, and induce a current of gold from the East (where an immense stock of the metal, unused as money, was in existence), which would have balanced the silver

* The following paragraph concludes an argument in support of the contention which the Commissioners pronounce to be fallacious, and is probably one among other similar expressions of opinion referred to in this place. "Now, what was the principle at work from 1803 to 1876, which gave its efficiency to the fixed ratio of exchange for the gold and silver money of France, but the principle of the 'intrinsic ratio'? It was because that principle was always at work that the coin of one kind which, valued at $1 : 15\frac{1}{2}$, became redundant, disappeared, and went to foreign countries, where its intrinsic value gave it its full effect in commerce, or was held by its owners until a turn of the wheel of fortune restored it to its full intrinsic value in the French currency and at the fixed ratio. We therefore venture to maintain that while the law of France fixed a *ratio of exchange* for the gold and silver of its domestic currency, it never did fix and never pretended to fix a *ratio of value* as between gold and silver metal even in France; much less, as is now asserted, did that law fix for seventy years the exchange value of gold and silver in foreign countries lying beyond the scope of the French currency system" (*National Review*. September, 1886, p. 19: Article, "Bimetallism," by the author).

supplied by Germany, and have maintained the equilibrium of the fixed ratio? The answer is, that the reason why the Latin Union did not accept the silver offered by Germany, was because its system had no inherent capacity for attracting the counterbalancing supply of gold.

If the courses of commerce were bringing this stock of silver into the system of the Union, they would have brought gold from the East likewise; but the impending influx of silver from Germany had no connection with commerce, and for that reason it was hopeless to look for a supply of gold from any quarter wherewith to meet it. It is, in fact, the force of commerce, and not the force of a monetary law, which lays down, when gold and when silver, and what quantities of each, shall be supplied to a bimetallic currency. It is also clear that the monetary law must be able to keep both kinds of money in circulation, in order to exert the influence claimed for it over the currencies of foreign countries. Foreigners will not coin their gold or silver into a bimetallic currency unless they can buy commodities with the money so coined. If this cannot be done, the attraction ceases, the cause does not act, and the effect (an influx of money into the currencies) does not follow.

The fact that the owner of silver or gold could coin his metal into the French currency proves nothing, unless he could also circulate it. What we require to see is proof that a legal fixation of the rate of exchange for gold and silver kept both in circulation within the territorial range of the law, and provided both kinds of money indifferently for the purchase of goods in the markets. Unless the system secured this, one or other of the precious metals, although it were coined into the currencies, would only circulate in small quantities. The withdrawal of the bulk of the undervalued metal which might be available for coin would leave its price unaffected in the markets generally, or only affected for the worse, and the inducement for more to come from abroad would not exist.*

The converse of the theory, which is thus described as "fallacious," is that the system of the Latin Union not only regulates the price of the precious metals over a large part of Europe, but in India and in Asia generally, and in other parts of the globe also, and that it is able to do this because the owner of silver or the owner of gold can coin either into the currencies of the Union and purchase commodities at the rate of $15\frac{1}{2}$ of silver to 1 of gold. Now, commodities are not purchased at a ratio, and what these words mean is, that foreign bullion coined into the currency would exchange, silver for gold at that rate, and that commodities would be procurable for either kind of money at prices fixed by that metallic par. But the conditions of the currency which the system creates are such that at any time, although coin may be minted, it cannot be used without loss for making payments, and consequently will not be employed to purchase commodities "at $15\frac{1}{2}$ of silver to 1 of gold." The

---

* Subsequent to the completion of this book, a letter from Mr. R. Giffen has appeared in the *Times*, February 1, 1890, which by a parallel argument based on statistical evidence, of actual gold and silver values, for long periods, both before and after 1803, supports the contention that the influence of the fixed ratio was extremely limited.

influence ascribed to the system in foreign countries would, therefore, not arise from the simultaneous commercial use of both metals in unrestricted quantities in a bimetallic country, but from the operation of a principle exactly its opposite, viz. the almost or quite exclusive use of one metal only. It is not "bimetallism," but an alternating silver or gold "monometallism," which exerts whatever influence is exerted by this sort of currency on the attraction of the precious metals from abroad. Prices in the bimetallic country would, if it were the turn, say, for silver to be the standard, become silver prices, in the regulation of which the other metal would play a merely nominal part, and the enlargement of the currency would be limited by the supply of the single-standard metal for conversion into money; in other words, the increase in the circulation would consist of money of one metal with a corresponding decrease in the supply of the other. But in point of fact, there are two causes why, and two occasions when, the precious metals should flow into a bimetallic currency. One is when the system acts towards lowering prices, and then one metal, or both, as circumstances may require, will be coined into the currency for the purchase of commodities, and their export to dearer markets; this cause can neither occur often nor operate for long. The owners of the appreciating metal will not convert it into the coin of the bimetallic currency during one day longer than they can use it more profitably within the limits of the Union than at home, and as an inducement for foreign countries to export the metal, it cannot have more than an evanescent effect. The "purchasing of commoditics" theory is therefore of very little importance in its bearing on the question of the enlargement of the measure of value.

It is the second of the two reasons which provides the stronger inducement to the import of foreign bullion of one metal into the limits of the Union; that is to say, the prospect of purchasing bullion of the other metal at a price lower than its market value in the place to which it is intended to export it. But this inducement, as is well known, can under no circumstances act on the price of gold and silver in one another for more than a short period of time. The undervalued metal is immediately withdrawn from circulation. No matter where it goes, it does not stay in the bimetallic currency. The would-be-purchaser of cheap gold with foreign silver finds that it has gone to a premium, and is out of circulation, and is no longer obtainable on the terms which would induce him to export silver for its purchase. This cause cannot therefore attract any material amount of metal into a bimetallic currency; and it is only in these two ways that the system can exercise the influence which is claimed for it as operating to enlarge the measure of value by bringing within the privilege of legal tender a larger quantity of either metal than would otherwise be the case, and increasing the circulation of metallic money.

If, when any given quantity of both metals had been coined at the proportionate weights of 1 to $15\frac{1}{2}$ in the bimetallic mints, the money of one kind was partly or entirely withheld from use, the price of the other in the market generally can in no way have been regulated by a nominal circulation and nominal exchange of both, since a seller of the cheaper metal could not stand out for a price for it in the dearer metal when there was no more of the latter in the bimetallic market for which it could be sold.

So far as the bimetallic method availed to keep the market price of silver in gold steady at the fixed ratio, its operation was confined to that amount of either metal which could be profitably exchanged into the other at that rate; and as the law which fixed the rate only ruled in the countries combined in the Latin Union, its efficiency outside those countries (if it had any), for regulating this price, depended on its coincidence with the natural or true market valuation. This true valuation of gold and silver in one another was fixed by the transactions of commerce, and the legal price of the Latin Union was, as a matter of fact, brought into conformity with the commercial price at the sacrifice of one of the fundamental principles of the system, that is to say, by the more or less complete exclusion of one of the two metals from actual circulation.

If, therefore, the sum of gold which may at different times have been the equivalent in value of greater or smaller sums of silver, was determined by a natural law, evolved out of the free action of commerce; and if the ability of the commercial classes to bring their gold and silver to the test of the bimetallic valuation, stopped short at the coinage of the metals, and found practically no field for its exercise in the free exchange of any amount of either kind of the money so coined, for the other sort; it seems as clear, as reason can make any proposition, that the utmost which can be said in favour of the influence of the French monetary law, is, that it *was* confined to the demand for the precious metals for currency purposes in the Latin Union, and therefore the theory of its more extended influence which the Special Commission favour, is untenable.

There is nothing in the investigations of the Special Commission to warrant the expectation that if the Latin Union were to revert to its former system, it would be able to keep unlimited supplies of both metals circulating in its currencies. We venture to repeat what has in many quarters been said before, that the reason why the advocates of the system of the fixed ratio desire the co-operation of the principal gold-using nations of the world, and stipulate that India shall not change her system—that is to say, shall not use gold legal-tender money—is, that without this assistance the countries working it would run the risk of becoming silver monometallic, and serve as a reservoir into which any amount of silver, that could be excavated at a cost sufficiently low to permit its exchange for commodities at a profit, might flow and remain there.

The Commissioners in their general report come to the conclusion that the circumstances connected with the supply of the precious metals do not sufficiently account for the altered conditions in their relative values which have come into existence since 1873 (part i. § 187). These conditions are briefly stated in the note added to part iii. of the Report by Sir Louis Malet (p. 107, § 7). "It will be observed that during the first seventy years of the century, although the quantities of the two metals produced varied in relative value from 3·227 to 1, to ·44 to 1, their value in the market varied only between 15·41 to 1 and 15·83 to 1 ; but between 1870 and 1885, with much less marked variations in relative production, the relative value of the two metals in the markets fell from 15·55 to 1, to 18·63 to 1, and at the time we write it is nearly 22·1. In the face of these facts it appears to me impossible to attribute the divergence of value between gold and silver to the comparatively slight change in the conditions of supply, irrespective of the altered conditions of demand." The Commissioners go on to say (part i. §§ 189, 192, 193), that looking to the vast changes which occurred prior to 1873, in the relative production of the two metals without any corresponding disturbance in their market value tending to keep the gold price of silver approximately stable, it was the operation of the bimetallic system which had been in force in the Latin Union, up to 1873, which kept the market price of silver approximately steady at the ratio fixed by law, viz. 15½ to 1 ; and that even if the Latin Union had been unable down to the present time to preserve silver from falling below the legal ratio, this would not prove that the influence which the system exerted on the stability of the ratio at 15½ to 1 was, up to 1873, otherwise than real. The utmost, that the Commissioners say, speaking unanimously, is that it does not appear to them *à priori* unreasonable to suppose that the existence in the Latin Union of a bimetallic system with a ratio of 15½ to 1, fixed by law between the two metals, should have been capable of keeping the market price of silver approximately steady to that ratio, established as the system was in countries the population and commerce of which were considerable. This admission, qualified as it is, is of importance ; for if it is warranted by the facts of the case, then the principle becomes established that it is in the power of law to fix value, and therefore to create it; since if it can make 15½ ozs. of silver of the same value as 1 oz. of gold it can make 13 or 14 ozs. also worth 1 oz. of gold. This creation of value would not be brought about—as in the analogous case of the creation of a value for home productions, by a protective tariff—through producers being secured from foreign competition, but would take place at a time when the production and use of the commodities thus affected would be unrestricted.

The conclusion above cited, as that which the Special Commissioners arrived at, on the power of the bimetallic tie to influence the prices of the precious metals in one another, involves no decision on the question whether the Latin Union, if it had since 1873 maintained the free mintage of silver, could have maintained its system at all. The Commissioners guard themselves from saying what would have happened if bimetallism had not been given up; they concern themselves only with what has occurred. But the facts of the case warrant the belief that if the Latin Union had not closed its mints to the free coinage of silver, a large part of continental Europe would have become silver monometallic without a hope of recovery or return to a bimetallic standard, as far as we can now see for perhaps a generation. England and her gold-using colonies, as well as the United States, Germany, Austria, with the addition of perhaps Russia, Holland, and the Scandinavian Powers, would have received the gold which under other circumstances might have run into the currencies of the Union. India would have used up her own store of gold metal, which is about ten times as much as would be required for the purpose, in establishing a gold currency, with the rupee exchanging at its market value in the sovereign. The South American republics might have been enabled to put their finances on a sound footing, with paper currencies convertible at par, but the Latin Union would have had no gold money. This is exactly what the Paris financiers did not intend should happen; and they therefore took steps to avert the imminent invasion of silver, with which the currencies of the Latin Union were threatened, by establishing a monometallic gold currency with full value of silver coins arbitrarily enhanced in value by a restriction on the supply.

When, therefore, it is asserted that the bimetallic system can be depended upon to influence prices by enlarging the volume of the standard of value, and stimulate trade by providing any required supply of capital for commerce, it must be shown why it failed, even to attract both gold and silver impartially and in quantities of convenient abundance within its range, and to keep them there in circulation as money. It must be shown that this failure arose from some other reason than the fact that it is neither the force of a monetary law, nor the strength of a bimetallic tie, but the conditions and methods of a free commerce working through a free exchange of either metal into the other in the form of legal-tender money which can secure these results.

That which gave its strength to the bimetallic tie was the quality of legal tender attaching to so much money of either metal as might at any time be in use in the Latin Union. Coined metal, as legal-tender money, has an artificial value bestowed upon it. Gold at the present moment has a higher purchasing power in Western countries than it otherwise would have, because it possesses a partial monopoly of employment as money, and silver for the same reason is affected in the same way in India; and so far as the bimetallic system made both metals legal tender in the Latin Union, to that extent it faciliated their use as media of exchange in trade; but that extent was not very great, and was measured by the difference in convenience between the employment of bullion and of legal-tender coin as money. The quality of legal tender is, of course, involved in the bimetallic tie; it was the latter which created the former throughout the associated countries, so long as the tie was maintained; but at the same time, if no plan for circulating money at a fixed ratio of exchange had ever been devised, and both gold and silver had been used as legal tender, at their full value in one another, they would have been as efficient as money, without the help of the bimetallic tie, as they were with its help, and perhaps more so. The opinion quoted above attributes to the fixation of a ratio of exchange that which really belongs to the function of legal tender residing in the coins which the law tied together. The tie was too inherently weak to bear the strain which the legal-tender quality of money put upon it when the amount of one kind became unmanageably great; with the rupture of the tie, silver ceased to be legal tender (except as token money) and losing its quality of legal tender it lost its market, its employment, and much of its value, and that which is essential to the recovery of its value, is its re-employment as full-value money in free exchange with gold, and towards gaining this end the reconstruction of the bimetallic tie will be no aid at all.

The grounds for the confidence which bimetallists feel in the power of their system to regulate the respective values of gold and silver are very clearly set forth in the "Theory of Bimetallism," a work of the highest authority on the subject.

"Under the bimetallic system the market ratio is not fixed by law. The laws regulating the currency are so framed that the demand is for silver when $15\frac{1}{2}$ lbs. of silver can be obtained for less than 1 lb. of gold, and the demand is for gold when more than 1 lb. of gold can be obtained for $15\frac{1}{2}$ lbs. of silver."*

What is the force under the action of which the situation thus described is created? When can $15\frac{1}{2}$ lbs. of silver be obtained for less than 1 lb. of gold, and when can more than 1 lb. of gold be obtained for $15\frac{1}{2}$ lbs. of silver? When this divergence from the ratio of value fixed by law for gold and silver arises, the action of the bimetallic law provides, it is said, a means for giving expression to the demand, and induces a supply of that metal which, by the valuation it prescribes, may be the dearer of the two. But this divergence is antecedent to the operation of the law; the law only begins to act when some other cause has placed the precious metals in a relation of value to one another which differs from the legal valuation. This force, or other cause, which causes the divergence, is clearly no other than that residing in the commerce of the world, and the occasion when it

* "Theory of Bimetallism," chap. x. Cassell and Co.

creates the divergence arises when its valuation of gold and silver is not that described by the formula 1 : 15½. Sir David Barbour goes on to explain how the operation of natural laws, acting under the regulating influence of the currency law, adapts the supply of either metal to the demand for it, which the system limits and prescribes, and so, under certain conditions, preserves a fixed ratio between gold and silver. It is not quite clear what the qualifying sentence, "under certain conditions" (p. 46), is intended to imply; but what is stated is, that the currency law controls the natural law, and that the former preserves a fixed ratio between gold and silver. This it cannot do, because the condition of relative cheapness, varying from the price set on one metal in the other by the law, comes into existence before the law begins to work. The operation of the monetary law is called into play and controlled by a pre-existing condition of values. If the law in this case preserves a fixed ratio between gold and silver, we are asked to believe that, while commerce fixes the conditions under which the law must act, it is the law which determines the results which the force of those conditions produces. Commerce decides that gold is cheaper one day than another in silver; but law decides that on both days they shall exchange as money at 1 : 15½. As a matter of fact, they do not so exchange when the commercial and legal valuations differ. The exchange at the legal rate is on these occasions maintained by an abandonment of a fundamental element in the bimetallic system, viz. the circulation of both kinds of money in unrestricted quantities. Commerce steps in and puts a restriction on the circulation of one of them, the more valuable of the two metals, and withdraws it from the bimetallic country where it can only be used at a loss, to be held in reserve, or taken to other places where it will fetch its real value. On these occasions the money of the more valuable metal may totally disappear from circulation. This occurred many years ago, and the collapse of the system between 1873–78 arose from the certainty that it would occur again. It is therefore a misuse of language to speak of "a system of currency which by the operation of natural laws tends, under certain conditions, to preserve a fixed ratio between gold and silver."

When the fixed ratio was preserved, it was the natural law which preserved it; when it was unfixed, it was the natural law which caused it to vary; when the currency was supplied with an abundance of one metal, and with but little of the other, it was the natural law which determined the proportions in which each kind of money should circulate; and when there was no money of one kind at all in circulation, it was the natural law which suspended the action of the monetary law, and converted the bimetallic into a monometallic system. The currency law was always subordinate to the natural law, and so far from regulating the values which the latter prescribed, had no tendency or influence but that which it received from it. The qualifying sentence, "*under certain conditions*," practically concedes the point at issue, for what the bimetallic system must do in order to fulfil its promises, and the requirements of those whose acceptance it seeks, is to preserve a fixed ratio of exchange between gold and silver money used indifferently in unrestricted quantities under *all* conditions of their relative market value. This the system never has succeeded in doing, and the reservation contained in these words implies that it never can be depended upon, with confidence, to do so.

As bearing on the contention that commerce, not law, regulates the market price of the precious metals in one another, the following passage from "The Theory of Bimetallism," p. 9, may be usefully examined. "The total amount of gold and silver in existence at the present day cannot, of course, be accurately known; but according to Tooke and Newmarck, in 1850 there was in existence 15½ millions of pounds (troy) of gold, and 374½ millions of pounds (troy) of silver. Gold being at that date worth 15½ times its weight in silver, it follows that the value of the gold was to the value of the silver, nearly, as 5 to 8, or, in other words, silver discharged $\frac{8}{13}$ths, and gold $\frac{5}{13}$ths, of the duty of metallic money."

If gold was worth silver at the rate of 1 lb. to 15½ lbs., then it was not worth silver at the rate of 5 lbs. to 8 lbs. The latter formula, although it may represent the proportion existing between the stock of silver and the stock of gold, rated in silver at its market price, does not describe an actual value, nor does it prove that gold carried through $\frac{5}{13}$ths and silver $\frac{8}{13}$ths of the duty of metallic money, for no one can say how much metallic money was in circulation in the world in 1850, nor consequently what proportion of it was gold, and what proportion of it was silver money. In no other way than by ascertaining this fact is it possible to make any assertion as to the amount of commercial work done by gold and silver money respectively in 1850, or at any other time; but it is possible to predicate this much from these figures, viz. that the value of gold and silver was not as 5 to 8, because if it had been, their exchange value as money would not have been 1 : 15½. It is also quite certain that gold did not perform $\frac{5}{13}$ths and silver $\frac{8}{13}$ths of the work of metallic money, because if this were the case, 5 lbs. of gold and 8 lbs. of silver money would have bought the same, or nearly the same, weight or quantity of the same kind of merchandise in markets where both gold and silver were capable of being freely used as money; and this was not the case.

The interference of the bimetallic law, which compelled, where it was in force, the use of gold and silver money at an exchange rate of 1 : 15½, at the penalty of the more or less complete exclusion of one or other metal from circulation; and the inability of India to use gold money, added to the rudimentary character of the monetary systems of semi-civilized countries, are circumstances which combine to make it impossible to state with any approach to certainty the point at which the relative value of gold and silver would have been found, had all the world been free to use them both indifferently as money at their true market rate of exchange. With so great a variation between the exchange rate which prevailed in practice where both moneys were used under the most favourable circumstances then existing, and that suggested by a comparison between the stock of gold, and the mass of silver metal in the world, it is the height of rashness to assert that any such relation of value between the two metals as that of 5 to 8 actually existed, still less to assert that it was a working relation of value, and that gold performed

$\frac{8}{13}$ths and silver $\frac{8}{13}$ths of the duty of metallic money. The fairest inference which can be drawn from these figures is that the 15½ millions of pounds of gold in the world in 1850, being worth 232¼ millions of pounds of silver, the portion of the stock of silver in the world (374½ millions of pounds), which was in excess of the rated value of the stock of gold, or, in round terms, 142 millions of pounds, was at the time hoarded or otherwise rendered useless for commercial purposes, and therefore had little or no influence on the relative values of gold and silver either in the form of bullion or of money. This estimate of the world's supply of gold includes the hoarded treasure of India, which, in 1850, would have amounted to some millions of pounds troy. It must therefore be reduced by a considerable amount in calculating its purchasing power; how much more also must be deducted from the sum of 15½ millions of pounds (troy) is mere matter for conjecture, as we know nothing of the stocks of gold metal hoarded in other parts of Asia, or in other quarters of the globe. We also know nothing of the extent of the silver store which in the same manner was withdrawn from commercial use; but that the mass of either kind of metal so discarded must have been of great magnitude is proved by the market price of 1 : 15½ being out of all correspondence with the relative proportions of their masses.

The value of silver in gold, with which alone this discussion can concern itself, is that evolved by their exchange into one another as money, or by the exchange of both as money, for commodities in commerce; that value was, approximately speaking, in

1850, and up to 1873–78, 15½ to 1; and if any other theoretic valuation is elicited by such a method as gives the equation of 5 of gold to 8 of silver these figures, even if they had any claim to reality, would be irrelevant, as it is only in terms of money that relative values find expression, and the money value of gold in silver was during that period 1 : 15¼. So long as corn, wine, textiles, and similar commodities exchange in equal quantities for 1 lb. of gold money and 15½ lbs. of silver money, those figures give the true value of gold and silver either as bullion or as money in one another. In "The Theory of Bimetallism," p. 62, a different principle is laid down. "It has already been shown at p. 9 that in the first half of the present century the value of the silver in the world exceeded the value of the gold, and that silver discharged a larger proportion of the duties of money than did gold, the ratio being about 8 to 5. In these circumstances, if the bimetallic theory be wrong, a constant market ratio could only have been preserved between silver and gold if the production of the two metals had been in the proportion of 8 to 5; in other words, if the production of each metal had been exactly proportioned to the extent to which it discharged the duties of money." And again, "From 1841 to 1850 the ratio of production was nearly 8 to 8, and yet the ratio of value was maintained at 15½ to 1. From 1851 to 1860 the ratio of production was not far from 8 to 28, and yet the ratio of value was still maintained at 15½ to 1. From 1861 to 1865 the ratio of production did not vary greatly from 8 to 23. And from 1866 to 1870 it was 8 to 18, and yet the ratio of value remained at 15½ to 1." Here it is asserted that 5 lbs. of gold were worth 8 lbs. of silver in 1850, and the argument implies that various valuations arose as between the precious metals, between 1841 and 1870, ranging from 8 to 8, up to 8 to 28, and these values of gold and silver in one another were regulated by the action of the bimetallic law, and kept at a market value of 1 to 15½, instead of coinciding with the proportions in which they were produced from the mines. But this line of reasoning ignores economic principles and actual facts; it overlooks the position in which money in use stands to commodities, and includes in the operations of money in commerce a vast mass of the precious metals which is not employed as money at all. The argument as it stands, involves the conclusion that gold and silver money held to one another in 1850 a natural relation of value stated at 5 to 8, and had an actual market price in one another of 1 to 15½, the absurdity of which no one can fail to perceive.

If the value of gold money in silver money depends on the varying productiveness of gold and silver mines in every ten years, it is clear that that relation of value can only arise through the action of commerce, and depends on the extent to which they are respectively used for effecting exchanges of goods; and it follows that if the precious metals are used for such purposes in proportions corresponding to the quantities of each excavated from the mines, their values in money will assume those proportions also; and that if they are not so used, the money values expressed by the formula of their relative production will not come into existence; and that if the fresh supplies of metal are partly so used, and partly discarded from use, the relative money value of the two metals will depend on the extent of the use irrespective of the extent of the disuse. The relative market price of the two metals does not therefore arise from the bimetallic law imposing its value on the relative volume of the produce of the mines, but on the proportions of that produce which may from time to time be used as money in commerce. All that we have a right to infer from such a circumstance as that, during the thirty years, 1840-70, when the production of gold and silver varied between 8 to 8 and 8 to 23, and sometimes more widely, the ratio of exchange remained constant at 15½ to 1,* is that the commercial classes employed either metal in such proportions, the remainder being withdrawn from use in various ways, that a purchasing power was bestowed on either metal which gave one in the other the market price thus described; and if for any reasons commerce had used both metals in proportions corresponding to those of their production, no law could have maintained the ratio of exchange at the point of 15½ to 1.

It must also not be forgotten that while production may have varied in the manner above stated between 1840 and 1870, the whole stock of the precious metals did not vary in their relative proportions in anything approaching the annual variations in productiveness of the mines. The annual increment, which has been made at any time, even at times of an unusual productiveness, to the existing stock of either gold or silver is but an exceedingly small fraction of the whole stock of either metal in

* " Theory of Bimetallism," p. 63.

existence. The Special Commission, in its Final Report (pp. 7 and 13), state as follows: "The value of the silver produced in the world, from the end of the fifteenth century to the present time, is estimated by Dr. Soëtbeer at upwards of £1,951,000,000. If an allowance be made of one-fourth for loss and wear, the annual supply, even at the present rate, represents an addition of less than 1½ per cent. to the existing stock." And again, "Dr. Soëtbeer's estimate of the production of gold since the end of the fifteenth century is £1,553,415,000, and an annual supply of £20,000,000 would consequently be about 1¼ per cent. on that stock, while the actual diminution in the supply, which has taken place during the last fifteen years, would only amount to ¼ per cent. per annum." The average annual increment to the supply of gold and silver has even in modern times been but small and very considerably less than the average annual additions to the stock of commodities which industrial activity and enterprise have brought into the markets for the purpose of being exchanged by means of that portion of the stock of precious metals which has been in use as money; and therefore the fact of a varying productiveness accompanied by a constancy of ratio during thirty recent years is not a sufficient foundation to support the theory that it can only be the bimetallic law which regulates the market price of the two metals in one another.

Inasmuch as the whole stock of the precious metals is always potentially available for use as money, the relation of the price of silver to that of gold does not depend on the increase or decrease in their production which may occur every ten years, but upon the volume of commodities taken in connection with the volume of gold or silver which is at any time in actual use as money. It is evident that a very considerable portion of the world's stock of the precious metals is not used as money at all, and the experience of the last few years proves beyond any question, that an increased purchasing power may fail to induce an increased supply of the metal which has risen in value for use as money, although there is beyond any doubt an ample stock in reserve from which such an additional supply could be furnished.

We thus see that however great the annual additions to the stock of the precious metals may have been, the market price of one kind of money in the other has been determined by the relation existing between the whole stock of the precious metals (in respect of which the fresh supplies are an insignificant quantity) and the increased volume of commodities brought into the markets for sale; and also that the annual supply of gold and silver has infinitely less effect on their relative value or on their relation of value to that of commodities than the complex and often obscure causes which tend to the withdrawal of large amounts of both from commercial uses, in which it would at first sight appear certain that those owning the material for money, would hasten to employ it. As instances of complex and obscure causes, those which at present prevent the rehabilitation of silver as full-value money, and which draw off many millions sterling of gold from the West, to be buried out of sight in the East, are convincing proofs of the influence which this class of causes exercises on prices and on the exchanges.

The inability of the bimetallic law to exercise such a restraining influence over the values of the precious metals as the author of the "Theory of Bimetallism" ascribes to it, may fairly be considered to have passed out of the region of discussion. If the system had possessed such power, it would have been well able to deal with the invasion of cheap silver from Germany and America, with which the bimetallic countries were threatened in 1873; but those who knew the system and its capabilities best, practically admitted that it was powerless to cope with the difficulties which were then created by redundant supplies of silver, and they made no attempt to employ its latent forces at a time when, if they were realities, their help was most needed.

The bimetallist, in asserting the dominant influence of his monetary law over the natural law, and in claiming for his system that it creates a demand for the precious metals which evolves the necessary supplies for employment as money, in effect contends that it secures an indefinite expansion to the circulation of metallic money; since, if it failed to do this, such an enlargement of the standard as would suffice to give stability to prices and to prevent violent fluctuations in the relative values of gold and silver could not be obtained. If, for instance, with a growing commerce, 50 millions sterling were the annual increment necessary to prevent a fall of prices, and the demand, in order to keep silver and gold in actual (not merely nominal) circulation, were 25 millions sterling of each kind of coin, any lesser supply, or that supply in different proportions, would obviously fail to secure a constancy in the money price of commodities or a constancy in the exchange rate for gold and silver. In order to meet these two requirements, commerce must have exactly the supply it requires, delivered in the proper proportions, and at the moment of demand. But suppose that instead of 50 millions being forthcoming annually, the supply were in some years 20, in others 30, and in others 40 millions, and never the proportion of equal values, then not only would the system fail to meet the necessities of the case, and fail to provide such a supply of metallic money, as commerce might require, but it would limit the supply to an amount smaller than that which would be added to the circulation were no bimetallic law in existence. If instead of 25 millions of gold only 15 millions were the amount of the annual increment, then only 15 millions of silver would be the increase of that kind of money either, for the hypothesis is, that in order to maintain the legal ratio the supply of both metals must come in equal values of either. Commerce would in that case get only 30 millions when she required 50, and prices would fall correspondingly. If more silver than 15 millions were brought into circulation, then a corresponding value of gold must be withdrawn, or the ratio of 15½ to 1 could not be maintained, and this partial withdrawal of the undervalued coin would conflict with the maintenance of an unrestricted supply of both kinds of money to the currency. The bimetallic system then puts a limit on the supply of metallic money to its currencies corresponding with the amount of the dearer metal which may be available for use; or if it puts no limit on the supply, then it operates to provide money of one kind only to the greater or less exclusion of the other kind. Whether the quantity so supplied may be able to maintain prices depends on its own price in the other metal in those markets where no bimetallic law interferes with the free exchange of one into the other, or of either into commodities. If, for instance, silver were the kind of money supplied exclusively to bimetallic countries (as would have been the case if the system had been maintained after 1873–78), the greater the supply the cheaper silver would become in gold. At the same time gold being, from its comparative scarceness, the standard of value both in bimetallic and other countries for silver as well as for commodities, the price of goods in the former or bimetallic countries, stated in silver money, would be regulated by the gold price of goods in the latter countries; and instead of any stability of prices being obtained, fluctuations would increase rather than diminish, because commodities would be sold for the cheaper metal, silver, which from its abundance would be less constant in its purchasing power than the dearer metal, gold, from which both would take their value, and the ratio of $15\frac{1}{2}$ to 1, as a working ratio, would at the same time be totally lost.

That the limit placed on the supply of one metal to a bimetallic currency for *actual* exchange into the other is fixed by the supply of the more valuable of the two, and therefore constitutes a real and not an imaginary defect of the system, may be inferred from what occurred in 1870–73. There were then large stocks of silver in Germany and America ready to be coined into the currencies of the Latin Union, but they were refused admission under the apprehension that they would drive the gold out. If, as is asserted, the bimetallic law can attract either metal into its currencies, by its influence over the natural law, we might have expected that the Latin Union would have taken the supply of silver offered to it from abroad under a belief in the efficacy of its system to draw gold from the East, where the metal was hoarded in quantities sufficient for the purpose of maintaining the equilibrium of the fixed ratio. That the bimetallic law does not possess the influence over the natural law ascribed to it then became clear enough, for although the supply of gold existed, it was not available, because commercial and other considerations prevented its employment in the bimetallic currencies, with profit to those who held the stock in India, at a rate of exchange with silver of 1 to $15\frac{1}{2}$. This monetary law therefore, although it is said to be able to convert a natural ratio of 5 to 8 into one of 1 to $15\frac{1}{2}$, wholly failed to move gold from the East into Europe when a comparatively slight alteration of value would have been the result. The supply of coin to the currencies of the Latin Union was on this occasion diminished by the volume of rejected silver, because there was not an equal value of gold offered, for coinage into them, at the same time. If along with this mass of silver which Germany intended to send into France an equal value of gold had been at the same time presented for coinage, the Latin Union might have proved itself able to enlarge the measure of value to any necessary extent, to have supplied all the currency of both kinds required, and to have maintained the fixed ratio of exchange; but such a supply of gold was not forthcoming, and there was no power residing in the bimetallic system to induce it from any quarter. As the system therefore cannot be depended upon to provide *all* the metallic money which commerce may at any time require, it follows that the supply is subject to limitation, and this limitation is fixed by the point of value at which it becomes unprofitable for those outside the system to exchange their gold and silver for one another at the rate fixed by the bimetallic law.

In this case another weak point in the bimetallic theory comes into view, which is, that a rise in prices in terms of the cheaper metal is of an advantage to producers or to traders. Arguing on the hypothesis that an increasing demand for gold and an increasingly inadequate supply, give to gold money an increasing purchasing power, the value of silver will continue to decline, and its command of commodities will be reduced also. It will be conceded by bimetallists, that the ratio of value for gold and silver money depends on the quantities of either which are respectively in use, actually or potentially, at the same time. If there is, compared with the commercial use for it, but little gold and an abundance of silver, although only a small portion of the latter is in use as money, its value in gold will be low and its purchasing power low also. If therefore it happens that the supply of silver goes forward uninterruptedly while the supply of gold remains stationary, there will be in the bimetallic currencies a preponderance of the metal which is the cheaper and less efficient for purchase. However much may be added to the currency, the whole stock of silver will buy no more than before, the gold price of commodities will remain the same, the silver price will rise; with, say, 25 per cent. added to the silver constituent of the currency, a napoleon would buy 25 francs and 25 francs' worth of goods. It has become a matter of experience that such a condition of the exchanges under a fixed-ratio system would drive gold out of circulation, and the rise of prices which an increasing volume of the bimetallic currencies is expected to bring about would be a rise in terms of the cheaper metal, and as this (*e.g.* silver) would be exclusively in use, the increase in the tale of money would be discounted in the decline of its value. The increase in the price of commodities would indicate no real increase of value. An abundant currency of cheap silver would neither stimulate production, nor give wages a higher purchasing power, nor benefit anybody. The mistake of supposing that an increase in the volume of a currency which is obtained in the falling money, brings about the same results as an increase obtained in the rising money is that which underlies the bimetallist assumption that the cheaper metal may be substituted for the dearer, silver for gold, and trade go on with as much assistance from currency as if the latter metal were in circulation in unrestricted quantities. Every merchant tries to exchange his goods away for something which will bring him in more value than he parts with, if he gets gold, and gold is rising in value, he succeeds; if he gets silver, and silver is falling in value, he fails in doing this. A rise of prices, in order to indicate a rise in values, must be a rise in terms of the dearer not of the cheaper metal, of that which will hold its own against commodities, and which from superior stability of value will give merchants a reasonable hope of securing profits before a decline in its purchasing power brings on a rise of prices.

When, however, both gold and silver money are used at a rate of interchange fixed entirely by commercial considerations, neither will acquire that artificial enhancement of purchasing power which a monopoly of use as money invests the metal so employed, and which the fixed-ratio system bestows alternately on either metal; nor will any limitation be placed on such a supply as commerce may require. Both gold and silver would, in this case, be provided under exactly the same conditions as those under which commodities are brought into the markets, and in quantities solely regulated by the terms of a profitable exchange. The additions made to the world's stock of both kinds of money, and the enlargement of the measure of value, would be indefinitely great. Prices would be under a constant tendency to rise, the rise would be gradual, because the presentation of the money metals for coinage would, in the long run, be behind the demand; but such a rise of prices would indicate a real rise of value, because the money, in terms of which values would be described, would only be supplied within the limits of commercial profit. As there would be no artificial value for one money in the other, so there would be no artificial value for money in commodities either, and there would therefore be nothing of the character of an artificial inflation about it.

CHAPTER VII.

GROWTH OF THE RATIO.

Mons. de Laveleye's opinion on the control of the ratio by law as opposed to commerce examined—History of the use of money proves that the real ratio of value is solely commercial—Silver and gold values in ancient times—The ratio in mediæval times—The ratio in modern times—Equalizing effect of commercial exchanges on the relative values of gold and silver money.

LEADING bimetallists to some extent admit it to be a fact, that commercial forces are inextricably connected with the action of the monetary law upon which their system is based, the importance of conceding this point in the letter at least, as distinguished from the spirit of their argument, becomes of importance to the defence of their case in proportion to the light which continued discussion throws upon its economic weakness. As the facts connected with alternations of the ratio from the earliest historic to the present times afford evidence that it grew out of natural and not out of legislative causes, it will not be considered irrelevant to the general argument to state in this place how little support the legal as opposed to the commercial theory of the regulation of the exchanges derives from the circumstances of this development.

Mons. de Laveleye, writing a few years ago about

the action of legislation on the relative values of gold and silver expressed himself as follows.*

"The value of money metals is controlled by the continued and obligatory absorption of them at the mints at the rate fixed by the law ... The State creates the greater part of the value both of gold and silver, for it creates a sure market for them. When the coinage is free, when the mints of France deliver 200 francs for every kilogramme of standard silver, and 3100 francs for every kilogramme of gold, these metals will not sell for less. Here, therefore, is a market always open at the legal rate, and this is not true of any other merchandise. ... *Now, the demand which rules the market of the precious metals is that which acts at the mint; as the Minister Gaudin said, in the year XI. (1803), the market value of the precious metals is the mint price. The State, therefore, which creates the demand can fix the price.* ... The variations in the relative value of the two metals of which history tells us, have been the result of legislation, and not of the more or less abundant production of the mines of silver or of gold. The French legislator of 1803, in fixing the ratio of equivalence between the two metals at 1 to 15½, was merely acting in conformity with historical precedents, ... he was not violating economic laws."

But more recently the same authority has spoken as follows: "*Bimetallism does not pretend, as its adversaries say, to fix the commercial value of gold and silver*, as has been perfectly demonstrated by Mr. Gibbs in his excellent article last July in the *Contemporary Review*, which was quoted yesterday after-

* "International Bimetallism," pp. 15–18. London, 1881.

noon, and which I am happy to quote once more. The French law of the year 1802 decrees as follows: 'To every person bringing to the mint 1 kilogramme of gold $\frac{9}{10}$ths fine, this same kilogramme shall be given back to him transformed into 155 gold discs of 20 francs of which the total shall be reckoned at 3100 francs; and to all persons bringing 1 kilogramme of silver $\frac{9}{10}$ths fine, this same kilogramme shall be returned to him coined into 40 five-franc pieces, of which the total shall be equal to 200 frs. *The debtor may tender these gold or silver discs at his option, and can obtain for them a full receipt for his debt.*' That is the law. A Government which coins money is not a buyer of values, it does not guarantee that these discs will keep their commercial or relative value. If money should fall in value, the State is not bound to its own people, and still less to foreigners, to pay back in gold the silver crowns; what the law does is to transform gold and silver into money of legal tender. But as it opens, in the mints of the Great Nations, an unlimited market for gold at 3100 francs the kilogramme, and for silver at 200 francs the kilogramme, it is evident that no one will sell his silver or his gold at a less price. *So the legal ratio will become the commercial ratio, in conformity with the economical law of demand and supply.* The demand of gold and silver at the legal ratio will be unlimited, because with gold and silver coined in legal tender you can buy hundreds of milliards' worth of land, houses, ships, manufactures, railways, shares, and debentures of every kind in all the countries of the Monetary Union." *

* Address by Mons. de Laveleye, at the International Monetary Congress, Paris, October 13, 1889. The italics are the author's.

There is a material difference between the definition of a system which is said to control the value of the money-metals by its mint law, and one which describes the same system as not pretending to fix the commercial value of gold and silver. The new position which is thus taken up is at least a change of front, if it does not involve an abandonment of an old one. In defending it, however, the bimetallists still retain their hold on the *fixed ratio* as their strategical basis; but are they both tenable together? If the commercial ratio regulates the legal ratio, is the latter not superfluous? and if it does not, is it not injurious?

The quotation above given from Mons. de Laveleye's address, states three points. (1) That bimetallism does not fix the commercial value of gold and silver; (2) that gold and silver being equally legal-tender at 1 : 15½ that circumstance does fix the value at that point, since a payment of silver at the mint equivalent of gold constitutes a legal acquittance of a debt incurred in gold, and therefore 20 francs become of the same value as 1 napoleon; and (3) that the legal ratio becomes the commercial ratio in virtue of the establishment of this legal equivalent.

The first and third propositions, taken together, would seem to mean that the mint ratio, *i.e.* the legal ratio, waits upon the commercial ratio, but this inference is neutralized by the second proposition, which says that it is the law, not commerce, which constitutes a fixed sum in silver the equivalent in value of a fixed sum in gold. The fallacy in the argument lies in the *petitio principii* that no one will sell his silver or gold at a less price than that fixed by law; an assertion which is opposed to evidence.

In another part of his address Mons. de Laveleye says that, "in France for seventy years no one took any heed whether they were going to be paid in gold or silver," which is very true, as far as it goes; but if it had been also stated that on occasions and during long periods of time the owners of gold and silver took very great heed not to pay away either one or the other according to the circumstances of the rating, it would have been impossible to arrive at the conclusion that under the fixed-ratio system no one would sell his silver or gold at less than the legal price. In the third proposition, Mons. de Laveleye calls this establishment of a legal equivalence, "the economic law of demand and supply," but that is certainly not an *economic* supply which is limited to such an amount of money as can without loss to its owners be exchanged at a rate fixed by law; if gold is not placed in the currency at 15½ francs because it is worth 20 francs, what becomes of the *economic supply?*

That which gives a direction to the movement of the precious metals for use as money from one place to another is their relative efficiency for purchase, or in other words, the ratio of value which they bear to commodities, and this valuation, as has been said before, determines their value in one another. This theory of the regulation of value for gold and silver cannot be reconciled with such a theory as that above cited in any way. Where exceptions exist to this rule, they are occasioned by the arbitrary action of monetary laws which, by placing a restriction on the supply of metal for use as money, limits the flow of capital to commerce, and interferes with that relation of value arising between money and goods under exchange which might otherwise subsist.

Thus we see at the present moment the supply of silver available for money unable to assert its true relation of value with commodities, because it is largely excluded from use as money. Not a single one among the leading commercial nations is now using both kinds of money in quantities unrestricted by law. As their real relation of value to one another is fixed by that which either of them holds to commodities, no true or fairly stable rate of exchange can arise between them, nor is it possible under such circumstances to predicate what the ratio for gold and silver might be, if free play were accorded to the action of commerce on their values.

The alternating value of gold and silver depends on variations in the demand for either acting on the supply, and if by currency restrictions that supply is artificially limited, the exchange rate will become much more sensitive to such variations than if the supply were capable of increase on the shortest notice. That it is always easier to disturb the equipoise of a small than of a large mass in suspension is as true in the monetary as it is in the physical world. This is one of the principal arguments in favour of a dual currency, and it is a sound argument when the laws under which such a currency acts place no limitation on supply, either by requiring the two kinds of money to be exchanged at a legal rate, or by fixing a legal-tender limit for the use of one of them.

The history of the growth of the ratio proves that if gold and silver money are let alone they will find their true level of value in one another, as quickly as time and distance permit; that as one or the other has a higher purchasing power in different places it will go where the returns to its expenditure are largest, and the nearer the approximation may be which commerce obtains to absolute freedom in the use of both kinds of money, the more permanently will the ratio of value become established.

Roughly speaking, the commercial area of the ancient World lay in a region which had for its boundaries on the north, modern Lombardy, the Danube, the Black Sea, the Caspian, and the country stretching from the latter sea to the northern spurs of the Himalayas; Persia and India with Ceylon would form its eastern, the southern coast of Arabia with Egypt and northern Africa its southern, while Spain and Gaul were its western borders. Practically it was the trade carried on within these limits which, between the fifth century B.C. and the fifteenth century of the Christian era, fixed the values for silver and gold money which prevailed during that period. Delmar* is doubtless correct in assigning to the fourth century B.C. the commencement of commercial intercourse throughout this area. The wars between the Persians and Greeks, waged at one time in Europe, at another in Asia, gave an impulse and a diffusion to the commerce carried on between the nations occupying the coasts of the Mediterranean and those inhabiting western Asia, which it had never known before.

There is good reason for believing that in very ancient times silver was, from its scarcity, more valuable than gold, but in the course of a period, perhaps of the duration of a thousand years, this condition of

* Delmar, "History of the Precious Metals," p. 237. London. G. Bell and Sons, 1880.

values was reversed. In Europe the ratio is said to have stood at 1 of gold to 13½ of silver in the year B.C. 708, and in the fourth century to have become 1 to 14 or 15.* At the subjection of Phœnicia by Darius in B.C. 517, the Syrians were required to pay tribute to the conqueror in silver, which in Persia is stated to have been $\frac{1}{13}$ of the value of gold, while in India at the same time it was ¼. The supply of silver from Spain, Attica, Thrace, and some other sources, had between the fifth century and the Christian era increased, while it is probable that some sources of gold supply in Arabia, Nubia, and Asia Minor had either ceased, or their yield had very much fallen off, while at the same time the Asiatic supply was not more than was required in Persia and India. At the beginning of the Christian era the activity of commerce had caused such a dispersion of the more valuable metal as to establish a ratio in the Roman Empire of about 1 of gold to 12 of silver, which lasted with some variations from the year B.C. 54 to A.D. 161, that is, for about two hundred years.† In India the ratio must have been gradually widening, as at the end of the sixteenth century it had become nearly 1 to 10, while at the same time in England it stood at 1 to 11. This approach to equalization is fully accounted for by the progressive importance and value of the commerce, which had passed between eastern Europe and India, from the beginning of the ninth century, when the Venetians allied themselves with the Turks in order to convey the produce of India and of the further East, by routes through Egypt and through Syria, into Europe.

* Demar. *op. cit.*, p. 237. † *Ibid.* p. 240.

That the principles above stated are those upon which the growth of a ratio must proceed, whether its tendency be to narrow or to widen, is confirmed by what we know of the causes which produced alterations of the ratio in the East in the last three hundred and fifty years, during which trade has been conducted with but little interruption by the Portuguese, the Dutch, and the English, with India, China, and Japan. In this trade the circulation of money has always been (with the exception of the fifty-four years which have passed since gold was demonetized in British India) free and unrestricted, and coins of the two metals have passed for one another at their commercial values. In the East this system of exchange has always prevailed.* Japan was at the time of its discovery, in 1545, entirely secluded from the western world, and apparently carried on but little commerce with its nearest neighbour China. Mines in the islands supplied the people with such quantities of gold and silver as they required. The ratio of value was therefore at that date in Japan purely local, and stood at 1 of gold to 6 of silver.

During the next eighty years the Portuguese, by selling Japanese productions at an enormous profit in China and Europe, and exchanging their silver for Japanese gold, which in Spain and England was rated at that time at from $1 : 10\frac{3}{4}$ to $1 : 11\frac{1}{10}$, brought the Japanese ratio under the influence of the stocks of gold existing in other parts of the East and in the West, and the value of gold as against silver rose to at least $1 : 10$, and is stated to have risen higher.

* The following statistics are for the most part abbreviated from the " Gold Treasure of India." London, 1884.

In 1624 the Portuguese were banished from the Japanese islands, and the Dutch trade placed under restrictions, which protected the currency of the country from foreign influences, and the ratio fell, according to information quoted by Delmar, to its former figure of 1 : 6 or 7. Sir Rutherford Alcock ("Japan," vol. i. p. 281) states that at the opening of the ports to British commerce in 1859, the ratio was 1 : 3.

So in China, the ratio at the end of the sixteenth century was 1 : 10; while in Europe, which was then beginning to feel the influence of the importations of American silver, it stood at 1 : 12. Silver and gold, which are indigenous in China, would necessarily find their way there from Europe only in small quantities, and both the action of trade and the somewhat indirect courses in which it was carried on with China would not tend to induce speedy or large importations of either metal into that country. As late as 1776 the ratio was said to have been only 1 : 12, while in England it stood 1 : 15½ at nearly the same time.

The effect of the American treasure on the stock of the precious metal in Europe was not complete until the beginning of the eighteenth century. During the earlier years of Queen Elizabeth's reign (cir. 1560) the ratio of silver was 1 : 11$\frac{4}{8}$. In 1600 the ratio calculated at the mint prices for standard gold and silver was 1 : 11. In 1604 (2 King James I.) it had risen to 1 : 12, and in 1717 (3 King George I.) to 1 : 15$_{1\frac{9}{24}}$.* The "Treatise on the Coins"

* The ratios which Lord Liverpool gives in his "Treatise on the Coins" are somewhat higher than these, which are calculated from MacCulloch's Tables and the Silver Commission's Report, 1876

informs us that during the sixty years following the accession of King James I, silver fell in the gold valuation 32 per cent., and these figures show that between the years 1600 and 1717 it had fallen more than 37 per cent.

In the reign of the Emperor Akbar (*cir.* 1590) a gold coin weighing 91 tolahs 8 maashas (*i.e.* 1100 maashas) was equal in value to 100 round gold mohurs, each of which was worth 9 rupees, and weighed 11 maashas (*i.e.* 1½ of a tolah). The ratio obtaining between gold and silver on these terms was 1 : $9\frac{1}{11}$, assuming that the silver rupee weighed a full tolah, which was likely to be the case, as at that period a rupee and a tolah were names indifferently used for the same weight. As in England, in 1600, the ratio was 1 : 11, the difference to a purchaser buying a pound of silver with gold would have been $1\frac{2}{11}$ lbs. in favour of his doing so in England rather than in India, and this proves that up to that time gold had been accumulating in India rather than silver, while the contrary had been the case in Europe.

More than a hundred years later, in the year 1717, Sir Isaac Newton, who was Master of the Royal Mint, stated that "in the East Indies a pound weight of fine gold may be worth twelve pounds of fine silver," while in England it was worth $15\frac{2}{4}$ lbs. of silver. The diffusion of the American silver had reached India by the beginning of the eighteenth century, but the existing stocks of gold which had been in process of accumulation during many centuries were still sufficiently large to give silver a higher value as against gold in India than in

England, and to act as an encouragement to the exportation of silver from the West to the East.

In Bengal, a gold mohur was issued by the Indian Government in 1769, and ordered to pass as legal tender payment for 16 sicca rupees. The intrinsic value of this coin was estimated to be equal to the nominal value of it, or as nearly so as was deemed necessary to render it current at the prescribed rate; but from causes arising out of the state of confusion which then prevailed in the Indian currencies, its circulation was confined during the next twenty years almost entirely to Calcutta. It was no doubt overvalued in silver at the Indian rate of valuation, as it was bought up by persons making payments to Government, and used for that purpose in preference to the silver coin. The ratio of value thus set up between the pure gold in this mohur and the pure silver in the sicca rupee was about $1 : 15\frac{5}{17}$.

The prevailing ratio in the north of Europe about the year 1770 was $1 : 14\frac{3}{4}$. In 1793 a new gold mohur and a new rupee were struck, the former of which was directed to pass for sixteen of the latter. As the gold mohur contained $189\frac{463}{1000}$ grs. of pure gold, and the rupee contained $175\frac{331}{350}$ grs. of pure silver, the ratio obtaining between the coins was $1 : 14\frac{13}{30}$. In Europe the ratio at the same date was $1 : 15\frac{2}{50}$. In 1818 another gold mohur and another rupee were issued, the ratio of value between these coins was almost exactly $1 : 15$, while in Europe the ratio was $1 : 15\frac{50}{100}$. A slight alteration was made in the value of the rupee in 1833, which need not be noticed here, as two years later the currency of the East India Company's territories was remodelled and placed on its present footing.

When two kinds of money are in free circulation together on the basis of their intrinsic value, the ratio of value between them obeys the same law as the ratio of value existing between either of them and commodities in commerce. It follow as a necessary consequence that the use of both metals as a common measure of value in effecting the exchange of commodities in commerce always exerts an equalizing influence on the relation which they bear to one another over the whole area of their employment. If the price of a commodity is high in one part of the world, people who export goods to that quarter will increase their exportations, in order to get a larger share of the redundant money circulating there, and by bringing it home exchange it for goods costing more labour than those they had exported. High prices in one of two countries trading together, and low prices in another, indicate a difference of level which is sooner or later rectified by the export of produce to the dearer or the import of money into the cheaper country, or by both means. This being the case, the money of two countries trading together is in respect of the commodities which they exchange, always approximating to the character of a common measure of value, and therefore the exchange rate for gold and silver money on both sides tends towards assimilation rather than towards divergence. This process of equalization will go on until the same equivalence of the inferior in the more valuable metal is established in both countries trading together, by commerce deciding how much of goods shall be given for so many pieces of silver, and for so many pieces of gold, and, *ex vi termini*, how many pieces of silver for the same value of gold. It is wholly superfluous to assume that commerce needs the assistance of a legal ratio for the exchange of gold and silver money in order to bring them to their true level of value in one another; and it becomes as clear as evidence and reason can make it, that the variations in the relative value of the precious metals, of which history tells us, have not (except in a great minority of instances) been the result of legislative action, but of a free supply of the money-metals acting in connection with the amount of work which they have been called upon to carry through; and at the same time that such influence as legislation in our modern currency systems has exercised, has resulted sometimes in an artificial limitation, sometimes in an artificial inflation of the currency, either metallic or fiduciary, and has therefore been the reverse of beneficial in its action on the prices of commodities, and consequently on the relative values of gold and silver money.

CHAPTER VIII.

SUMMING-UP.

Until commercial ratio of exchange is ascertained, fixed ratio cannot be established—The system of the fixed ratio will not create a correspondence between supply and demand of the precious metals—Nor will the supply correspond with the wants of commerce, but will be affected by external systems of currency—For the objects of bimetallism the monetary law must be universal in its application—Difficulties of obtaining universal acceptance for monetary law stated—Arising from variations in supply acting on prices of commodities—Which subjects monetary to influence of commercial ratio—India and the East—Objections from point of view of Asiatics—Risks involved by including India in a bimetallic arrangement—Case for bimetallism as stated by either party; burden of proof lies with bimetallists—Initial steps towards reviving bimetallism described—Discretion with the bank to refuse to pay gold not admissible—Practical result of system on bank reserve stated; its conversion into a silver reserve—Theory that bimetallic ratio will impose itself on the world examined—Remonetizing gold in India secures a natural ratio of exchange—Conflict of eastern and western ratios will limit supply of money to western currencies—Commercial supremacy of England affected—Process of apportionment of stock of money to bimetallic countries—Its results on bank reserves foretold by past events—Commissioners' opinion on possible results of fixation of ratio—Some practical objections to system extracted from the Report—Bimetallists unable to prove their case—Mr. Goschen's opinion and Mr. Gladstone's opinion support preceding arguments.

THE strong point of the bimetallic case is the confidence which its supporters feel in being able to create a commercial value for gold and silver in one another, corresponding to the legal valuation prescribed by their system. This commercial value is really only a question of supply and demand, and until it is determined by economic conditions the legal ratio of exchange must be purely experimental.

The argument for bimetallism, in this part of the case, may, we think, be fairly stated as follows: "If it can bring into use as much silver coin as commerce requires, the demand will balance the supply. Nothing more than this can be attained under any system; as much silver will be used in the world as can be used, and its price, either in the exchange with commodities or with gold, will be its top price, and that price will necessarily be the fixed-ratio price, since in response to the demand evoked by the system, the supply of silver will not exceed this demand, because if it were to exceed it there would be no use for the surplus metal, it would be valueless, the miner who produced more silver than commerce might require would have his pains for his reward."

No doubt it is true that when this state of things is brought about, and the supply of silver for use as money and other purposes never exceeds the requirements of commerce, then given sums of money made of either metal will buy equal quantities of the same commodity, and the commercial and legal valuation of gold and silver when priced in terms of one another will coincide.

For the moment we speak of the supply of silver as being in question by way of simplifying the argument, although, of course, what is true of silver is equally true of gold, and the theory of bimetallism applies as much to one metal as to the other.

The questions at issue are these: Will the bimetallic system create this equilibrium of supply and demand, or will it result from the operation of trade? In the former case the amount of gold and silver in use will be regulated by the law of the fixed ratio, and the whole of it will be amenable to the system which rests on that law. And next: Will that amount at all times and under all circumstances be exactly that which commerce requires? Or will there exist at the same time outside the bimetallic system, stocks of gold, or of silver, or of both, which will not only be uninfluenced by its monetary law, but which will, by their action on the relative values of the precious metals, control the system itself, and set limits to the mass of either kind of money which may at any time be in use in the countries where it prevails? Shall we, in fact, see gold and silver always exchanging in any required quantities at the regulation price both in bimetallic countries and everywhere else besides? Or shall we see occasions arise when the value prescribed by the market in other countries comes into conflict with the fixed and legal rate of exchange, and the system at once ceases to attract as much gold and silver money as commerce may require, and its currencies in a few days or hours lose their character and provide trade with a great deal of coin of one metal and with very little of the other? In the latter case the bimetallic currencies will only take up both metals in those proportions, in which, having regard to commercial considerations, they can be profitably used, and exchanged for one another, *under the terms of the bimetallic valuation.*

The theory of bimetallism is that "the law does not arbitrarily fix the relative market price of gold and silver; that it merely legalizes a system of currency which by the operation of natural laws tends, under certain conditions, to preserve a fixed ratio between gold and silver." * This ratio, then, has to be created, and this creation is to be the act of natural laws as opposed to monetary laws. But it is an essential characteristic of a natural law that it acts always and everywhere in one way; it follows, therefore, that the monetary law, which is the instrument with which the bimetallic system is to do its work, must pervade all places and prevail at all times consentaneously with the natural law. The natural law, from the fact of its universal application, comprises within its operations the whole supply of the precious metals throughout the world; the monetary law, to be equally efficient, must do the same.

There is now no legal fixed ratio such as the French law of 1803 laid down, nor is there any agreement among bimetallists as to the figure at which it is to stand. As long as some recommend 15½ to 1, others 18, others 20 to 1, it is obvious that no rate will become the legal rate until it is first recognized and accepted as such by the mercantile classes, who are expected to buy and sell their commodities (as a bimetallist would say) at that ratio. The legal rate, if it is to exert an universal influence, must clearly wait on the evolution of the market rate. Let us suppose for a moment, and for

* "The Theory of Bimetallism," p. 46. Cassell and Co.

the sake of argument, that the market rate has been ascertained and the legal rate fixed in accordance with it by a law which the principal commercial nations of the world agree to accept. It is not any part of the scheme that the desired stability of value between given sums of gold and silver should be established by a wider agreement than this, but on the contrary it is proposed that the constant point, the pole-star of value, should be first fixed in its place by international legislation among Western peoples, and it is assumed that it will then become, by its own inherent infallibility as a guide, the cynosure of all the monetary systems of the rest of the world; and that by this means the monetary law will obtain a range of action coinciding with that of the natural law; or, as we have said elsewhere, it is expected that the monetary law, which is the outcome of the natural law, will regulate it; that effect will control cause!

Let us go on to suppose that the monetary law is introduced, and is accepted by the inhabitants of one quarter of the globe comprising countries which we will call bimetallic, and that in another quarter of the globe are found the silver-using countries, who use silver money almost exclusively, but at the same time, treating gold as a commodity, employ it for purposes of purchase, and that among them it is readily taken in exchange either for silver or for goods at a varying rate depending entirely on commercial conditions. These nations are expected to acquiesce in the provisions of the monetary law, which may lay down that 10,000 coins of gold, and 100,000 coins of silver are of the same value, and that one gold coin shall exchange for 10 silver coins.

Suddenly an invention is discovered by which gold can be produced at half the cost of labour previously expended on it, and as 1 lb. of gold procured 10 lbs. of silver in bimetallic countries before, so now ½ lb. of gold can exchange for the same weight. The gold miners therefore can now, with the same labour as before, get as large a value of silver, and all the advantages in the purchase of commodities which 1 lb. of gold procured for them in the bimetallic region, and ½ lb. of gold besides. There is clearly a market for this extra half-pound of gold (multiplied into an indefinite number of pounds by the activity of mining enterprise), in the silver-using countries. It is not imperatively necessary that each of these extra half-pounds should exchange for 10 lbs. of silver, because nearly the whole cost of their production has been recovered by the sale of the first half-pounds in the bimetallic countries; nor would these extra half-pounds be sent to the bimetallic countries because the half-pounds of gold already sent there avail to purchase all the silver which the full pound could procure before. It is no part of the hypothesis that the supply of silver increases with the cheapening of gold, or that 1 lb. of gold would procure twice as much silver as it did before, or that 1 lb. of gold, and under the new valuation 20 lbs. of silver, would procure twice as much merchandise as 1 lb. of gold and 10 lbs. of silver procured before. The case assumed must be taken in all its parts, and with all the consequences it involves; and if a new relation of value is set up between gold and merchandise, it is evident that its value must fall both in commodities and in silver, and the bimetallic hypothesis fails. For the purposes of the illustration, gold must be assumed to have retained its original market value in the bimetallic country, although it had become twice as abundant throughout the commercial world as it was before. In the silver-using countries, the gold miners would find a ready market for the extra supply of gold at 6, 7, or 8 lbs. of silver to the half-pound and thus a ratio of value for the precious metals would be created outside the bimetallic countries which would be different from that in force within them, and from day to day cause fluctuations in the fixed ratio. The system would break down from its own inherent inability to resist the influence of the new supply of gold on prices in the silver-using countries. The 6, 7, or 8 lbs. of silver which could purchase ½ lb., of gold in those places would be used for that purpose, and each half-pound of gold would be used to buy 10 lbs. of silver for transportation to the silver-using region, and the bimetallic countries would tend to become gold monometallic, and the legal ratio would cease to act with the disappearance of one factor in the equation; or what is equally likely to happen, it would be found, from the circumstance that the values of the precious metals in each other are fixed by the quantity of any particular commodity which a given value of can buy; that ½ lb. of gold and 10 lbs. of silver would procure a certain amount of merchandise in one place, and ½ lb. of gold, and 6 or 8 lbs. of silver, the same quantity of the same merchandise in another place, and the purchasing power of the metals in the dearer and bimetallic countries would necessarily fall and accommodate itself to their purchasing power in the silver-using countries; because traders always buy in cheap markets and leave the dearer markets alone until prices fall in them to the lower level. In this case the bimetallic ratio would give place to that evolved by the free action of commerce in countries lying beyond its influence.

At the present time £100 sterling buys more wheat grown in India, Russia, and the Argentine Republic, than it can buy of English-grown wheat, and the price of the latter therefore tends to fall to that obtaining in those countries. If England were a bimetallic country, then £100 or its legal equivalent in silver, would, according to bimetallic principles, have the same purchasing power. But India, South America, and other silver-using countries have been able in the case assumed to obtain gold at a cheaper rate in silver than the bimetallic rate, and the market rate in those places would differ from the legal rate. It would therefore follow that the same amount of corn would be sold for slightly different weights of gold and for widely differing weights of silver in bimetallic and in silver-using countries respectively; or, which is the same thing, a lesser weight of foreign than of English silver would suffice to buy the same weight of gold. This would necessarily throw the whole system into confusion, and the legal ratio of the bimetallic countries would for the reason given above, adapt itself to the commercial ratio fixed by the values of corn and commodities generally in the precious metals in silver-using countries, and would be in practice abandoned. Unless, therefore, the system of the fixed-ratio can embrace all the gold which in the illustration is produced by the new method more cheaply than before; and it is evident that it cannot do so; then the monetary law not only fails to control the natural law, but fails even to act in correspondence with it. Its universal influence vanishes, and a conflict of ratios arises which can only result in the subjection of the legal, and the supremacy of the natural valuation of gold in silver.

The expedient by which the bimetallists now propose to avert such an eventuality is to bring the currencies of the principal commercial nations of Europe and that of the United States of America under their system, and so prevent the presentation of a redundant supply of silver, from any quarter outside their Union, in their own market for the precious metals. Some countries, all of them silver-using countries possessing in the aggregate stocks of silver of untold magnitude, will constitute the quarter from which such an invasion of silver may be expected. The bimetallists hope to disarm this invasion by fixing, in virtue of the force of their monetary law, a universal price for silver in gold, which shall extend to the silver-using countries.

If they can bring the stock of silver existing in those countries under the control of their system, a universal bimetallism may be established; if they cannot do so, the new Union will be exposed to exactly the same risks as the old, and it will not be in the least degree guaranteed against a repetition of the collapse of 1873. We express this opinion with complete confidence, and we believe that those bimetallists who understand their own principles will admit, that without the co-operation of the silver-using countries of the world a revival of the bimetallism of the Latin Union is impossible.

In order to comprise so vast a supply of silver in the bimetallic system, as will suffice to fix the price of one metal in the other permanently and universally, *India and other silver-using countries of the globe cannot be left outside it, or neglected.* In that case we shall have to deal with the inhabitants of many countries who live under the influence of a great diversity of commercial customs and social habits of immemorial antiquity. The novelty of the bimetallic scheme, the contrast it offers to any financial methods to which they are accustomed, and the prejudice which its Western origin is calculated to excite, are difficulties in the way of its acceptance in Asia that will not be easily, if at all, overcome.

If the mercantile classes among Western nations, to whom the principles of currency are familiar, look askance at the scheme and withhold their support until experience has given them some ground for confidence in its success; how much more may Asiatics be expected to do the same? The confidence, which must be implanted in men's minds, that if they deposit their money in banks worked on this system, they will certainly receive its equivalent in value back again, will be as slow to take root in the East as it appears to be in the West. It is difficult to imagine what the first steps in this direction are likely to be which would have a chance of success in Asia; and as far as we have seen, the bimetallists do not trouble themselves with working out the *modus operandi,* but are contented to repeat their two cardinal maxims : (1) that if all the principal commercial nations join in the convention, the fixed-ratio price will be the market price ; (2) and if the owners of gold and silver in Asia try to exchange the metals for one another at any other rate, there will be no exchanges at all.

It will be sufficient to speak of India as typical of Asiatic countries generally. India provides us with the point of view from which all Asiatic nations will regard the system in which they must be included if it is to succeed at all. No government in that country has hitherto passed laws fixing the price of gold and silver in one another. The precious metals have always throughout the East, either as money or as bullion, exchanged at their commercial value. The mercantile classes in India, than whom there are not in the world more shrewd or sagacious traders, know very well that the relative values of gold and silver are regulated by the same conditions as any other merchandise, and they certainly do not believe, with some modern bimetallists, that those values * follow a specific monetary law which supersedes the regulating influences of commerce, or that the "value of money-metals is controlled by the continued and obligatory absorption of them at the mints at the rate fixed by law."† If they were told that "the State creates the greater part of the value of both gold and silver, for it creates a sure market for them;"† and that "the State which creates the demand can fix the price;"† and that "the variations in the relative value of the two metals of which history tells us, have been the result of legislation, and not of the more or less abundant production of the mines of silver and gold;"† they would regard such theories as contradicted by experience, and when urged as the ground for legislative interference

* Publications of the International Monetary Association, No. 5, p. 10.

† Mons. de Laveleye's "International Bimetallism." London, 1881.

with the free exchange of different kinds of money for one another at the market rate, they would appear to them as specious and delusive arguments put forward by the English with some sinister purpose connected with the abstraction of gold from India. The assertion that a fixation by law of the value of the two kinds of money in one another is indispensably necessary to a circulation of gold money, would be at once disposed of by notorious facts. The Indian people would fairly argue that as gold money can, and does, circulate at its real value in silver among them, there can be no good reason for creating an artificial value for it by law. An absurd belief, suggested by the popular idea that hoarded treasure constitutes wealth, commonly prevails among the uneducated classes that the English export their savings in the form of bullion or coin to their own country from India. As ignorance is a factor in politics, with this and similar delusions Government must reckon, if it proceeds to pass laws regulating the exchange rate for gold and silver money, as such a proceeding would give an appearance of reason to the suspicion that the English were endeavouring to lower the price of gold in silver, and so procure more of it at the same silver price as before, in order to send it out of the country.

To the statement just made, that the precious metals have always in the East exchanged as money at their commercial value; an exception must be made in respect of the copper currency of British India (if copper may for the sake of argument and for the moment be classed as a precious metal), to which the people of India would point as a proof of the inability of the Government to circulate gold and silver money at a fixed rate of exchange. There exists in British territories in India a token currency of copper issued by the State which, according to the variations of the value of copper metal in the market, is rated at a more or less arbitrary valuation in the rupee currency. About ten or fifteen years ago, when copper was worth £90 a ton, token copper money to the nominal value of 100 rs. would be worth at the market 37 rs. The same quantity of coin, allowing for the fall in the gold value both of copper and rupees, is now worth perhaps 27 or 28 rs. The Government copper currency is therefore driven almost entirely out of circulation, and the people use instead a currency of coins made of rough lumps of copper, some square, some round, rudely fashioned and stamped with a few characters, which the mints of some of the native states or perhaps private speculators supply. As a greater quantity of copper in the form of these coins can be obtained for any given sum of silver coin than the same will suffice to purchase of the copper coins of the Imperial mints, the latter are necessarily largely discarded. The legal copper currency of British India is no doubt inadequate in amount, and this is partly because its intrinsic value is low; for the same reason it is but little used; and nothing would be gained by increasing its quantity, for no larger supply of it than is now provided would be made use of by the people as long as its real and its currency valuation differ so widely, and while it is exposed to the competition of full-value coins, although the latter are not legal tender. The same result would be experienced in the case of gold. If gold money were rated at a higher than its market value in silver money; if, for instance, ten sovereigns were rated to exchange for a hundred rupees, while twelve sovereigns were the market value of that sum of silver money, a smaller value or weight of gold would exchange for a hundred rupees, than if the two kinds of money were circulating at their true rate of value in one another. In such a case, if any gold money were circulating at all, which is not likely, it would be, as the copper money is in a similar case, thrown out of use, and the people would use gold as money in other forms than that of legal-tender coin, because they would get a greater weight of metal for any given sum of silver at the market than at the mint. And on the other hand, if twelve sovereigns were rated to exchange for a hundred rupees when ten sovereigns were their market value, then no one would exchange gold money for silver, except by private contract, and at the market instead of at the currency rate.

It must not be forgotten that if the system of the fixed ratio for exchanging gold and silver money were introduced into India, the Government would entirely depend for gold as well as silver metal for coinage on supplies voluntarily brought to the mints by the people themselves; and unless the legal and the commercial valuation coincide, it is evident that but little metal of either kind will be forthcoming for the purpose. The objection would certainly be made to a bimetallism on the principles of the Latin Union, that if the Government cannot circulate copper money over-rated in the rupee currency by more than 300 per cent., they will not be able to circulate a gold currency undervalued in silver money at 25 per cent. or any other figure; and if gold is made the standard and silver becomes undervalued, then the volume of the currency will be still more disproportionate to the requirements of the people than it is now, and all the evils which low prices bring upon commerce and industry will follow. How such objections are to be met, or what inducements can be offered to the people of India to put either gold or silver, in unrestricted and sufficient quantities, into circulation on the terms imposed by the system of the Latin Union, it is for the bimetallists to show.

Those who are acquainted with the credulous and suspicious character of the people of India, can understand the panic which any attempt to disturb the relative commercial values of silver and gold by legislative interference would excite. It is beyond doubt that a contraction of the rupee currency would be the result of an apprehension that Government was bringing its power to bear on the regulation of values; and that the paper currency would be speedily returned into the issue department and disappear from circulation. "If the values of silver and gold are to be fixed," the Indian trader will argue, "then the values of rupees and commodities will next be taken in hand, and the less coin we use the less we shall lose, and the more goods we shall buy with what we do use." In this event the rate of interest would rise, rupee paper (of the public debt) would fall considerably, the returns to capital employed in developing the industrial resources of the country would diminish, the repayment of loans borrowed for business purposes (and a large part of the agriculture of the country is carried on with borrowed money), would become a heavier burden, the revenue of the country would be collected with less ease than is even now the case when the people are paying some hundreds of millions of rupees a year in extra taxation levied to meet the "loss by exchange," the progress of the country would receive a material check, and the financial credit of the Government would be seriously shaken. These are some among the "fresh and grave difficulties" which, as the Special Commissioners very truly report (Final Report, p. 85), would be provoked by the inclusion of India in a bimetallic convention on the principles of the Latin Union.

But let us suppose that India is excluded from the Convention and the existing prohibition which her monetary law places on the use of gold legal-tender money is maintained, then we have to consider the effect which the Indian monometallic system with a silver standard, considered in relation to the propensity which her people have always, and at present more than ever display to import and hoard gold treasure, will exercise on the bimetallic currencies of the West.

It will no doubt be urged that the commercial instincts of Eastern peoples will secure their adhesion to a system which provides them with the only terms on which their gold and silver can be exchanged. We repeat that the price has first to be established; and in the process of doing this, constant fluctuations in the rate of exchange will occur. Nor will it be forgotten that under the system as it was established in the Latin Union, this price, even when fixed by law, was inconstant. Sometimes one metal, sometimes the other, became undervalued by the standard of the fixed ratio; and this circumstance will be held to prove the existence of a commercial value in disagreement with the legal valuation, and that in past times, that which caused the disappearance of the undervalued metal from bimetallic currencies was the prevalence of a commercial price for one metal in terms of the other, outside the bimetallic system, different from that prescribed by law for use within it. The people of India, therefore, and other nations similarly situated, will naturally wait to see what commercial valuation will be evolved out of the remonetizing of silver as full-value coin in Europe, and whether it coincides with the price fixed in gold by law, and if it does not they will assuredly stand by the former as giving the only terms on which they will exchange their gold and silver.

It has been said that monometallists, like the professors of an orthodox religious creed, feel above any necessity for defending the reasons for their belief. Those, however, who are unwilling to disturb the existing currency system of the United Kingdom, have ample reason for their disinclination to change, and are quite able to prove the truth of the convictions upon which they act. This country has prospered greatly during the last seventy years in those respects, in which a sound currency system is a material aid to prosperity. The report of the Royal Commission leaves no room for doubt that our commerce and industries would be exposed to grave risks and various disadvantages by the substitution of bimetallism for our own system. Gold monometallists at present hold the field. Those who wish to drive them off must show that they are able to do so, and that if they were to succeed in doing so, the country would be better off under the system which they wish it to adopt than it has been in the past. It is for those who assert the positive to explain in what manner the fulfilment of their predictions will be brought about, not for those who deny their propositions and reject their prophecies to prove the negative. It is enough for the latter to say, "You can give us no grounds either in reason or experience to go upon in accepting your theories, but much to the contrary. If you wish us to believe what you say, the burden of proving that you are in the right lies with you." Whether they will be able to do this will appear from what follows.

For the bimetallists, the most encouraging expression of opinion which the Report of the Special Commission contains is to be found in § 193, p. 59, and is as follows:—

"Nor does it appear to us, *à priori*, unreasonable to suppose that the existence in the Latin Union of a bimetallic system, with a ratio of $15\frac{1}{2}$ to 1, fixed between the two metals should have been capable of keeping the market price of silver steady at approximately that ratio."

The arguments for and against this view may be stated concisely as follows:—

1. The bimetallists allege that under the system of the Latin Union the monetary law regulated the commercial law;

2. That the bimetallic tie held silver and gold together at a ratio of $15\frac{1}{2}$ to 1;

3. That when the tie was broken, silver fell

BIMETALLISM STATED.

in value to 20 : 1 in gold, *i.e.* to its commercial value as distinct from its bimetallic value;

4. That therefore the bimetallic tie maintained the price of silver, *i.e.* raised it to a higher value than it otherwise would have had, and brought its commercial into coincidence with its bimetallic value, and that if the tie were restored it would do so again;

5. That this effect was caused by the bimetallic tie creating a demand for silver and regulating the supply in correspondence therewith, and this ceased with the rupture of the tie.

Another view of the case is—

1. That about 1873 a great supply of silver came into the market (how or why the supply came is not, for the moment, to the purpose), for which there was no demand, and which was certainly not evoked by the action of the French monetary law;

2. That an ordinary supply, the bimetallic system could take up and dispose of;

3. That so large a supply as this was too much for it to manage;

4. That the attempt to manage it would have practically broken down the machinery designed to circulate a dual currency of full-value coin in the Latin Union, by driving out gold as money from its system;

5. That the managers of the system therefore refused to make the attempt, and the machine was stopped working, and the bimetallic tie was ruptured.

Now, in the case just stated, was it the cheapness of silver which broke the bimetallic tie, or did the rupture of the tie cause the cheapness of silver?

Did the monetary law control the commercial law, or did the commercial law control the monetary law?

Bimetallists say that the cheapness of silver was subsequent to, not antecedent to, the rupture of the tie; that if the tie had been maintained the cheapness of silver would not have supervened.

To this the answer which may be made is—

Abundance of silver for which there is no demand for money involves a fall in its value. Under the circumstances of 1873 abundance and cheapness became interchangeable terms. It was the magnitude of this redundant supply of silver which compelled the managers of the bimetallic currencies to refrain from attempting to deal with it, which in fact broke the tie. As abundance and cheapness of silver are in this connection synonymous terms, it was the cheapness of silver which caused the rupture of the tie.

But the other side say that it was the rupture of the tie which caused the cheapness of silver.

The decision on the issue thus raised must go by the answer to a third question. "If the bimetallic tie could have prevented the cheapness of silver, which occurred as a consequence of its rupture, why was it not maintained to do so?" The answer is obvious,—because it could not do so.

It follows therefore that as an occasion has arisen (1) when the system failed to regulate the supply of silver, and the metal was forthcoming in quantities wholly irrespective of any demand originating in the bimetallic system; and (2) silver fell to a low valuation in gold which the monetary law failed to arrest; and (3) the monetary law proved unable to exert any regulating influence whatever on the commercial value of the metal in gold;—so a like occasion may occur again.

If the advocates of bimetallism claim the confidence of the public in their ability always and under all circumstances to secure the stipulated equivalent in one kind of money for any given amount of the other, they cannot expect to acquire it by fixing a ratio of value by their own mere motion. The Convention must first prove that their rate is that which may be expected to prevail, because experience shows that it is the true rate. But this experience and the resulting confidence in the bimetallic system require time and opportunity to come into existence. Unless this confidence is complete and assured, the supply of either kind of metal may at any time fall short. The Convention will in vain protest—"If our ratio is universally adopted there can be no other." The mercantile classes will answer: "We should first like to see how generally or how partially it is adopted, and whether any currencies circulate outside your system which may any day wreck it." A man will hesitate to pay 100 sovereigns into a bimetallic bank if he feels any doubt whether he will get them back again. If he takes notes for them and pays away the notes for their legal equivalent of silver, he must feel certain that the sum he receives in silver will at any future time bring him back his 100 sovereigns, or goods which are valued at 100 sovereigns and not less. Whether or not such a result is certain to occur, is the matter of doubt which underlies the general suspicion of bimetallism.

The collapse of that system in 1874–78, is the most striking incident in its history, and it does not tend to create an assurance of this certainty.

"Let us try the experiment over again on a larger scale," say the bimetallists. "If all the principal commercial nations join together to fix the price of gold and silver in one another, general confidence will take the place of partial suspicion." But this confidence must have a commencement. It must take root somewhere before it can grow and flourish. The initial steps taken to set the system at work will therefore be carefully watched for any signs of failure. Public opinion will remain in suspense. Men will wait to see how the large accumulations of unused silver which are available for a revival of the bimetallic system are brought into use without expelling gold from circulation, how silver which is 25 or 30 per cent. cheaper in gold than it was fifteen years ago, is to be brought up to par.

An adjustment of the proportions of the metallic money in each country corresponding to the fixed ratio (as will afterwards be explained), must be arranged. If the ratio is fixed say at 16 : 1, there must be a close approximation in the volume of each kind of coin in circulation in every one of the associated countries to those figures, otherwise the ratio would be merely nominal. We shall, of course, be told that it is an entire misapprehension of the bimetallic principle to suppose that it is necessary that any of the associated countries should hold a stock of metal divided between gold and silver in proportions corresponding to the terms of the fixed-ratio; that in France the napoleon exchanged for 20 francs, irrespective of the relative weights of the mass of either kind of coin in circulation; that as long as any one can get notes for either silver or gold at that rate, no one need trouble himself to find out whether the silver coin in circulation is sixteen times heavier in mass than the gold coin. But under the French system it was not regarded as a matter of the last importance that gold and silver money should always be obtainable indifferently on the sale of commodities in any required quantities, or that gold money should always be forthcoming for notes or for silver money. To prevent the currency being deprived of its gold constituent, or the amount of gold in circulation in France being suddenly reduced, the Bank of France retained the power of cashing or of refusing to cash notes drawn in terms of silver with gold coin, at its discretion. This practice, however, would not do for England. It does not appear to enter into the calculations of those who wish to introduce the system of the Latin Union into England, that producers, manufacturers, and traders will reject a valuation which to be real must at all times be ready to stand the test of a free exchange of metallic money. If a gold mohur is to be worth 16 rs. (the two coins being of equal weight), or if 16 ozs. of silver money are to pass for 1 oz. of gold money, then there must be at hand a sufficient quantity of either kind of coin to insure the actual exchange whenever it may be demanded.

The essence of a true bimetallism is that creditors, that is, the holders of notes, should always be able to demand from their debtors, that is, the banker who has received their deposits, payment in whichever metal they may choose to ask for. In this country, therefore, and necessarily in all countries associated with England in a bimetallic convention, the system will not be tolerated for a day unless the paper currency which it may bring into use is absolutely convertible on demand in either gold or silver at the option of those presenting notes for payment. It is for the bimetallists to show how the reserve against which the notes are issued is to be kept full of both kinds of coin up to the limit of the whole issue of notes.

It is nothing to the purpose to say that 20 francs could always procure a napoleon under all variations in the relative quantities of gold and silver coin in France. Though this may have been true of one napoleon, it was frequently not the case when half a million, or even smaller sums in gold, were asked for in exchange for notes. Throughout the Latin Union the necessity for keeping the mass of each kind of coin in correspondence with the proportions prescribed by law was obviated by the authority which the Bank of France possessed of refusing to make payments of gold if it thought fit to do so, on the principle, that the five-franc piece was a full legal-tender coin. This circumstance and the consequent inability of the mercantile public to obtain gold from the Bank of France in any desired quantity at all times; and the certainty that the Bank of England will always pay its notes in gold, the fact that gold can always be obtained in England by those who hold bills drawn in this country, and the certainty that gold could not be so obtained in France, has greatly contributed to make London the centre of international finance.

Bimetallists argue that their system can bestow by law a value on silver and gold, which they do not otherwise possess, somewhat in this way. "Governments," they say, "would not impose the ratio they adopted, but the adoption of a certain ratio, let us say 15½ to 1, would be automatic and perfectly natural, and consequently it would impose itself on the commercial world" (Appendix ii., Final Report, p. 271, § 11).

Some propose to fix the ratio at 15½ to 1, under the belief that silver will appreciate to the point at which it stood before the causes which lowered its value in gold came into play. Others think that it should be fixed nearer the present point of value, because such a valuation would cause less disturbance of the existing relative value of the two metals, and because it would be unfair to the general public to increase considerably, by law, the value of silver for the benefit of those who happen to hold large stocks of the metal.

That the precious metals have an economic value regulated by supply and demand, and that the price of one in the other depends on these conditions in connection with the work thrown upon them as money in exchanging commodities in commerce is a circumstance which bimetallists appear to regard as quite secondary to the influence which they expect their system to exert on the price of one metal in the other. They feel sure that the action of the law will regulate the supply and demand, and thus fix the price.* They seem to take no account of the requirements of commerce in choosing a ratio. Given the ratio, 15½ to 1, or 20 to 1, which of the

* "International Bimetallism." London, 1881.

two is immaterial, commerce will require just as little or just as much of both kinds of money as can be brought into the system on the terms they may dictate in fixing the ratio. If the establishment of a true ratio of value in this manner were possible, if when adopted it would necessarily impose itself on the commercial world, then it stands to reason that the monetary law has power to prescribe the quantities of every kind of merchandise which is bought and sold all over the world; for unless the ratio thus adopted were identical with that evolved by the operations of commerce, it certainly would not "impose itself on the commercial world."

The question will then arise, Which side of the world is to constitute the predominating market; by which will the universal price, the ideal of bimetallism, be fixed; by the East or by the West? Bimetallists, being Europeans, of course answer—by the West; but Asiatics will be of a different opinion. If the ratio which the Convention may fix upon is the commercial ratio, no conflict of ratios need occur, but if it is some other ratio, how can the actual rate be ascertained? Mr. Grenfell says (Qs. 4267–78), "Before you can say what the relative value of gold and silver is you must demonetize gold, and when you have done that, you will have some *other thing* than the money standard to tell you what the relative value is. At the present time, the privilege of the law having been conferred on gold and taken away from silver, the ratio is 20 or 21 to 1, but you cannot say what the natural ratio would be unless you demonetized gold first. Then you consider that, having gold as the sole standard here, puts a fictitious value upon it? I would call it an artificial value."

Herein we find an opinion given on two points, viz. that (1) in order to ascertain the real or market value of one metal in the other, both must be put on the same footing; and that (2) to make one metal the standard of value to the exclusion of the other gives the selected metal an artificial value. But it is not necessary to demonetize gold in order to put both metals on the same footing. This result can be obtained equally well in another way, that is to say, by using them both on the same terms, by exchanging them for one another at the relation of value which each holds to a third factor—that "other thing" than the money standard which will "tell you what the relative value is;" this third factor in the equation is—merchandise in commerce. Secondly, if to employ one metal as the standard gives it an artificial value, and a purchasing power higher than it would otherwise have, this quality arises from the favoured metal being secured against the competition of the other in the business of exchanging commodities. Under the bimetallic system this security from competition in favour alternately, of one metal or the other is less complete, than it is in the case where a single standard is used. If gold, for instance, becomes really more valuable at the market than it was before, and is undervalued at the fixed ratio, and is therefore withdrawn from the currency, silver is secured from competition for the time being, that is to say, until circumstances alter, and by a fall in the value of gold, as measured in commodities, the legal and commercial valuations coincide, and it becomes possible to circulate gold again without loss. The enhancement in the value of silver may not be so great from this cause as it would be if the use of gold as legal-tender money were absolutely forbidden, but the effect of the undervaluation of gold and its temporary disuse as money is not to cause the values of the two metals to approach the equation prescribed by the fixed ratio, but rather to drive them apart, to lower the value of the discarded metal, and to raise that of the metal in use. In any view of the case, therefore, neither the constitution by law of one metal as the standard, or of both as the standard at a fixed rate of exchange, provides a means of ascertaining the commercial or natural value of gold and silver money in one another. Under both systems, although in different degrees, the free action of trade on the determination of this value is hindered; whereas, if both are used as money at their true commercial rate of exchange in one another, any artificial enhancement of the purchasing power of either is avoided, and their true relation of value in one another is ascertained with infallible certainty.

Mr. Grenfell's opinion involves the necessary conclusion that the "natural value" we are in search of must be created by the ebb and flow of the precious metals from the shores of each country to those of every other engaged in international trade. Unless there is a general resumption in the use of silver money in quantities unrestricted by law, how is this tide to be set in motion?

Meanwhile the ratio will vary from day to day.

It is by no means a wild prediction that the Eastern ratio will turn out to be the most important factor in determining the figure at which the market value will stand. The stock of silver in Asia is beyond all comparison greater than that held by European nations. The proportion of silver to be found in that part of the world, to that of gold, is high, while in Europe it is comparatively low. On the other hand, Asia, and especially India, holds a vast stock of gold which is almost entirely unused, while in the West the stock of gold is all in use. The amount and value of the mass of either gold or silver available as a contribution of fresh metal to the currencies of a bimetallic convention is certainly very great, but how great it is not possible to say. The extent of the area over which the possession of both metals is dispersed, the varying quantities in which they are held by different nations in Asia, the facility with which they can nowadays be transported from place to place, the conservative habits of her numberless populations, a prescription of thirty centuries, which throughout that quarter of the globe is universally in favour of the exchange of different kinds of money for one another at the varying rates which the competitions of the market from day to day evolve, all combine to give to the East a preponderating influence in the adjustment of the relative values of gold and silver.

If the ratio adopted by the Convention does not happen to be the commercial ratio, but if, for instance, 15½ or 16 to 1 is chosen with a view to avoid recoinage of existing silver currencies, the conflict of ratios will at once begin. The West will say, "We will give you no more than 16 ozs. of silver for 1 oz. of your gold;" the East will answer by buying as much gold from the West as it can pay for at that rate and take it away. It is nothing to the purpose for bimetallists to deny that this will happen, because the Indians or Chinese will have no use for the gold when they get it. In face of the fact that India alone of all Asiatic countries has been making purchases of gold on these terms for the last fifty-four years, to a value exceeding 130 millions, it is incumbent on the bimetallist to show cause why Asia will cease to draw gold from Europe, America, and other places where the metal is either used or produced, in the future as she has in the past; especially if her gains in doing so become, under the arrangements of the Convention increasingly great. If the people of India buy and hoard gold when it costs them more than 20 rs. a tolah, will they not do so when they can get the same weight of the metal for 16 rs. ? Why should they let their gold go at 16 ozs. when they do not let it go at 20 ozs. ? Until they see some proof that silver has ceased to fall, why should they step in to improve its value by selling their gold at a loss to themselves? As long as it continues profitable to the nations of Asia to draw gold from the West, what reason is there for the belief that gold and silver will flow backwards and forwards between the two hemispheres, and that the currencies of bimetallic countries will be replenished by contributions of both metals from Asia. Let the ratio fixed by law be that which the conditions of commerce prescribe, and the conflict will cease with the disappearance of the cause of contention; but with Asia knocking at the doors of the Western banks for all the gold which she can afford to buy with her surplus exports, so long as the ratio adopted by a bimetallic convention is not identical with the valuation of commerce, that convenient abundance of both kinds of coin which is essential to the existence of the system can never be depended upon. It therefore still remains to be proved that the bimetallic contention—that if the principal commercial nations of the world join in fixing a rate of exchange for gold and silver, that that rate will fix their price throughout the world—has any real foundation in fact. We can find no reason for this belief, the bimetallists appear to put their trust in it, as *à priori* certain. Their confidence is not the result of either experience or successful experiment. On the other hand, reasons have been given why the mercantile classes will remain unconvinced of its soundness, and as long as they are so, neither in Europe or in Asia will they acquiesce in the system or yield up their gold and silver to the banks or State treasuries which may be engaged in working it.

When bimetallists tell us that a ratio if it is once agreed upon by all the principal commercial nations of the world will so universally rule that no one will ask for more silver for his gold or *vice versâ* than the Convention may prescribe as its price, because he will get no more if he does, and that therefore all mankind will hasten to exchange 16 ozs. of silver, or any other quantity agreed upon, for 1 oz. of gold; are they not jumping to a conclusion rather than arriving at it step by step? They trust, in fact, to the general acceptance of the law to act on the imagination of men and to beget that kind of confidence which only comes of experience. In such matters action proceeds on facts not on fancies, and the facts are all against the theory that the force of law will avail to maintain the fixed rate of exchange at all times and under all circumstances without diminution in the supply and circulation of both kinds of coin indifferently. The only experience which can be appealed to, shows clearly enough that the actual exchange of gold and silver money under the French system was often merely nominal, and that the conditions under which the system was worked in France, if reproduced in this country, would lead to intolerable inconvenience, and involve the certain destruction of the financial supremacy which England at present enjoys.

The public confidence in the immediate as well as in the final success of bimetallism in England must rest upon some kind of foundation in ascertained facts; but in the absence of that, let us try to make a forecast of the manner in which the system would be introduced among us. Let us imagine the currency becoming bimetallic, and the Bank of England taking the lead in working it. The Mint would issue as much gold and silver coin of the prescribed weights as the metal sent in by individuals and bullion dealers might suffice to fabricate. The Bank would receive silver bullion as it now receives gold bullion, and would issue notes against it in terms (it may be presumed) of the pound sterling for its value at the ratio agreed upon. From figures in the reports of the Special Commission it appears likely that the stock of unused silver in the middle of the year 1888 exceeded 208 millions sterling in value, and from the difficulty of obtaining complete accounts, the amount may be very much more. The impulse which the introduction of an extended bimetallism would give to the silver-mining industry might increase the stock available for the experiment to an unmanageable amount. The coinage of this mass of silver would doubtless be spread over all the associated countries, but it is quite certain that the stock of silver to be found in each country would not hold a relation of value to the stock of gold held in the same place, at all corresponding with the terms of the fixed ratio. Suppose the ratio to be fixed at 16 to 1, and let it be granted for the sake of argument that all the silver is in weight sixteen times as heavy as all the gold in the possession of the Convention; that circumstance would not warrant the acceptance of the equation of value determined by the fixed ratio, until the metals held by each individual country were adjusted to that proportion. Germany might hold $\frac{3}{5}$ths of the value of its currency in gold, Austria might hold her currency in exactly the opposite proportion, England might hold next to no silver at all, and France more than she knew what to do with. For each country to provide itself with the necessary supply of metallic money, a great movement of coin and bullion must inevitably take place and go on for a long while, which it would be the business of the exchange banks, of bullion-dealers and others in possession of stocks of the precious metals, to direct. This they would do in the ordinary course of their business, and necessarily with a view to making a profit in doing so. Thus, while an enormous mass of silver and another of gold were being placed where each was most wanted, there would be added to the ordinary variations in exchange, which arise from international indebtedness, another set of variations in the exchange rate of gold and silver resulting from this process of dispersion of the precious metals over different parts of the world in their proper proportions. While this was in progress, these variations would be incessant, and every change, however trifling, would be the occasion for a demand for one metal on payment with the other, for operations in the exchanges with foreign countries, or to be hoarded against a rise.

The paper currency which, in consequence of a greatly extended use of silver under the new system, would be in circulation in larger quantities than is now the case, would become the real test whether the two kinds of money hold to one another on any given day the value prescribed by law. Let us suppose that, with a circulation of 170 millions sterling, 10 millions consist of gold coin and 160 millions of silver coin, and that owing to the inconvenience of handling silver, 100 millions of silver are reserved as the metallic support to that value of notes, and that out of 10 millions of gold in circulation, 5 millions of gold coin are held in reserve against an issue of notes to that value. On bimetallic principles bills would be discounted, money would be lent, or paid away by the passing of notes issued against either the silver or the gold reserve indifferently. On the same principles there would be no reason why the notes for 105 millions should not be drawn in terms of the pound sterling and made payable on demand in either or both kinds of coin at the option of the bearer. There would then be 105 millions of notes in circulation, with only 5 millions of gold in reserve to cash any value of them for which gold might be demanded. If for any reason a suspicion arose that the exchange could not be kept at the par of the fixed ratio, a run would be made on the bank for the dearer metal, and if that metal were gold the whole of it would be withdrawn from the reserve, and for a similar reason the remaining 5 millions would be taken out of circulation also, and there would remain only silver either in the Bank of England or in the country, and the Bank would be broke through a run on it for gold. This is exactly the catastrophe which comes into view, at the end of every discussion on the practical working of the scheme in detail. Whenever a forecast is made stage by stage of the process by which the results of the system are to be obtained, monometallism of the cheaper metal invariably makes its appearance in the distance.

This is no imaginary eventuality. In 1860, and again in 1876, something very similar occurred in France. On the former occasion the larger part of the bank's reserve was held in silver, the proportions being a little over 3 of silver to 1 of gold. Silver was appreciating, and to avert a withdrawal of its reserve of silver, the Bank of France exchanged 2 millions worth of silver with the Bank of England for 2 millions worth of gold, and thus brought the stock of the metal most in demand to a higher figure, and replenished the supply. The case we are now considering is that of an appreciation of the smaller stock of metal—the gold held, *ex hypothesi*, by the Bank. But to what quarter could the directors of the Bank of England turn for help? What country would take 50 or 60 millions of silver off its hands in exchange for the same value in gold, and so by increasing the stock of gold in the Bank's reserve help it to meet the demand, and to redress the defect of value in favour of silver?

Again, in 1876, the Bank of France held the larger part of its reserve in the appreciating metal, gold; it held 50 millions sterling in gold to 20 millions sterling in silver. To have allowed this gold to have been taken away and silver substituted for it would have forced the country into a system of monometallism, with silver as the standard, and no such exchange as that of 1860 could have been effected on any large scale without bringing into the reserve a quantity of the least desirable metal for which there would have been little or no demand and use. The alternative which was adopted was the abandonment of the bimetallic system, and the substitution for it of gold monometallism, with silver circulating in limited quantities at an artificial rate of exchange.

The mere apprehension that such a situation might arise would prevent the required confidence in the ability of the Bank to work the scheme ever taking root, still less growing into a conviction in the minds of the mercantile class; and until this confidence is first secured the system cannot even make a start.

The bimetallist members of the Commission are of opinion that if the average ratio of two or three years were taken, to the neglect both of the ratio of $15\frac{1}{2}$ to 1 and of that which happened to be the market ratio at the date fixed for the re-introduction of the bimetallic system, a stable ratio might be maintained, provided that the principal commercial nations of the world would accept and strictly adhere to bimetallism at the suggested ratio. They are not agreed as to the inclusion of India in any such arrangements; nor can they give an opinion as to the view which would be taken by Australia and other of our colonies with reference to the formation of a bimetallic union. As large producers of gold, they might naturally take objection to it, and it would be a serious matter to introduce a different system of coinage in the mother-country and our larger colonies (Final Report, part ii. p. 85).

In support of their case they argue that fluctuations of exchange between countries having different standards would cease so far as those fluctuations depend on the varying relation which silver holds to gold; that the adoption of bimetallism would tend to check, diminish, or prevent a fall in prices so far as it may be due to an appreciation of gold; that if the fall in the gold price of silver has caused a fall in the price of commodities produced in, and exchangeable between gold-and-silver-using countries respectively, this cause would cease to operate when once a stable ratio between the metals were established; that if it be true that the fall in the gold price of silver unduly favours Indian manufacturers in their competition for trade at home and with silver-using countries, there would be no extension of this fostering influence; that if the production of gold continues to diminish, or ceases, the enlarged basis for credit which the bimetallic system would afford, would lessen the risk of the system of credit (which now rests on a gold basis) being disturbed by an appreciation of gold. How far these theories and anticipations are reliable the reader can judge from the preceding arguments; there are, besides, to be gathered from the Report of the Commission several practical objections to the bimetallism of the Latin Union, among which are the following :—

(1) Some unprecedented discovery of one or other of the precious metals might make the maintenance of a constant ratio difficult. (2) The burden imposed on the Indian exchequer, due to the fall in the value of silver, would become permanent. (3) If the gold price of commodities has fallen in consequence of the fall in the gold price in silver, that fall, other things remaining the same, would become permanent, and the benefit of a rise in the gold price of silver would be lost. (4) If the financial position of England is in any way bound up with the fact that her currency is monometallic, and her standard a gold one, that position would be imperilled. (5) Any change in the English system would give rise to apprehension of further changes, and such an apprehension cannot be treated as a trivial circumstance or as one to be lightly regarded. (6) Under the bimetallic system contracts to pay in one or other metal would be common; this practice would send the favoured metal to a premium, and produce considerable financial disturbance. (7) If one or more of the associated nations were to recede from the Convention, the arrangement would be disturbed, and England might have to go back to a monometallic system, and find herself in a worse position than if she had maintained her existing standard. (8) At present this country is not dependent, in respect of her currency system, on any other country, and this condition of freedom

would cease if she became a party to an international agreement. Dangers arising from this connection would be aggravated by the engagements that the country might be required to enter into regarding coinage currency and other internal financial arrangements. (9) In some of the associated countries the banks or governments might make it their business to accumulate gold for objects of their own, in spite of the bimetallic agreement, and if a fear of the Convention breaking down arose, a struggle for gold might set in between the members of the Union, which would deprive gold-using countries of their customary supply. (10) As in France, between 1830 and 1845, the currency was almost entirely silver; and as from 1846 to 1865 it was almost entirely gold, with the result that in 1845 an *agio* was taken on gold coins; so it might happen on the most extended international agreement, that from time to time in some of the associated countries a premium would be charged on either gold or silver coins, and an *agio* on any part of our coinage would be a serious evil.

As has already been said, the burden of proving their case rests with the advocates of bimetallism. How its principles can be placed on any scientific basis at all, or how they can be stated plainly and consistently without disclosing conditions which prove their unsoundness, is what those who profess them have as yet failed to show.

It will not be considered irrelevant to the foregoing argument if two expressions of their views, which Mr. Goschen and Mr. Gladstone have at different times made public, are reproduced in this place. Mr. Goschen's opinion was quoted from a report of the International Monetary Conference held in Paris in 1881, by Mr. J. H. Norman, in a paper read before the London Chamber of Commerce, in January, 1888, from which the following extract is made :—

"Remarking on facts submitted by Mr. Feer-Herzog and a proposition made by Mr. Horton, Mr. Goschen said, 'What Mr. Horton has asked was that the Conference should pronounce on the utility of the relation irrespective of the present possibilities or impossibilities of establishing it. Now he did not consider it necessary to give a categorical reply to a question thus hypothetically put; but if the character of the question were changed by the question of principle being no longer separated from the question of execution, he would modify also the character of his answer, and would not in that case hesitate to affirm, as Mr. Feer-Herzog had done, *the entire and absolute impossibility of the establishment of a fixed ratio*, and this for many reasons of a scientific and economic nature, which he need not enter into in detail.' Again, at the same conference, he is reported to have said, 'I merely desired to combat the theory of the economists who demand the universal adoption of the single gold standard, a measure which in my view might be the cause of the greatest disasters. I maintain my assertions in this connection absolutely. I believe that it would be a great misfortune if a propaganda against silver should succeed, and I protest against the theory, according to which this metal must be excluded from the monetary systems of the world. But from my words no opinion ought to be deduced in favour of the adoption of the double standard—*a system to which my colleagues and myself are entirely opposed, and which has against it the public opinion of the nation which I have the honour to represent*. As for the desire which has been expressed that the hope be left open that some day a fixed relation may be established between gold and silver, and an international value given to them, the English delegate declared that in his view it was impossible to realize this, impossible to maintain it in theory, and that it was contrary to the principles of science." *

Mr. Gladstone's views are given in the following letter, which appeared in some of the daily papers about the middle of the year (1889).

"Replying to Mr. R. L. Everett, of Rushmer, Ipswich (who sat for the Woodbridge Division of Suffolk from 1885 to 1886), who requested that the right hon. gentleman would receive a small deputation of his supporters in Suffolk on the money question, as connected with the distress existing among the agricultural classes in the county, Mr. Gladstone has forwarded the following letter:—

"'Dear Sir,

"'I am very reluctant to send you a reply which may be thought to indicate indifference to the circumstances of depressed interests in land, whether they may be those of landlords, farmers, or labourers, for I fear that these last also have, in some parts of the country, been undergoing a diminution of wages very much to be lamented.

"'But the special calls at the present time put it

* Extract from the International Monetary Conference, August, 1878. Washington Government Printing Press, 1879.

wholly out of my power to enter orally upon any full or profitable discussion on a subject which is in itself complex, and the adequate illustration of which from contemporary facts would require an expenditure of time beforehand such as it is out of my power to make.

"'I know that the circumstances of agriculture (in which I have every reason to feel a deep interest) vary materially, not only from time to time, but also in one portion of the country as compared with another; and, while I regret that in Suffolk you should find it your duty to record an increasing depression, I trust that that county may soon share in the relative improvement which is, I think, observable in various parts of the country. I cherish this hope all the more, because the great coal and metal industries, which for many recent years shared the depression of agriculture, or even suffered still more heavily, now show signs of revival.

"'In no case can anything but mischief arise from referring distress to causes which are not its real source. The standard value, which is the great instrument of exchange, is itself a commodity, and, being such, is itself subject to fluctuations. Such fluctuations are economically an evil, and every wisely governed state should seek to have for its standard of value the commodity which is the least subject to fluctuation.

"'That commodity, as I conceive, is gold, and to adopt any other standard, or to add to gold any other metal more subject than gold to fluctuation, would be to increase the fluctuation, and therewith the consequent inconvenience or distress. If the change were made which should of itself lower the value of sterling money, in which debts are payable, this would be an additional and most formidable mischief.

"'Thirty or forty years ago it was very commonly thought that gold had undergone a very heavy depreciation. There is now an opinion that it has been artificially and very largely forced up in value. My belief has been all along that any increase or any decrease of value which has taken place has been within very narrow limits.

"'I cannot deny that the action of certain great Continental States may have had a limited effect in raising the exchangeable value of gold. Such action has arisen, I must suppose, from a desire to attain an approach to the best possible standard; and, while I regret the inconvenience which may be due even to a minor change of value, there will be a future compensation in the results of a policy that extends the area over which the best and most stable standard is in use. I also observe that incidental contraction may be counteracted by incidental expansion. It is at this time thought by many persons that South Africa is about to make a material addition to the available gold currency of the world. I personally am aware of no sufficient reason why we ourselves should not effect a moderate addition to it by the gradual introduction of a carefully limited system of issuing notes smaller in value than £5. But I am convinced that any search for industrial relief of whatever kind from legislative alteration in the basis of our exchanges, great and small, which is gold, would be a barren and hopeless quest, diverting men for the time from efforts after practical thrift and improvement, and ending in substantial, perhaps in bitter disappointment. As your letter appeals to me on a subject of wide public interest, you are entirely free, if you should think proper, to publish this reply.

"'Allow me to remain, dear sir,
"'Faithfully yours,
"'W. E. GLADSTONE.
"'London, July 8.'"

Both these high authorities affirm different parts of the contention of the preceding argument. Mr. Goschen pronounces "the entire and absolute impossibility of the establishment of a fixed ratio." He considers that the exclusion of silver from use as money would be a great misfortune, from which it may be inferred that in his opinion an extension of its use by legitimate means is in every way desirable. Mr. Goschen's opposition to a double standard is disclosed in this extract, and the double standard he was then speaking about was that of the Latin Union. There is nothing in this extract which implies any opinion either favourable or otherwise on the question of a dual currency of full-value gold and silver money, with gold as a standard of value, such as that to which the reader's attention will now be invited.

Mr. Gladstone's opinion is seen to be that, in an investigation such as this is into the causes of the industrial competition of Asia in European markets, "nothing but mischief can arise from referring distress to causes which are not its real source"—to the exchanges, for instance, instead of to cheap labour and cheap production. The theory which the foregoing arguments are partly directed to establish is also affirmed, that "the standard of value, which is the great instrument of exchange, is itself a commodity, and, being such, is itself subject to fluctuations." And the superiority of a gold standard over any other is emphasized in the following words, "That commodity, as I conceive, is gold, and to adopt any other standard, or to add to gold any other metal more subject than gold to fluctuation, would be to increase the fluctuation." An explanation of the economic reasons why this superiority would assert itself in India as much as elsewhere, will occupy the remainder of this book, and it will be found indirectly to derive confirmation from that part of Mr. Gladstone's letter wherein he speaks of there being found a future compensation for the inconvenience which may be due even to a minor change of value, "in the results of a policy that extends the area over which the best and most stable standard is in use." As one of the objects in the proposed reform of the Indian currency is to extend the use of gold money throughout India, and its regulating influence on prices and the exchanges to more remote parts of the East, the arguments employed to establish the principle upon which it proceeds (apart from all details of execution and practice), may well claim, in view of this expression of opinion, the reader's attention.

CHAPTER IX.

Antiquity of the trade of India and of use of coined money—Descriptions of merchandise supplied by Indians—Balance of trade in favour of India settled by treasure—Trade between India and Palestine—Trade with Phœnicia and Egypt and shores of Mediterranean—Drain of gold to India from the West in historic times—Sources of supply in Asia—Asiatic trade of India—European trade with India in Middle Ages—Estimate of gold treasure now existing in India—Accumulations up to 1835—Accumulations since 1835—Estimate of coin current in British India—Statistics of coinage—Exportation of coined money—Effect of trade by land into Asia on stock of coin in India—Tale of coin *per capita* in use in India.

As introductory to the consideration of a scheme for remonetizing gold throughout the territories under the direct rule of the Queen-Empress in India, and thus to bring a portion of the gold treasure which has been for centuries accumulating in that country within reach of the commerce of the world; and in order to provide a statistical basis for arguments directed to prove the various advantages which would accrue to the people of India from such a reform in their currency, a recital of the economic causes of these accumulations, and an estimate of their magnitude, as well as a computation, made as close to fact as the circumstances of the case permit, of the silver coin now current in British India, will be admitted by the reader to be both relevant and necessary.

In order to estimate the stock of gold now existing in India, it is necessary to recall briefly the circumstances and causes of its accumulation. They were commercial and no other. No gold has been brought into India from beyond its borders, as gold was brought into Europe from America in the sixteenth century by conquest or rapine. A large portion of that which India possesses was obtained by the exchange of such of her productions, as among the Indians were superfluities, but were at the same time not only highly prized by the nations of Western Asia, Egypt, and Europe, and were obtainable from no other quarter except India, or from the further East by means of the Indian trade. The rest of the Indian store of the precious metals came from sources of supply in parts of Asia beyond India, and from mines in the country itself.

The antiquity of the trade of India is the surest measure of its importance and of the volume of the precious metals which was continually rolling on to its shores. The semi-religious code of the Hindus, called the Institutes of Menu, of an ancient though uncertain date, speaks of a class of "men well acquainted with sea voyages, and of journeys by land, and of shipbuilders, and of sailors as many as navigate rivers." To a particular caste of Hindus was assigned the business of conducting trade, and upon them was enjoined the necessity of making themselves acquainted " with the productions and requirements of other countries, with various dialects and languages, and with whatever else has direct or indirect reference to purchase and sale."*

* Irving, " Commerce of India."

The use of coined money, and the economy which may be effected in its use by means of bills of exchange, and the insuring of goods against loss in transit, are known to belong to a remote age of Indian commerce, and indications of other kinds which we find of the activity of this commerce, although rare and scattered over a long period of history, tend to the conclusion that India has been for many centuries the final depository of a large portion of the metallic wealth of the world.

During thirty centuries, Phœnicians, Jews, Assyrians, Greeks, Egyptians, and Romans in the ancient world, and Turks, Venetians, Portuguese, Dutch, and English in modern times, have carried on a commerce with India. The industrious and simple habits of the people, a genial climate, and a fertile soil rendered them independent of foreign nations in respect of the necessaries of life, while their secondary wants were few. Of the latter, tin, lead, glass, amber, steel for arms, and perhaps coral, and to a small extent medicinal drugs, complete the list of imports from Europe and Western Asia, while Arabia supplied frankincense for use in the temples. On the other hand, India provided Europe with wool from the fleeces of sheep bred on the mountain range which formed its north-western limit, an article of commerce as famous in the days of Alexander the Great as it is now. The same region supplied the onyx, chalcedony, lapis lazuli, and jasper, then esteemed as precious stones, a resinous gum (similar apparently to the shellac of our own day), furs, assafœtida, and musk, embroidered woollen fabrics and coloured carpets, which were as highly prized in

Babylon and Rome, as their modern reproductions are in London and Paris at the present day. But the most valuable of the exports of India was silk, which is said, under the Persian Empire, to have been exchanged by weight with gold. It was manufactured in India, as well as obtained for re-export from China. Next in value to silk ranked cotton cloths, ranging from coarse canvas and calicoes to muslins of the finest texture, as fine and delicate, no doubt, as that which at the present day is compared for tenuity to the dew of the evening. Oils, brass-ware, a liquid preparation of the sugar-cane, salt, drugs, and dyes, certain aromatics used by the ancients in mortuary and religious ceremonies were procured from various parts of the country, while pepper, cinnamon, and other edible spices were in so great request, and therefore of such high value in mediæval and modern Europe, as to give the name of the spice-trade to this portion of the commerce with India.

Under these circumstances the balance of trade would clearly be in favour of India, and that could only be settled by treasure exported from Europe and other parts of Asia which were commercially indebted to her. India desired nothing which foreigners could give her but the precious metals. Of gold and silver India was in need, and in one age of the world the redundant treasures of the silver mines of Spain, Attica, and Thrace, and of the gold-bearing rocks of Midian, Southern Arabia, and Ethiopia, as well as gold dust gathered from the beds of the streams of Lydia, and in another age the mineral wealth of Peru and Brazil passed in large quantities into India in exchange for such merchandise, as that country and her neighbours in the East unfailingly supplied.

King Solomon perceiving that the trade with the East speedily enriches the nation which obtains its control—Egypt no doubt being to that monarch the visible evidence of this fact—addressed himself to appropriating a share of it for the Jewish people by creating facilities for traders with the East, both on the land and sea routes. He built Tadmor (Palmyra) at a distance of one hundred and twenty miles from the Euphrates, on the edge of the Syrian desert, probably also Baalbec (Heliopolis), and Hamath (Epiphania), as store cities, or resting-places for caravans travelling from Persia and Babylon and the head of the Persian Gulf, and as emporia where the camels' burdens could be sorted and arranged for distribution. From these cities merchandise would be carried to Tyre, Aradus, and other Phœnician ports on the Mediterranean, to the cities in the valley of the Orontes, to the port of Seleucia, or by way of Edessa and the valley of the Euphrates into Asia Minor. Solomon's foresight in protecting these caravan routes bore fruit in the great trading centres of Mesopotamia. Babylon, Ctesiphon, Seleucia, Ossis, and Borsippa, at different times, between his age and that of the Roman emperor Severus, flourished on the profits of their commerce with the East. At the capture of Palmyra by the Emperor Aurelian (A.D. 273), as well as at the sack of Ctesiphon by the Mussulmans under Khaled in the year 637, there was found in either city an immense treasure of precious stones, gold, silk, cotton goods, and other commodities which could only have been obtained by trade with Persia, India, Ceylon, or countries still further eastward. The seaborne trade was equally an object of solicitude to the Jewish monarch. His fleets made periodical voyages to and from the head of the Red Sea in the Gulf of Akaba, and the ports in the Persian Gulf. We know from Holy Writ that "Ezion-geber, which is beside Eloth, on the shore of the Red Sea, in the land of Edom," was the Syrian port for the arrival and departure of the fleets sent on these voyages. Their cargoes were carried by caravans to Petra, and distributed some to Egypt and others to Rhinocolura, a port on the Mediterranean in the angle between Egypt and Palestine, for transhipment to Europe.

In the account of King Solomon's magnificence is found almost the earliest historical record which has come down to us of any great supply of gold which is likely to have been available for commercial uses. Where trade was carried on, there gold would be carried to and fro in the ordinary course of business. The revenue in gold which Solomon collected is described as amounting to 666 talents, which has been estimated to be of the value of four millions sterling, besides the gold which traders brought with them into his dominion (2 Chron. ix.). This argues the existence of a wide-reaching and flourishing commerce, which grew up during forty years of peaceable and settled government, maintained over a territory extending from Anti-Libanus to the Red Sea, and from the borders of Egypt to the Euphrates. The system of Solomon's rule was doubtless directed to securing peace and order in his dominions, and thus to give free play to the commercial instincts of the Jewish people. It would attract into his territory industrious and mercantile men, and from all quarters would be brought into his cities much of the metallic wealth of neighbouring countries. In an age of disorder and misrule such a polity would produce exactly the results described in Scripture; gold would become abundant, and silver be of "no account," and be "made as common as stones." But the commerce which these conditions fostered must have resulted in something more than an accumulation of the precious metals; these, like other goods in trade, in order to multiply, must have been the subject of exchange, and as a considerable part of the commerce of the Jewish people was carried on with the inhabitants of Persia and India, a share of the supply of gold which this commerce dispersed wherever it penetrated must have fallen to the latter country.

The Phœnicians took an active part in this trade, both by land and by sea. They transferred merchandise from the coasts of India to Tyros and Arados, contiguous islands lying off the Arabian shore of the Persian Gulf, now known as Bahrein and Mahang. From this port, as from Gerrha on the mainland, which geographers describe as one of the richest cities of its day, Arabian caravans conducted the trade by land through the inhabitable tract now occupied by the State of Nejd to Petra; while part of the merchandise was taken by sea and river to various points on the Euphrates, and from thence into the Syrian cities, where it was distributed in the manner above described. As the Phœnicians organized a trade which had its centre at Tyre, and penetrated to the west coast of Spain, to Carthage, Egypt, and other parts of the Mediterranean on the west, and to India, Ceylon, and probably as far as China on the east, India obtained the precious metals from every part of the then commercial world which contained a source of supply.

The conquest of Tyre by Alexander the Great and the foundation of Alexandria revived the Egyptian trade with Arabia and India, and the successive decline of the Jewish, Phœnician, and Persian powers in Western Asia gave to the people of Egypt and Arabia a monopoly of this commerce for about nine hundred years, between his death and the conquest of Egypt by the Mussulmans in the year A.D. 640. During the Roman occupation of Egypt the foreign trade of that country reached a point of prosperity which in those days was considered unusual. Heeren quotes from Strabo, who was a contemporary of the Emperor Tiberius, that as many as one hundred and twenty ships of burden engaged in the Indian trade had been seen lying in the roads of Myos Hormos at the same time; and an incident is recorded in the history of the reign of the Emperor Aurelian, about two hundred and forty years later, that after the reduction of Palmyra he was obliged to turn his arms against Egypt to suppress an insurrection which was supported by Firmus, a merchant of that country, with a fortune which he had made in the Indian trade. These circumstances show that at that period of the world's history the external commerce of India was both valuable and extensive, and could only have become so from the country possessing in an ample store of the precious metals the means of making the exchanges which a large commerce involves. That this was the case may be inferred from the narrative of Cosmas Indicopleustes, an Egyptian traveller, who in the sixth century B.C. compiled from the information of one Sopater, who had visited India, an account of Ceylon, in which it is stated that traders from that island obtained gold metal in exchange for merchandise at the port of Adule, on the Red Sea, and from Yemen, in Southern Arabia.

An overland route of great antiquity conveyed one branch of the commerce of the East into Europe from the direction of the Caspian Sea. Up to that locality it followed two lines of route, one mentioned by Herodotus, which conveyed gold from the Imaus range and the western frontier of China (Thina), and the peltries collected by the tribes between those mountains and the northern shore of the Caspian, through the country of the Scythians and Sarmatians to the north shore of the Black Sea, where the Greeks had already in his time placed trading-stations; the other to have united at a pass situated under the 35th parallel north latitude called the Caspian Gates, two caravan routes, one starting from Western China and the countries situated between the Himalayas and the southern shore of that sea, and another travelling from India in a direction nearly west from Kandahar.

Another route appears to have passed from India through Media, or through Northern Assyria, into Asia Minor, and to have supplied the wares of Asia to the colonies which the city of Miletus had, between the seventh and fifth centuries B.C., planted on the shores of the Euxine, from Sinope to Dioscurias.

Heeren's researches leave no doubt that commercial relations brought into communication with one another, in a remote age, the nations and tribes of Northern India, North-western (or, as it is commonly called, Central) Asia, Persia, Mesopotamia, and the territories now forming Southern Russia.

Pliny, writing during the first century B.C., states that the trade of Italy with the East, carried off annually a stock of gold and silver which Delmar estimates at a value of £70,000 of our money.* The same author alludes to the prohibition which during the declining years of the Roman Commonwealth was placed on the export of the precious metals, but which it was found impossible to enforce under the emperors. So well was this peculiarity of the trade known in modern times, that in the charter granted by Queen Elizabeth to the first English East India Company, in the year 1600, it was stipulated that the associated merchants were "to import, within six months after the return of every voyage, as much gold and silver as shall be equal to the value of the silver exported by them." This regulation was, from the nature of the case, but feebly enforced, and soon repealed. As early as the year 1674–75, the accounts of the Company showed that out of their exportations to India, to the value of £550,000, £400,000 was entirely bullion.

India thus exercised an influence over the commerce of the ancients, which from the nature of her exportations enabled her to accumulate a store of gold and silver derived from various parts of the world lying beyond her own borders, during a period of more than a thousand years preceding the general collapse of the trade with Asia, which resulted from the decline of the Roman Empire from the conquest

* "History of the Precious Metals," p. 191.

of Western Asia, Northern Africa, and Spain, by the Arabs, and from the occupation of Eastern Europe by the Turks.

India, however, was not entirely dependent on Western Asia, and Europe, Arabia, and Africa, for a supply of gold. The inhabitants of the countries situated to the west of India, those of Central Asia, Thibet, China, the Straits of Malacca, and the countries on the eastern coasts of the Bay of Bengal, traded with her people : and as in ancient times the inhabitants of those regions possessed gold and silver, it is not only probable, but historically certain, that they put their treasure to its most profitable use, that of effecting commercial exchanges, and thus contributed an additional supply to the stores of the precious metals accumulating in that country.

Ctesias, a Greek physician, who lived at the Persian Court about B.C. 400, speaks of that which is the oldest recorded trade route connecting the countries lying between the Caspian and India on the west, with Tartary and China on the east, as being frequented by caravans of a thousand or two thousand men travelling through a desert, which must be that now called by the name of Cobi, and returning in three or four years, their beasts being laden with gold. Ptolemy, the geographer, writing in the second century of our era, speaking of probably the same route as that described by Ctesias, says that merchants travelling from Parthia and Bactria followed a road which lay under the same parallel of latitude as Byzantium (42°) to the country of the Seres (China), from the capital of which people that metropolis was seven months' journey. This route is probably still

used, as it was more than two thousand five hundred
years ago by those visiting the countries beyond the
sandy desert which stretches eastward from Aksu
and Khoten. Heeren identifies both of these towns
with places bearing Greek names in the itinerary of
this route. The narrative of the mission sent to the
Amir of Kashgar by the Indian Government in 1873–
74, speaks of some of the envoy's staff witnessing
the annual arrival of tribute at the capital, either presented in person or despatched by the governors of
distant districts in the province; the tribute and
offerings consisting of the productions of each locality.
Among them the Governor of Khoten "led in a
caravan of 450 camels laden with carpets, silks,
cottons, felts, tents, metal dishes, and other local
manufactures; 2 arabas (carts) each carrying 1500
jings (equal to about 1800 lbs.) of gold and silver," and
some other contributions of less consequence; thus
the drain of 240 centuries has not exhausted its beds
of gold.

Herodotus speaks of a tribe on the banks of the
Jaxartes among whom utensils of gold were as common as Pizarro found them to be among the Mexi-
cans on the discovery of America. Strabo and Arrian
describe what can be nothing else, when stripped of
the guise of fable, than the practice of excavating
gold from beneath the earth by a people who in-
habited the borders of the desert of Cobi and wore
clothing of hides, a peculiarity in which they are
imitated by a remote Himalayan tribe at this day. As
these gold-diggers were periodically robbed by visitors
using horses and carts to carry off their spoil, we
may conclude that they were armed traders from

India, who relieved them of the fruits of their labour. The satrapy of India, which included as much of Afghanistan, Kashmir, and the Punjab as the Persian monarchs could keep in subjection, was esteemed a dependency of great importance, by reason, among others, of the gold dust in which its tribute of 360 talents was paid, a fact which can only be accounted for by the importation of gold into that region from Central Asia, whence Ctesias and Herodotus record that it was usually brought in the age of Darius Hystaspes.

Considerable quantities of gold appear to have been obtained by superficial mining in the hills of the Deccan, from very ancient times. The inscription on the great Temple of Tanjore is quoted to prove that in the eleventh century A.D., gold was more common in Southern India than silver. The Hindu princes of that part of India, as masters of the territory which had produced and at that time retained large quantities of gold, fell victims to the cupidity of the Mohammedan conquerors of Northern India, who during and subsequent to the fourteenth century transferred to their own capital of Delhi a considerable part of this treasure.

Turning to Ceylon, we find that a trade passed through the hands of the Singhalese, during many centuries, which could only have been organized by a people which held control of ample supplies of the precious metals.

Although the age which produced the Ramayana may be much more recent than that to which the Hindus ascribe its composition, its antiquity is unquestionable; and the description in that epic of wealth in gold, both manufactured and in use as money, possessed by the people of the countries mentioned in it, among which Ceylon was the most conspicuous, proves that the precious metals must have been generally diffused among the nations of India from a very early period of their history; and as the supplies from local mines were limited, they can only have obtained their gold and silver from foreign countries.

Megasthenes, the ambassador of Seleucus Nikator, who visited India about B.C. 300 and travelled to Ceylon, describes the island as producing gold. Pliny speaks of the people of Ceylon finding gold among their hills; and the ambassadors sent by the King of Ceylon to the Emperor Claudius (*cir.* A.D. 41–54) excited curiosity and wonder by their description of the luxury and magnificence of their monarch, to which a lavish use of gold, not only in personal decoration, but in the enrichment of buildings, largely contributed. That both Southern India and Ceylon obtained gold and silver from China may be certainly inferred from the fact of that country having always possessed and generally exported those metals, especially gold, of which India has received from that quarter large supplies; while the Greek names of Chrysa and the golden Chersonese, applied to the Burmah and Siamese coast and to the Malayan peninsula, attest that those regions were as famous for the production of gold at the commencement of our era as they are now for its possession and use. And gold, as has already been stated, came into the island many centuries before our era, from Arabia and probably from Ethiopia also, through trade with the Red Sea ports.

The gold, silk, furs, and similar commodities brought into India from the mountainous region on its northern border and beyond, appear to have been collected at Taxila, the modern Attock, at the junction of the Indus and Cabal rivers, and thence distributed throughout the interior of the country. One course of trade was directed to a point on the Jumna in the neighbourhood of the modern Delhi; following the Doab of the Ganges and Jumna it probably descended the former river to Palibothra (which is believed to be now represented by the city of Patna); the capital of the Prasioi, with whose king, Sandracottus, Seleucus the King of Syria made a treaty about the year B.C. 302. At that time this people had extended their dominion over countries now comprised in Bengal between Sirhind and the mouths of the Ganges, and between the Himalayas and Central India. They flourished for about a thousand years from B.C. 500 to some date between A.D. 400 and 600. The existence of a powerful nation during so long a period of time argues the maintenance of a strong government, of a durable and highly organized polity, conditions which promote the growth and extension of internal and external commerce, with the necessary result of attracting the precious metals from foreign countries.

Another line of trade started from Taxila, and went down the Indus to Patala on the delta of that river, whence it was conveyed by the coast to the seaports in the Persian Gulf.

It appears likely that a land route for merchandise passed from Taxila through North-western India to Ozene or the modern Oojein in Malwa, and to a city called Pluthana, and to another called Tugara in Central India, whose sites are uncertain. The seaport for that part of India was Barygaza (Broach) at the mouth of Nerbudda, whence an active trade was kept up with both coasts of the Persian Gulf in correspondence with the commerce in the precious metals from Europe, Arabia, and Egypt, which the Phœnicians conducted by means of their trading stations in the Arabian waters; and with the inhabitants of the Assyrian and Mesopotamian cities, who forwarded their wares by caravan and river to the mouths of the Euphrates.

The materials from which Ptolemy, the geographer, compiled in the second century A.D. his itineraries afford proof that in the age of Alexander, and certainly during many preceding centuries, a great commerce was carried on between India and Ceylon on the one hand, and Burmah, Siam, Malaya, and the coasts and islands lying to the south and east of the Straits of Malacca as far as China on the other. Nearchos, exploring under the orders of Alexander the coasts of the Persian Gulf, found a settlement where Muscat now stands, in communication with Limyrica (the Malabar coast of India) and Ceylon. Commodities are described in the "Periplus" as being conveyed down the Ganges and thence sent to Limyrica; and the author of that work (writing cir. A.D. 64) mentions a town called by the same name as that river, situated near its mouth, which served as a trade emporium. Merchandise from the east coast of the Bay of Bengal would, at most seasons of the year, be carried into or past the Ganges, according to the part of India, eastern or southern, which might be its destination, and two streams of trade would thus unite on their way to the Coromandel coast, the chief port of which was situated at the mouth of the Cauvery.

From Ceylon, commodities collected from the mainland of India and from countries to the east of the bay were distributed along the western coast by vessels issuing from many different ports between the southern cape of India and the delta of the Indus. Heeren quotes Agatharcides, who wrote about one hundred and fifty years before our era, as noticing the importance of Patala near the mouths of the Indus in the trade between India and Arabia. Callienc (Callian, near Bombay) is mentioned in the "Periplus" as a port which had recently decayed after a long career of prosperity. Barygaza, or Broach, has already been noticed. Musiris, in Limyrica, where stands the modern Mangalore, was resorted to by Greek traders at the commencement of our era for the purchase of silk. The "Periplus"* (quoted by Irving) describes silk as being brought to that port from Thina (which is believed to indicate Northwestern China) by caravans to some point on the Ganges, and necessarily by that river to the sea, and thence to Ceylon. This and other commodities from the same region may either have travelled round the sea coasts of Asia, viâ the Straits of Malacca and the Bay of Bengal, to that island, or have been conveyed by land and river transport from Northern India to the mouths of the Ganges, and thence have been taken by the Coromandel coast, which was well provided with small but convenient ports, to its destination in the southern sea.

* The "Periplus of the Erythrean Sea" is believed to have been written in the reign of Nero, *cir.* A.D. 64, by Arrian, an Egyptian Greek.

Cosmas Indicopleustes, in the sixth century B.C., notices the activity of the trade along the coast of Limyrica, and describes it as issuing from Ceylon, which was the principal emporium for that part of Asia, and being transported in vessels belonging to numerous ports on the coast, which he names—among which Nel-kynda (identified by Heeren as the modern Neliceram) and Arrhota (Surat) still exist—to the Persian Gulf.

In this way the merchandise of China, Southern Asia, and India, fell into the courses of commerce through which the seamen of Arabia and Egypt and the caravan traders of Assyria distributed it throughout the Roman Empire.

The Oriental trade was not restored in mediæval Europe until about the year 800, when the Venetians, allying themselves with the Turks, revived the use of the route through Egypt. The Venetians laid the foundations of the great carrying trade, upon which the Italian republics flourished for seven hundred years between the ninth and sixteenth centuries. The conquest of Constantinople in 1204–5, by the Latin crusaders, the acquisition by the Republic of territory on the mainland of modern Turkey, of Crete, and other important islands and places of advantage for trade in the Levant, made her commercial supremacy paramount wherever the sails of European merchantmen were seen.

Venice provided Germany, through the intervention of the merchants of Augsburg, and countries lying nearer Italy, with Oriental productions, principally obtained by means of her navies sailing from the coasts of India to Egypt, through which country a system of land and river transport was organized

R

to Alexandria, whence they were re-shipped across the Mediterranean.

Ormuz, in the Persian Gulf, Aden, and apparently Kosseir in the Red Sea, were the principal stations for the Venetian sea-borne trade with India, and these they secured by a formidable navy of armed commercial vessels. From Alexandria they re-shipped the merchandise for distribution along the coasts of the Mediterranean, or for transport to Venice and Genoa, whence it was exported into the interior of Europe. The Venetian occupation of Cyprus, for nearly one hundred years during the fifteenth and sixteenth centuries, gave them facilities for organizing another route for the conveyance of the Indian trade by the Euphrates, and by land from that river through Syria to the ports on the northern coast of Palestine. The total destruction in the Indian Sea in the year 1508, by the Portuguese admiral, of a combined Turkish and Venetian fleet, which those two powers had equipped for the purpose of extinguishing the rivalry of the Portuguese in the Indian trade, and the appropriation by the same people of the Venetian stations at Ormuz and other places in the Gulf, deprived the republic of her carrying trade in Eastern waters; while the greater security and cheapness of the voyage round the Cape of Good Hope involved a simultaneous disuse of every overland route, either through Egypt, Syria, or the country between the Caspian and Black Seas, and reduced the commerce of the Italian and Levantine cities to unimportant dimensions.

Genoa, in the time of the Greek emperors, obtained an influence at Constantinople which gave her the command of the Bosphorus, and ensured her the monopoly of one branch of the commerce of the East, which came by an overland route of great antiquity from the direction of the Caspian Sea.

Caffa, a port on the Sea of Azof, was the destination of the caravans bringing merchandise from Northern Asia and India (by routes already described), whence it was carried into Central and Western Europe by the Genoese.

The appointment of Albuquerque, in 1506, as governor on the part of the King of Portugal in the Indies, speedily confirmed the value of Vasco de Gama's recent discovery of the sea passage round Africa to India, by substituting that nation for the Venetians as the carriers of the Oriental trade.

In the year 1595, the merchants of Amsterdam fitted out their first India fleet of armed trading ships, to contend with the Portuguese for a share of this commerce. The destruction of the city of Antwerp, ten years before, by the Duke of Parma, had driven a considerable number of artisans, merchants, and others interested in trade, from the Low Countries to take refuge on the banks of the Thames.

It is from that time that England, as well as Holland and Portugal, began to freight ships for the voyage round the Cape with a certain amount of merchandise, but with disproportionately large stores of silver and gold, derived from the recently discovered sources of supply in Central America, and to bring to Europe in exchange cotton, pepper, silk, and other rarities and articles of luxury from the coasts of India.

This route has only during the last fifty years been partially given up in favour of the more rapid means of transport which ocean steamships, a railway, and a ship canal through Egypt now offer to a commerce carried in the vessels of every nation of the world which owns a mercantile marine.

This sketch * of the commerce of ancient and mediæval India setting forth the causes which have induced an accumulation of the precious metals rather than a dispersion of the supplies indigenous to the country, is a necessary introduction to an estimate of the stock of gold now in the possession of the people of India, and to the discussion which follows of the most appropriate means for bringing it back into the courses of commerce, and rendering it available as an effective addition to the volume of gold money in use throughout the world.

No materials exist for an estimate of the quantity of gold which may have gone to India from Europe, Western Asia, and from Africa, between the fifth century B.C. and the discovery of America in the fifteenth century of our era. Delmar is of opinion that "during the dark ages of Europe gold and silver flowed back from the Orient by the hands of the Arabian and afterwards of the Italian traders, and found their way to Europe;" † and he attributes this to the occurrence of an era of great prosperity in India and China, when prices, falling to a lower level in Europe than in Asia, induced a current of the precious metals westward. Whether this condition of prices existed or not, treasure would not flow from the East to the West as an incident in the commerce of the period, unless the East owed a

* Abbreviated from that given in "The Gold Treasure of India." London, Kegan Paul, Trench and Co., 1884.

† Delmar, "History of the Precious Metals," p. 190. London, G. Bell and Sons, 1880.

debt on the balance of trade to the West. It has already been shown that from the nature of the commodities under exchange from either quarter such a balance could not have arisen against India at one time more than at another. This period of depression in Europe is not particularly defined, but it may be that referred to as occurring between the third and seventh centuries A.D., when "all communication between Europe and Asia was lost." In this case the trade may have well-nigh ceased; but, if so, no great value of treasure would have been carried either way, and no presumption would arise that on the balance the East parted with any considerable part of its metallic wealth to the West, for western nations would have had nothing wherewith to purchase it, and eastern nations would have had no score run up against them which could only be discharged in gold or silver. But as the metal which went from Europe to India was, previous to the discovery of America, chiefly silver; and as that country drew her gold supply, so far as regions to the West are concerned, from Arabia and Africa, the value of gold which can have been absorbed by India from this direction must, in comparison with the quantity which has subsequently gone there, have been small. The same author estimates that gold to the value of £112,062,500 sterling went to the East from Europe and America between the years 1565 and 1835,[*] and has never been re-exported. Up to 1809 the estimates of the flow to Asia are taken by Delmar from Jacob (vol. ii. pp. 68, 126, 197, 214). From 1810 to 1831 the estimates are formed on statistics published by Jacob and

[*] "History of the Precious Metals," p. 194.

Macgregor (Jacob, vol. ii. p. 322; Macgregor, iv. pp. 404, 410, 454), and from 1832 to 1835 they are derived, so far as concerns India, from official reports published by the British Silver Commission of 1876.* The figures in detail are as follows:—

Period.	Amount of Gold.
1565 to 1599	£3,500,000
1600 to 1699	8,312,500
1700 to 1809	88,000,000
1810	250,000
1811 to 1831	10,000,000
1832 to 1835	2,000,000
Total	£112,062,500

How much of this India took, and how much China, it is not possible to say, but having regard to the comparative importance of the trade of the two countries with Europe, it is not too much to assume that 70 millions of this treasure was the share which India appropriated and retained. Any portion which found its way to other parts of Asia would have been of comparatively trifling amount. Japan, Malacca, Burmah, Siam, were sources of supply for Europe, and therefore to assign 50 millions as the share taken by China and other places in Asia outside India is probably to overstate the figure, and to reduce the importation into India below the mark. To this must be added the proceeds of her own mines, and gold obtained by trade from Central Asia, China, Burmah, Siam, and other Asiatic sources. The sources of gold supply in Asia itself were in all probability more fertile than those situated in Arabia, Africa, Asia Minor, or Greece, and were more accessible to the Indians. The

* "History of the Precious Metals," p. 195.

ancient books of that people, and occasional notices of their country in classical writers, refer to their wealth (which in those days meant stores of the precious metals) as exceeding that of Western nations. Having regard to the activity of the internal trade of India, her external commerce, both by sea and land, with other parts of Asia, her trade with Europe and with Egypt, which extends back to a remote antiquity, and has been matter of history for more than twenty centuries, and looking also to the character and magnitude of the exportable productions of the country, the industrious habits of her people, the shrewd and enterprising spirit of the trading classes, their numerous cities and towns, the density of the population, the variety of their occupations and amusements, the large armies maintained by their rulers, and the comparatively high degree of organization which their political and social system had attained to, we find all those conditions united in India, which in all other countries are accompanied with a plentiful use of coined money. If therefore so large a treasure of gold as 70 millions was taken from the West into India between the discovery of America and the year 1835, it is by no means extravagant to estimate the treasure drawn by India from various parts of Asia, together with the proceeds of mines within the country itself at an equally large figure. What the latter sources of supply provided must ever remain uncertain, but having regard to commercial considerations, and other circumstances already described, an inference drawn from them that India had in thirty centuries accumulated a stock of gold metal of about the same dimensions as that which she has obtained from Europe (after allowing for re-exportations) in fifty-four years is so reasonable as to have more than probability in its favour. This estimate is corroborated by one said to have been made in the year 1835, when gold was demonetized in India,* which placed the stock of gold then in the country at about 140 millions. As an independent calculation made at a time when the facts of the gold stock in India were more obvious than they have since become, it confirms this conclusion in a remarkable manner. From the year 1835 onwards we have reliable statistics compiled by the Indian Government of the movement of the precious metals to and from India, accounts brought up to April, 1889, show that there has been exported into India since the former year, and never re-exported, a gold treasure to the value of **£130,292,758.** In these accounts of the import and export of gold, 10 rs. were estimated as the equivalent of each £1 sterling of value up to the year 1871; since then the estimates have been made at the market price of gold bullion in rupees on the day of importation. The value above given as that of the stock of gold acquired and retained by India since 1835 has therefore been obtained by reconverting the silver figures into gold figures at 10 rs. to £1 sterling up to 1871; and for each year between 1871 and 1886 at the rate of exchange taken for the purposes

---

* Douglas, "Currency of India." Glasgow, 1886. This estimate necessarily accounts for gold known to have been taken away from India, and was derived from contemporary observation; and there can be no doubt that any gold treasure taken away by invaders, such as that carried off by Mahmoud of Ghazni in the eleventh century, and by Nadir Shah in 1738, was only an insignificant fraction of the stock then held by the country.

of the annual budget of the Indian Government. From 1886 onwards the accounts show the weight of gold bullion in tolahs, from which the values of the net importations have been calculated at £3 17s. 9d. per ounce.

There is thus lying in India a stock of gold bullion wholly useless for commercial purposes, and increasing at the rate of nearly 3 millions annually, of the value of not less than **£270,000,000** at the market, being probably two and a half times as great as all the gold money in circulation in the United Kingdom.

Any estimate which may be made of the number of coins in circulation in British India must be confined to those issued from the mints at Calcutta, Bombay, and Madras since the year 1835, when the currency now in use came into existence. The mint at Madras was closed a few years ago. A considerable quantity of coin is fabricated in the mints of the independent native powers of a different standard weight and value from the rupees of the Government of India. The amount of coin of this kind circulating in the territories of the Queen-Empress cannot be ascertained with any approximation to accuracy, but as these coins are seldom seen in use, it is probably inconsiderable; at the same time there is reason for believing that hoarded silver coin is generally laid by in this form, because it is of less use as current money than the standard coin, and, being unalloyed, sells more easily as bullion. While this kind of coin may be neglected in an inquiry into the volume of the currency in use in British India, it must not be forgotten that its omission leaves the estimate thereof rather understated.*

Before the year 1835, the East India Company coined rupees for use in their own territories in great quantities, but it was not until that year that the Company's coins were stamped with the effigy of the King of England. When, therefore, the new coinage was introduced, it consisted of coins fabricated from new silver, bearing the king's head, and coins (generally inscribed with Persian legends) of the East India Company's previous currencies, which, in order to further their removal from circulation, were received at the Government treasuries in payment of taxes. Many years passed before they were entirely disused, and they are occasionally still to be met with.

In 1835, therefore, the Government of India started with a few millions of currency of the new pattern, and a stock of coins of the old pattern, which, as fast as they could be collected, were re-minted in the new form. Viewing the king's head, or authorized currency as that of British India, we find that it consisted at the end of the first five years of its existence (1835–40), of 166,173,710 coins made from new silver, and 73,335,180 coins made by the recoinage of the obsolete currency.†

In speaking of currency, it should be stated that the East India Company had four authorized currencies, the Bombay, Madras, Furrukhabad, and Sonat rupee, equal in value to one another; and a

* In the following calculations fractional silver coins are included in the rupee currency.

† Besides a considerable quantity of obsolete coin in process of withdrawal from circulation.

fifth, the Sicca rupee, 1/16th more valuable. In 1836 the Sicca rupee was demonetized; the others, being of the same value as the new rupee, continued to be legal tender, were declared open to recoinage without seignorage, and were not reissued when received at the Government treasuries.

In every five years, large, and in most periods increasing, quantities of coins have been fabricated from fresh silver, while the increment to the currency from the reminting of obsolete coins has gradually diminished, as it necessarily would. It must not, however, be forgotten that having regard to the currency bearing the sovereign's effigy as the only currency of British India which can be dealt with statistically, every rupee of the obsolete currencies which has been coined into it is a clear addition to its volume. This cannot be said of the current coins which, becoming light weight by wear and tear, are recoined.

These are returned into circulation to the same number as they are withdrawn for recoinage, the deficiency of weight being made up by new silver added at the expense of the State. The recoinage, therefore, of light-weight current coin neither increases nor diminishes the volume of the currency.

The Indian coinage accounts discriminate between rupees made from new silver on the one hand, and those made from obsolete (uncurrent) coins and current coins worn down to a point below legal-tender weight on the other. The details of the recoinage of the two latter classes of coin are not given. If the amounts of obsolete coin, and of light-weight current coin, respectively, which are brought under recoinage were separately stated, the whole value of the coins issued from the mints might be more accurately ascertainable than is now possible. Obsolete coins recoined, become an effective addition to the standard currency; current light-weight coin recoined, having been reckoned at the time of its original issue, will not in this calculation be counted again on recoinage. As in the recoinage the proportion which obsolete coin holds to current coin is not officially stated, this omission of detail is one of two or three circumstances which make it quite impossible to state exactly what the amount of coin is which is in circulation in British India.

The following figures will show from the published accounts of the Government of India the tale of rupees coined from new silver between the commencement of the issue of the existing currency in 1835 and April, 1889, and provide materials for an estimate of the proportion which in the reminting, obsolete coin has borne to worn current coin, the former being and the latter not being an addition to the volume of the standard coin in use. The sum total of money coined from new silver, and from obsolete coin, is (subject to a deduction on account of coined silver exported beyond India) that which constitutes the volume of the silver currency of British India.

It will afterwards be seen that the tale of rupees (including fractional coins, half and quarter rupees) supplied by the mints to the inhabitants of British India since 1835 to the present year (1889) amounts to 3,326,510,921.

There were coined * in the mints of British India the following tale of rupees from new silver, with one exception † :—

	Rupees.
Between 1835–1885	2,750,534,130
In the year 1885–86	102,855,660
,, ,, 1886–87	{ 46,165,370 31,837,783 †
,, ,, 1887–88	107,884,240
,, ,, 1888–89	72,577,479
Total	3,111,854,962

Obsolete and worn current coin was also recoined to the following amount :—

	Rupees.
Between 1835–85	242,290,720
In 1885–86	4,624,410
In 1886–87	20,696,587
In 1887–88	1,365,901
Total	268,977,618

As has been said above, the coinage accounts do not discriminate between the recoinage of obsolete and of merely worn coin, but there can be no doubt that in the early years, during perhaps the first twenty years of the new currency, this recoinage constituted an effective addition to the currency, because it must have consisted of obsolete coins of the old issues, and have included little or none of the new coinage, as the latter would not in any appreciable quantity have become so much worn as to have fallen below legal-tender weight, and have been on that account reminted. In those twenty

---

* Third Report, Appendix B, Commission on Depression of Trade and Agriculture. The remaining figures are taken from the public accounts relating to India.

† The proceeds of the Gwaliar loan.

years the old silver recoined amounted to the following sums, and is reckoned in this estimate as new money put into circulation :—

		Rupees.
Between 1835–1840	... ...	73,335,180
,, 1840–1845	... ...	46,327,890
,, 1845–1850	... ...	33,638,470
,, 1850–1855	... ...	34,226,250
	Total	187,527,790

After 1855 the recoinage of old silver sinks from about 34 millions of rupees to about 11 millions during each of two periods of five years, then to 3½, then to 1½ millions in the five years ending with 1875. From this it may be inferred that the recoinage in these later periods was decreasing in the element of obsolete coins, and becoming more and more a recoinage of worn coins of the authorized currency. This is only to be expected, because the obsolete coins in use in British India would in every period of five years become fewer, while the number of worn and light-weight current coins would increase. But in the five years ending with 1880, the amount of remiuted coins rose to nearly 3 millions, in the next five years to over 24½ millions, and in the following three years to upwards of 26½ millions.

The recoinage of light-weight current coins and of obsolete coins has, as already stated, been excluded from the calculation after the year 1855, because it is probable that it consisted for the most part, although not entirely, of coin already accounted for at the time of its first issue ; but in the thirteen years commencing with 1875, it is evident that of the remintage a comparatively moderate proportion consisted of light-weight standard coin. Any other coins brought into the British mints for recoinage must therefore be held to be effective additions to the currency, since they must have come principally from the currencies of the native powers existing or extinct; and to a small extent perhaps from the remaining stock of the East India Company's old currencies, which up to that time had escaped recoinage.

The great increase of recoinage in these thirteen years corresponds roughly with a period when the expansion of the Indian trade was creating a great demand for fresh coin, and in this way the production of coins of this description from their hiding-places, and their coinage into the standard currency for use in the trade of the country is accounted for.* It cannot be supposed that in those years the current coin of British India became unusually reduced in weight by attrition, and there is no third source of supply from which coins for remintage could come. A part, therefore, of this recoinage must be considered as an actual addition to the currency of the country, for the same reason that the recoinage of the twenty years 1835 to 1855 has been so reckoned. The figures are as follows:—

	Rupees
For the five years ending with 1880	2,961,540
,, ,, 1885	24,607,900
For the three years ending with 1888	26,686,898
Total	54,256,338

Of this sum it may be taken that one-half, rather than any other proportion, represents the recoinage

* During the fourteen years 1873–87, the excess of trade or balance in favour of India amounted to nearly 50 millions sterling (Appendix viii., Final Report, p. 102).

of obsolete as contrasted with light-weight coin; for this reason that, whereas during the twenty years when the recoinage was confined exclusively to obsolete coins it was going on at an average rate of 9½ millions a year, during the next twenty years when it was chiefly composed of light-weight current coins, it only amounted on an average to 1⅓ million a year; if therefore in the next thirteen years the recoinage rises to over 2¼ millions per annum, the excess over 1⅓ million may be assumed to be obsolete coins. In round terms, half of the amount recoined (if not more than half) or 27 millions may be attributed to the recoinage of obsolete coin.

However near to actual fact the sum thus estimated may approach, it must fall short of exact correctness, and is the second element of uncertainty in the calculation. By the reckoning made in this way, the sum total of the silver currency of British India issued since 1835 would amount to 3,326,510,921 rs., in the following detail:—

	Rupees.
Coined from new silver	3,111,854,962
Obsolete coin recoined between 1835–1855	187,527,790
Half the recoinage of the 13 years, 1875–88	27,128,169
Total	3,326,510,921

This gives the closest approximation which circumstances allow to the total issues of coin, but to get the effective circulation a deduction must be made on account of coined money exported from India. The Government sends abroad to various dependencies of the Empire of India, annually, a considerable number of rupees to defray the public charges, and there are places in the Queen's dominions in the East, besides those politically connected with India, such as the islands of Mauritius and Ceylon, where the currency in use is the Indian rupee, and it is provided by private agency through banks and trading firms in the ordinary course of commerce. These exports are returned in the accounts as " exported treasure," without specification of coined money or bullion. No doubt bullion is sent, but how much is not discoverable, nor is there reason to suppose that it forms any large part of the treasure exported on private account, or any part of that exported on Government account; for the purposes therefore of this calculation all silver treasure exported to these places is reckoned as coined money, and the tale of rupees circulating in India according to the foregoing estimate must be correspondingly reduced. The countries to which the silver treasure thus assumed to be coined money is exported, are Africa or Mauritius and Zanzibar, Arabia or Aden and the Red Sea ports, Persia or the Persian Gulf, Ceylon, and certain other places in Asia, described without specification as " other countries."

The statistics of this exportation are not complete. For the six years 1835–40 inclusive, they appear to be entirely wanting. For the six years 1841–46 inclusive, the exports from Bengal of gold and silver are lumped together in the accounts, and are therefore omitted from this estimate. From 1847–66 as respects Bengal, and from 1841–66 inclusive, in the Madras and Bombay accounts, gold and silver are separately returned, but up to the latter year no detail of the places to which this treasure was exported is given; it is only with the year 1867 that this particular information begins. The amount of this exportation is therefore calculated, by taking

s

the silver treasure exported to the places above mentioned for the twenty-two years 1867–88,* and the proportion it bears to the whole treasure (of silver) exported; this, which is approximately ⅜ths, is held to be coined money; the same proportion is assumed to hold good for the silver treasure exported between 1841 and 1866, and ⅜ths of that is reckoned as coined money sent out of India. By this calculation the exportation of coined silver money of the Indo-British currency amounts to 436,576,568 rs.; deducting this sum from that of the coins issued from the mints as above given, there remain **2,889,934,353** rs. in actual circulation in the country. The amount of the exportation above mentioned for the twelve years, 1835–46, is the third element of uncertainty in this estimate, but the sum involved is, in comparison with the whole volume of the currency, of trifling importance. It would, by a proportionate computation, amount to a reduction too small to affect the force of any argument derived from the estimate thus made of the money in use among the people, and in the absence of any figures giving the actual exportation of silver treasure for those years, it is better to leave this uncertainty as it stands, than to attempt to correct it by calculations which to a great extent must be conjectural.

It is commonly believed that coined money goes out of India by land routes into other parts of Asia, but a little consideration of the circumstances of this trade makes it evident that the stock of silver available for coinage or actually coined in India, is not in this way reduced. Such

* The accounts of this exportation published up to 1889, are not carried to a later date than March 31, 1888.

exportations can only be carried through by traders who come into India from Beloochistan and Afghanistan, from Thibet through Nepal, or across the frontier of eastern Bengal and Burmah. They import furs, shawls, and woollens, borax, caoutchouc, fruits, spices, dyes, gums, resins, assafœtida, drugs, and some descriptions of raw produce of small value, which they exchange for salt, sugar, indigo, spices, opium, tea, cotton goods, metals, etc., supplied by the Indian markets. This trade is at most of small value, and has been decreasing during recent years; its total value was estimated for the year 1888–89 at about six millions, reckoning 15 rs. to the £1 sterling. The traders carry away a larger value of commodities than they bring into India for sale; for excluding certain kinds of exportations to our settlement at Quetta, the exports exceed the imports in value; they cannot therefore take away any but an insignificant quantity of coined money or bullion, and any silver which they do export is more likely to be in the form of ingots or coins of the native states made of soft unalloyed silver than of standard rupees. On the other hand, it is evident that the traders must bring some gold or silver metal with them, to pay for the excess of value of the goods they take away over that of the goods they bring; the amount may be small, but this landward trade so far as it affects the stock of bullion in India, tends to increase rather than to diminish its supply.

As the inhabitants of British India were returned at the last census at 199 millions, the volume of the circulation would stand in relation to the numbers of the population at 14·52 rs. *per capita.*

CHAPTER X.

SCHEME FOR REMONETIZING GOLD IN INDIA.

India most concerned in silver question—Amount of loss by exchange in ten years—The present time most suitable for resuming use of gold money—Cost of purchasing gold an increasing burden on India—Financial risks incurred by India averted by use of gold money—Evidence of the predilection of the people of India for gold money—Evidence of injurious effects on trade produced by disuse of gold money—Propensity to hoard gold would have no effect on supply of the metal for money—Use more profitable than hoarding—Inducements to hoard diminishing under British administration—Gold money as necessary to India as to England—Consequent rises of prices beneficial to India—The country can supply ten times the gold required for the currency—Reasons why prices are stationary in India—Silver currency inadequate; use of gold would not check coinage of silver—The disuse of gold acts as a restriction on industry—Silver purchased abroad with gold bullion less efficient as money in India than gold—Results of modern monetary legislation on trade—Silver token currency unsuitable to India—Dual currencies of gold and silver common in India—Plan for circulating gold money, and its effects—Similar methods considered on previous occasions—Opinion of the Duke of Wellington.

THE country most concerned in the settlement of the silver question is undoubtedly India. Although during the last thirty years the frontiers of India have been more than once disturbed by war, and parts of the interior of the country have been devastated by famines, yet the rule of the Queen-Empress has been rewarded in the order of Providence with a remarkable development in the prosperity of her people, who in respect of those matters which concern this discussion have created a new point of departure in the economic history of mankind by bringing their cheap labour into competition with the more highly paid labour of the West, and underselling with their low-priced wares the dearer productions of European industry. They are better fed, better clothed, better housed, and better taught, and enjoy (because by their own industry they are able to procure them) the secondary conveniences of life, to a degree which, to the generation now passing away, seems extraordinary. The increasing productiveness of the industries of the people is proved by evidence of various kinds, among which may be mentioned the foreign trade of the country, which has trebled since 1858, and is now equal to that of the United Kingdom as it stood in 1840; and the public credit of her Government, which ranks next to that of England when tested by the rate of interest at which money for the public service can be raised on loan. But for this condition of prosperity the extraordinary cost of procuring gold to discharge the obligations of the Government of India in England could not have been met out of the taxation of the people.

The financial connection which unites England and India is without parallel in the history of the world. Other nations besides England have held in subjection conquered races, and have levied a tribute from them. In the case of India no tribute is levied, the taxes are wholly expended on the government and in the interests of the people of the country. Money is borrowed for their use, *matériel* of peace and war, and services of various kinds, are procured for their advancement and benefit, for the payment of which their silver money is useless until it is first converted into its gold equivalent. Unfortunately it has become the custom of the last few years to speak of these payments as "tribute," whereas they have not a single feature which justifies the description. When a railway company can be said to pay tribute to the manufacturers who supply it with steel rails and steam-engines; when the military department of the State can be said to pay tribute to those who manufacture ordnance and firearms for it; when a trader can be said to pay tribute to the banker who discounts his bills and supplies him with capital for industrial investment; when the shareholders of a commercial company can be said to pay tribute to the directors and manager of their business; when the Treasury can be said to pay tribute to the stockholders in the public debt when it pays them their dividends;—then the people of India will rightly be said to pay tribute to the Crown and people of England in respect of the home charges of their government, and not before. They purchase certain articles in the open market, and using for payment a metallic currency which commercial causes have depreciated by the standard of the gold wherewith the payment is necessarily discharged, they are obliged to pay more than they would pay, were the value of their silver money higher than it is. This difference between what the people of India do pay and what they would pay, if their currency were properly constituted, is the disturbing element in

Indian finance; its amount is uncertain, but it is continuously on the increase; it is commonly called *loss by exchange*, and is the excess payment over ten rupees which the Secretary of State makes for every one pound sterling which he buys with Indian currency. In 1871 this difference for the first time rose to half a million sterling;* between 1873 and 1878 it varied between three quarters of a million and two millions a year. Since then it has risen year by year, and for the last year for which the accounts have been made up (1888-89) it has nearly touched seven millions of pounds. To avoid wearying the reader with statistics, it will be sufficient to say that during the last ten years† the people of India have been taxed in the amount of more than 402 millions of rupees, to pay for that part of the price of the gold money they have purchased, which exceeds ten rupees to the pound sterling. This, with occasional and unimportant variations, was, previous to 1870, the ruling price.

The prosperity of India (as has already been shown) is not involved in the cheapness of silver. Silver may rise in price against gold, and the domestic and foreign trade of the country will nevertheless continue to flourish. Her power of production and opportunities of sale, in which consist the potentiality of wealth, will not in the least degree be diminished, and, as will afterwards appear, the use of gold legal-tender money will be an important aid in the development of those two conditions of prosperity. Amazingly prosperous as India is, she

* These calculations are made at the conventional rate of 10 rs. = £1; the figures in the India accounts are in tens of rupees.
† 1879-80 to 1888-89 inclusive.

is living year by year up to the edge of her income; revenue can only follow on the footsteps of wealth, and in the case of a people with so few secondary wants as the people of India indulge in, proper objects for additional taxation are not easily found, and when found, are often so scattered as to make the cost of collection too costly for its imposition. The growth of the public revenues must therefore be slow, and for the present taxation has reached the limit of safety and prudence. For the Government to neglect the gold revenue which is within its reach, and to buy gold abroad at a fancy price in silver, in order to discharge its gold debt, and for this purpose to levy 60 or 70 millions of rupees of taxes from its own subjects at a time when they possess the material for gold money in much larger quantities than they can use, is very questionable finance.

Events, the occurrence of which is never absent from the minds of Indian administrators, may at any time and with scarcely any warning involve the empire in a European war, in which India would be isolated and cut off from the help of England; her seaborne trade would temporarily disappear, and the supply of a large part of her wealth would be intercepted at its source. If her frontier were attacked, her financial credit would be shaken, further borrowing would become hardly possible, and additional taxation equally difficult. It is therefore of the last importance that while peace and prosperity prevail such a reform of the Indian currency should be undertaken as may afford a fair prospect of reducing the enormous cost which the country is now put to in the purchase of English gold, and, at the same time, involve no risk of any countervailing disadvantage.

The dominant fact of the situation is that the gold price of silver has fallen 30 per cent. in the last seventeen years. From 1850 to 1872 the price of silver was always more than 60d. In 1873 it fell to 59¼d., and in the middle of 1882, the Indian banks were giving no more than 42d. The last great fall in the value of silver occurred in the seventeenth century. During the sixty years following the accession of King James I. silver fell 32 per cent., and during the next fifty years about 5 per cent. more. The ratio in A.D. 1600 was 11 to 1, in 1604 it was 12 to 1, in 1717 it stood at $15_{1\frac{2}{2}4}$ to 1.* As silver never recovered from the decline which it experienced in the seventeenth and eighteenth centuries, so in the nineteenth century we may be entering on a long course of years in which silver may hold a more or less permanent relation of value to gold of 10 to 1 instead of 15½ to 1.

That full-value silver money will again become current in Europe appears highly improbable. The use of gold money in India, as will afterwards be shown, will create a demand for silver which may exceed very considerably that of any previous period, coming from the same quarter; but the metal may be produced so cheaply that this demand will only suffice to arrest a further decline, and maintain its present price. Our arrangements in India should be adapted to a state of things in which silver can be placed on the market with a profit at 30d., or less, and the Indian rupee stand at 1s. in gold.

As long as gold appreciates against commodities, the foreign trade of India will not be affected by

* These ratios are calculated from McCulloch's tables, and the Silver Committee's Report, 1876.

mere cheapness of silver, except that silver prices in India may rise, and exportations to a certain extent fall off; but the Government has to look at the matter from the point of view of the taxpayer, and of those classes of men in India who, like the Government, are compelled to buy gold in England, but cannot increase their silver income in the least correspondence with the increasing silver price of gold. The State in India cannot, as a trader can, export valuable produce for the purchase of gold, the only commodity with which it can procure gold in England may become one of the least valuable of commodities, and bring in the smallest returns. The silver it uses for this purpose it can only obtain at the expense of the industry of its people. Each fresh million of rupees which it takes from them to defray the home charges will cost the labouring classes more of their labour than the last million. The value of that labour, or rather of the produce of that labour, may rise a little in the silver currency; ten seers of wheat may sell for $5\frac{1}{4}$ rs. instead of for 5 rs., but the larger sum will buy less gold than the smaller sum buys now. If the figures for the loss by exchange on 10 rs. be multiplied by millions, it is evident that no rise of prices which the near future is likely to see in India can compensate the people for such a tremendous drain on their industry as the increasing cost of the home charges occasions, while they get no advantage or return at all as a set-off against the loss they suffer.

The only chance which offers itself to the Government of India, of extrication from a predicament which circumstances may any day bring about, and which may place the country in a position perilously close to bankruptcy, is to make a beginning, and to make as much progress as it safely can from year to year, in utilizing the gold treasure now hoarded in the country, both for trade and revenue purposes.

Sir Evelyn Baring, who a few years ago was the financial member of the Council of the Viceroy of India, gave the following opinion in his evidence before the Special Commission: "There is no security whatever that the Government of India two or three years hence will not be bankrupt; none whatever in the present condition of affairs. Neither do I think it possible to separate completely the interests of the Government of India from those of the population of India. The first and greatest interest of the population, considered as a whole, is that the financial position of the Government, who are the trustees of the population, should be one of assured solvency" (Q. 7091).

And again, "I can only say that if I were Finance Minister of India, and I found the rupee go to 1s. (and there is no guarantee that it will not go to 1s.), I should not have any idea whatever how the difficulty was to be met; and that is the point I want particularly to insist upon before this Commission. I have heard a great many people say that the difficulty is one which the Indian authorities must get out of in the best way they can; but the practical thing that anybody who has to deal with the question has to consider is, How they are to get out of it. And with a rupee much lower than it is now, I have no idea how the Indian Government will be able to pay its way" (Q. 7102). Sir Evelyn Baring goes on to say that, although the extreme limit of what is possible in the way of increasing the revenue may not yet have been reached, he is of opinion (to make a general statement), that the Government would be unable to counteract a further considerable fall in the value of silver by any alteration of the existing taxes or by raising new ones (Qs. 7103-4).

If a gold currency were introduced into India, it could only affect the interests of the people for the better. Such a measure will not involve lower, but may induce higher prices both in silver and gold at home; while for their exportations merchants will get as high a gold price as the state of trade may allow. These exportations will take their value from gold, and whatever their price may be, it will be, as far as the money used for payment is concerned, the best price obtainable. Producers and traders cannot be worse off under a gold than under a silver regime, and there can be little doubt that they will be much better off, and with the increasing prosperity of the people the solvency of the Government becomes increasingly assured, and the substitution of a gold revenue for even a moderate portion of its present silver revenue will provide the Government with the means of paying in Indian gold its home charges without any loss by exchange. It will subsequently be shown that to levy part of the revenues of India in gold from those classes of people who sell their produce for gold, and to convert certain sources of revenue which are not derived from taxation, from silver into gold receipts, is a measure which it is quite possible to take, without adding to the burdens of the people.

The predilection for gold which is general throughout the world, rests on the same grounds which cause men to esteem it a superior money-metal to silver. Its rarity allows a large value to be contained in a small bulk, and the care which is for the same reason bestowed upon gold secures it to a great extent from loss or wastage. Thus the existing mass of metal is maintained almost unimpaired, and at the same time the increase made to it in response to a demand which is always in advance of the supply, progresses at a quicker rate than the stock of the metal diminishes by use. Ordinarily every million pounds worth of gold costs more to put on the market than the value in commodities which it exchanges for, and its value does not therefore fall from excessive production. The homogeneous character of the metal ensures the values of the component parts of any quantity which may undergo division, being in the same proportions to one another as their respective weights. Unlike other commodities, gold can be used over and over again with very little waste by attrition. These are the principal circumstances which contribute to invest money made of gold with a greater steadiness of value in the exchange with commodities, than any other article known to commerce.

These characteristics are just as efficient to make gold bullion and gold money objects of desire among the people of India as among the rest of mankind; and as silver, which is now exclusively used in that country as money, possesses them in an inferior degree, it is unreasonable to assert that for the Indians silver is good enough, or that they have less desire or less need of gold for money than Western nations. That the legal tender of gold would be welcome to the people of India is proved by the habitual use of gold as well as of silver money among their ancestors from a remote antiquity, extending certainly over the twenty centuries preceding its demonetization by the East India Company throughout their territories in 1835. The native princes at this day coin gold for circulation as money among their subjects, and there is no reason for supposing that there is less inclination among the inhabitants of the Empress's territories to use gold money than exists elsewhere. The current of gold which continuously sets towards India, and which since it has ceased to be used as money has not decreased in volume, proves that in that country custom continues to retain gold as a representative of value, and makes it quite certain that it would be employed in the most profitable of its uses, were it not that the monetary law of British India refuses to accord to it the quality of legal-tender money.

A currency commission which sat in India in 1866,* among the members of which were Sir William Mansfield, Sir H. Sumner Maine, and Sir William Grey, reported that gold coins of various descriptions were sought for in the provinces for trading purposes by merchants and bankers, and as a medium of reserve of wealth by the people at large; that the demand for a gold currency was unanimous throughout the country; that the opinion was general, almost unanimous, that the currency should consist of gold, silver, and paper.

Sovereigns of the Royal and Australian mints are

* Report printed by order of Parliament, 1868.

in circulation in India, although they are not legal-tender money, by the million, and are to be bought in every large town in the country, and their price in rupees is daily quoted in the principal newspapers. Sovereigns, in one sense, can be said to circulate in India, as they are always changing owners for those purposes to which money is applied. Gold coins of a particular description issued by the Emperor Akbar (A.D. 1555–1605), are imitated and sold at their intrinsic value, being fabricated on a recognized standard. Gold coins of the native states are procurable everywhere. No considerable firm of bankers or merchants is without a small stock of gold as a support to his commercial credit, and men of wealth, although not engaged in trade, keep gold bullion in some other form than jewellery in their possession. Obsolete coins of mediæval Europe or full-value imitations of them, as well as coins of the French, Turkish, Russian, and American mints, are frequently met with. In times of pressure these, as well as gold ornaments, are brought to the mints to be melted and assayed. The propensity to hoarding which the people of India display, is urged as a fatal objection to the circulation of gold money in India. "If the Indians import gold and hoard it when they cannot use it as money, they will continue to hoard it when it is coined, and its use as money legalized; will the issue of a legal-tender gold coinage prevent the money, when coined, being replaced in its hiding-places?" That this kind of objection has very little in it may be inferred from the following extract from the work entitled "The Finances of India," whose authors had opportunities unusually good for forming an opinion on the subject: "The opinion has been expressed that gold money is not used in India because the people prefer silver by reason of the small amount of their transactions. There is, however, no real evidence of this, the fact being that for three quarters of a century at least, gold coin has either not been legal tender, or has been improperly valued, so that either it could not come into circulation, or could not remain in circulation in competition with the silver rupee, which has always been the standard coin. Towards the end of the last century gold coins circulated freely with silver in most parts of Bengal, and about half the revenue was paid in gold."

As additional evidence of the inclination of the people of India to use gold, as an answer to the objection that a gold money is neither desired nor required by them, and in proof—if the statement were not too obviously true to require proof—that the interests of the whole country demand this reform of the currency, the following passages are quoted from a pamphlet by General Ballard, R.E., late Master of the mint in Bombay, written in 1868, in advocacy of a gold currency for India.

That the introduction of a gold currency would be merely restoring what existed up to the commencement of the present century the following extracts will show: " Gold coins were a legal tender up to 1835, when they were demonetized by an Act of the legislature, for what reason has never been made public that I am aware of—probably because they had almost disappeared, owing to our mint regulations. Hence bankers or merchants, who imported bullion for coinage, always gave a preference to silver. The Madras Mint Committee reported in

1813, that there was a great preponderance in the importation of silver bullion compared to gold. They say, 'In the territories subject to this Government gold has from time immemorial been considered the standard of value by which the pay of the troops, and the collection of revenue has been valued.

"'Objections have indeed been urged against the introduction of the rupee into the southern districts. It has been observed that in them gold has always been the measure of value, and that the introduction of the rupee would overthrow the whole system of native accounts. But such alterations have already been made in other districts without any apparent inconvenience, and even with positive advantage.' In 1827, when the new rupee was introduced into Bombay, Mr. Bruce of the Civil Service, and a member of the Mint Committee, thus wrote to that body—

"'I take the liberty of drawing your attention to the inconvenience which the public have for some years experienced from the disappearance of all gold from the circulation, and of submitting to your consideration the expediency of revising the principles by which the coinage of that metal is at present regulated, that is to say, of raising the existing mint proportion between its value and that of the silver coin, without which, as it appears to me, gold can never again be expected to form any part of the currency of this presidency. The present mint regulations must of necessity be tantamount to a perpetual banishment of gold from the currency.'

"Mr. Bruce then goes on to argue that the exchange rate for the gold and silver money of the East India Company's currency should be assimilated to the commercial rate, but he stops short of saying how this should be done.

"'As far as I can perceive, a revision of the mint rules would not involve any innovation of importance—at least none that could create any confusion in either public or private transactions; it would be nothing more, in fact, than a recognition by Government and the mint, of that rise in the value of gold which for several years has been practically recognized in the market of this presidency, while, by restoring a currency which facilitates mercantile speculations, and promotes the convenience of the community generally, it would be the means of conferring a great public benefit.'

"In 1864, the Bombay Reporter-General on External Commerce remarked on the extraordinary amount of the gold imports, observing that the question of a gold currency must come prominently forward if they continued.

"The use of gold in this part of India is more prevalent than in other districts, and especially the use of gold as a means of remittance, or for the adjustment of accounts, in fact as a substitute for money.

"The Currency Commission (1866) asked in their circular of questions sent to the Treasury officials (Q. 28) 'Does bar gold circulate in your district?' The answers from Bengal and Madras were about in the proportion of one affirmative to two negatives, from Bombay in the proportion of four affirmatives to one negative. But the answer from all districts is that gold in one shape or another is hoarded or used for ornaments.

"It is highly probable that the great extent to which gold is imported, and used as a substitute for money or as hoarded wealth, in the districts of which Bombay is the commercial centre, contributes largely to the fluctuations in which the money market of that part is not unfrequently involved. In 1865 (and on other occasions) when the rate of interest was 10 to 15 per cent., and exchange more than 10 per cent. above par, there must have been a store of gold amounting to at least three, perhaps to six, millions sterling available for coinage within a two days' journey from the mint, where it could have been coined in a week. I am not speaking of gold ornaments, but of sovereigns and gold bars, and hoarded gold, held as a reserve of wealth, which would immediately have been brought out to take advantage of the high value of money, and have given great relief to commerce by reducing the rates of interest and exchange. The monthly imports of gold sometimes reach half a million sterling, and, when money is scarce, could be disposed of to the greatest advantage by being passed through the mint.

"In almost all other countries the gold could be readily turned into money at the mint. In India this resource is not available.

"It is certain that commerce and trade are at times much hampered by this want of adaptation in our currency regulations to the habits of the native merchants and bankers. The monetary crisis in 1865, which commenced at Bombay and extended to other parts of India, would have been instantly, and probably completely, relieved if the mint rules had admitted the coinage of gold. This was shown by the following facts.

"Although sovereigns are not [a legal tender in India, and therefore not money in the strict sense of the term, yet, by a provision of the Paper Currency Act, they are received by the Department of Issue of Paper Currency, in exchange for currency notes, to a limited extent, at the rate of 10 rs. The limit is that not more than one-fourth of the total amount of the currency reserve shall be in gold. In 1865 this reserve was about £1,300,000.

"At the close of 1865 there was a great demand for money in the capitals of the Indian presidencies. This demand was for the legitimate purposes of commerce. Large quantities of raw produce were being brought to the seaboard for shipment, and rupees were required for transmission to the interior in payment for this produce. The banks and merchants of Bombay who held Government currency notes sent them to the Currency Office, to be exchanged for coin, because the merchants of the interior object to receive payment in notes.

"This drain became so serious that a steamer was chartered at Calcutta by Government to bring round specie. The Mint was working night and day, and turning out 500,000 or 600,000 pieces in the twenty-four hours. But this was not sufficient to meet the wants of the community, and they took advantage of the regulation allowing sovereigns to be tendered for notes. The notes issued against sovereigns were at once changed for rupees: the full amount of sovereigns allowed by law to be held in the Currency Department, viz. £300,000, was received in a few days. On the last day of receipt a tender of £70,000 from one bank alone was refused. These sovereigns, not being a legal tender, were of no use to the Currency Department at such a time. The reserve of rupees was reduced to £100,000, or one twenty-fifth part of the note circulation, the rest of the reserve being all in bullion or gold coin, and the Government bank of issue was on the point of being broken, not by a demand of gold for notes, but by demand of notes for gold.

"At Calcutta the full amount of gold allowed to be tendered to the Currency Department was taken up in the same way.

"The money market was only relieved by the importation of vast quantities of silver from abroad."

Sir Charles Trevelyan, who had a large experience of India, and is known to have favoured the resumption of gold money, has recorded his opinion that, "the natives of India have never acquiesced in the exclusion of gold from the currency."

Sovereigns are more frequently met with in the markets than other kinds of coin, because the certainty of their present value and their future stability as against silver and other commodities is more assured than that of bullion cast in any other shape. That gold will still be hoarded even when used as money is not to be denied, and the practice has this advantage, that it prevents violent fluctuations in the relative values of money and commodities on the occasions when an abundance of money is likely to depreciate the currency and raise prices, as a part of the supply is temporarily intercepted, and additions made to the circulation are more gradual than they otherwise would be. At the same time, if the hoards of the people take the form of legal-tender coin, they are more immediately available for commercial purposes and profitable use than they would be in any other form. That the practice of hoarding would restrict the contributions of the hoarded gold of India to a legal-tender currency is an assumption unsupported by a shred of evidence, and opposed alike to reason and experience. Gold is hoarded in that country for two principal reasons: (1) because it cannot be used as money; and (2) because it has for some years been rising in value against both silver and commodities, and therefore its owners, by mere abstention, have been gaining some part of the profit which they would have made by investing it in trade. If the desire of the people for gold money were gratified the first reason would disappear, and the second would disappear with it, since a general use of a portion of this stock of gold, as money, would arrest the appreciation of gold, and, as will afterwards be shown, the depreciation of silver also; their relative values would therefore converge, and any part of the gold employed in commerce would bring in larger returns than would be obtained from the unearned increment in its value which now accrues through a deficiency of supply. The people are willing enough to use any quantity of silver which they can obtain, as money, and although much of that metal which goes to India is doubtless hoarded, the supply of silver to the currency still goes on; nor would the supply of gold be stopped from such a cause either. The Hindus, than whom there are no traders more keen or shrewd, will use their stocks of gold so far as the conditions of commerce allow them to do so profitably, for the same reasons that they use silver for money; and they will have an additional inducement to do so in the knowledge that the merchant who pays in gold where his rivals pay in silver will command the market, and that the returns to any investment are more certain in their value when received in gold than when received in silver.

The days have passed for India when it was necessary for merchants to travel in large companies for mutual protection, when the building of walled enclosures for caravans to rest in, secure from the attacks of banditti, was an object for the benevolence of the wealthy; or when it was possible or profitable for a firm of traders to hire the army of one of the lesser native powers to escort its consignment of goods on a journey of some weeks across Western India. In those days merchants trading on the largest scale had a partial monopoly of the internal commerce of the country, and although combination to keep up prices is still largely the rule in every bazaar, facility of communication and a great and steadily progressive increase in the volume of the currency are rapidly acting as solvents on antiquated customs, and familiarizing the mercantile classes with the uses of competition in the creation of a market, and with the advantages of quick returns and low profits. Those who complain that their business has fallen off in the course of years, are feeling the effects of the extension of trade among yearly increasing numbers of those who are quite ready to profit by the European methods of business which the English administration—essentially a commercial rule—puts within their reach.

In the space of a little more than thirty years, over 15,000 miles of railway have been opened for traffic where not a mile existed before, and unnumbered thousands of miles of bridged and metalled roads have been made during about the same time on the system organized by Lord Dalhousie when he held the office of Governor-General of India, throughout and beyond the territories of the Queen-Empress.

Tradesmen in the small towns, instead of resorting to the cities in order to stock their shops, can now take off from the railways consignments of merchandise direct from the place of manufacture or production in small quantities for local retail sale; while the cart roads which act as feeders to the railway system are thronged with trains of waggons, which have been seen in particular places and at certain seasons to extend without a break over a distance of many miles in length. As impediments to the exchange of commodities and the circulation of money are rapidly disappearing, and not only adjacent but distant districts are brought into communication with one another, opportunities for the creation of wealth correspondingly increase. The proverbial thrift, the habits of industry, and the commercial spirit of the people, find room for play, and new centres of production and exchange spring into existence wherever the influence of British security and British trade is established and prevails.

As will afterwards be shown, the exclusive use of silver as money has acted in restraint of trade, and has prevented a possible development of the internal and also of the foreign commerce of India. Money has not been so abundant as it might have been, and prices have therefore not risen so high as they might have risen had a dual currency been in use during the last fifty-four years; and trade between India and gold-using countries, and with it the opportunity of exchanging her productions against the large stock of money in use in many markets, and dealing with many classes of purchasers, and its consequent occasions of gain, has been greatly hampered by the fiscal policy of the Government, which has withheld from the people the same measure of value and the same money-metal which are in use among their best customers abroad. A sound and complete currency is accompanied by exactly the same advantages in India as in Europe, and the statement that the commerce of that country has less need than our own, of the use of gold money, is one of those assertions in which men take refuge, when reason proves the absurdity of their arguments.

That a rise in prices, as a result of the re-employment in the world's commerce of the hoarded treasure of Indian gold, would occur, is highly probable, and in such a rise the productions of India would partake, not only in their gold-price, but in the value which they would command in the exchange with those of other countries. A rise of prices in the Indian markets would be a matter of no loss to the Indian producer, since it would argue an ability on the part of the home consumer to pay a higher price for the same article than he paid before; what he might lose in the foreign market he would gain in the Indian market. At the same time it would relieve the intensity of the existing competition between some Indian and some English commodities; this can only be reduced by a convergence between Indian and English prices. The longer the time during which India may be deprived of the means of increasing her material wealth by trading on equal terms with her commercial rivals, the longer will the quality of cheapness prevail in her productions, the longer will the competition of India last, and the more severe will it become.

That this gold treasure, of the value of 270 millions, is much more than the country will require for its gold currency need scarcely be stated. In former years the gold currency of India was not less than one-seventeenth part of the value of the whole circulation, and that the proportion was larger there can be little doubt. During the first thirty-two years of this century the East India Company coined gold and silver money in about the proportion of 1 to 17, but there was at the same time in the Company's territories a large circulation of gold coins provided by the mints of native powers, so large that up to that time about half the revenue used to be taken in gold. The currency of India at this day is estimated to amount to 2889 millions of rupees, and if one-tenth of this value is taken as the amount of gold coin which the people would use, or, say, 30 millions of sovereigns, this sum would be found sufficient for all purposes to which a gold currency in India is at present likely to be applied. Thus it is clear that India can not only provide all the gold required for her own currency without drawing a single ounce of metal from the West, but also retain gold to the value of more than 240 millions for the indulgence of that propensity on the part of the people to hoard the precious metals, which those who are opposed to the use of gold money in India predict will be fatal to its circulation.

The use of gold money in India would benefit English commerce by checking the importation of bullion into that country in two ways.

If gold is coined in India free of seignorage, the importation of gold in the form of bullion or coins will be discouraged, because the imported metal will be handicapped with the cost of transportation, and therefore would not circulate on so favourable a footing as the coins of the Indian mint.

The system of council drafts operates to diminish rather than to stimulate the exportation of silver to India, and when these bills are drawn against the gold revenue of the Government of India, they will have a similar effect on the exportation of gold. They will maintain a constant demand for gold, which will be met out of the gold resources of the country, as they are now met out of the rupee currency and the stock of silver bullion, and this will assist in maintaining the volume of the gold currency, and the uninterrupted circulation of gold money. Every million of sovereigns coined out of the stock of gold now in India, will contribute to satisfying the demand for that country, without drawing on Europe or America; and the stocks of gold available for the money of western nations will be, by the diminution of the existing drain of gold to India, *pro tanto*, replenished, instead of being, as some persons anticipate, still further reduced by a demand arising for gold coinage in addition to that for hoarding.

As every sum of revenue which may be collected in gold will immediately be spent in the current business of the Government, and as traders only take money for the purpose of parting with it again as soon as they can do so in some fresh investment, the movement of gold coins from hand to hand will be unceasingly active. Every process of commerce which guides the circulation of metallic money, will act with its full force in respect of the gold currency of India, for the reason that the £1 sterling of England (and the gold coin of the Indian mint will be identical with it in weight and fineness) is the most acceptable measure of value anywhere in use. It is the common and universal isobar of international trade and finance to which all values are referred. There can, therefore, be little doubt that the new gold money will not be exclusively used in the domestic trade of India, but will afford an effective addition to the stock of the World's gold money. This being the case, if the drain of gold from the West into India still goes on, it will in great part return again in the course of trade; but at the same time we may reasonably expect it to diminish, because those who now import gold because it is rising in value, will gain nothing by doing so when gold and silver are daily exchanging in India at their commercial equivalence of value; and because gold will, in consequence of its re-employment as money in India, tend to fall rather than to rise in value, both against silver and against commodities; and because gold will be more easily procurable in the country itself than it is now, without the expense of bringing it from abroad.

So far, then, from the apprehension being well grounded that the introduction of a gold currency into India will result in a permanently high rate of discount at the Bank of England, the exact contrary will be the case; the whole tendency of the scheme will be towards an abundance of gold money and a low rate of discount. Commerce may safely be relied upon to direct the stream of Indian gold on to those markets where it can be most advantageously used. Its courses in the long run invariably correspond with the general interests of all traders, and so far as, and at such times as, the gold of India may be of more value in London than in Calcutta, it will be to the profit of those holding Indian sovereigns to ship them abroad, and for the same reason the coins will in the reflux of trade come back to their original starting-point. The apprehension that an Indian gold currency, if it were once issued, would be immediately drawn to England and absorbed in our own currency, is no more reasonable than the prediction that it will be replaced as soon as it is coined, in the hoards from which it was taken as bullion. Either objection betrays a singular lack of acquaintance with the principles of commerce, and the use of money as applied to the creation of wealth. While, therefore, the reform of the currency will not in the slightest degree reduce the circulation of gold money in western currencies, it will under certain conditions of trade increase their volume, and at the same time it secures to the currency of India as full a supply of gold money as the commerce of the country can at any time demand, but these circumstances will be considered at greater length in discussing the working of the scheme in detail.

The insufficiency of the currency of India is one reason why prices instead of rising to cheap silver have scarcely moved at all during the last few years. Another is that it is only now that the full effects of that facility of communication which the railway system has during the last thirty years been providing for the people are beginning to be felt. The diffusion of industrial productions, and the diffusion of money which this facility has brought about, alike tend in the present condition of the country to keep prices stationary. Railways and metalled roads serve to convey the cheap produce of distant districts into the centres of distribution and thickly populated places, the price of produce is in consequence raised in the former, and lowered in the latter places; money in the same way becomes less abundant in some places by its dispersion over others where it has hitherto been scarce. In this way prices are equalized throughout districts and provinces, and a rapid rise resulting from a great absorption of silver metal for coinage is prevented. But if the length of mileage which is open in the railroad system of India is compared either with the area of the country or the density of the populations which it is intended to serve, it will be obvious that what has been done in this direction is only a fraction of what may be and will be done in the course of no long time, and the capacity of the industrial classes to use the money-metals for coinage will increase progressively with every extension of the means which the Government or the Railway Companies are now providing for the transportation of their productions, all over their own country and to distant markets abroad. So much of the petty commerce in country villages is still carried on by barter, and so much more is everywhere carried on by book debts bearing interest, rents and services are so largely paid in kind, and prices of the same articles in markets not far distant from one another still vary so widely, that if no other proof were wanting, the inadequacy of the currency of India to the work which it has to do could be no matter for doubt.

The proportion of coin and paper money to population in British India is rather less than £1 sterling per head. In France it is £10 10s. per head. At the rate for France the people of British India would require 31,342 millions of rupees. The country people in France are in the habit of keeping coin in their own houses instead of in banks, and in comparison with some Western nations make little use of bank-notes and cheques, and in this respect their customs are very similar to those of the people of India. At the same time the wages of unskilled labour and the cost of the necessaries of life are much less in India than in France, and this gives a scale whereby the difference between the expenditure of the masses in both countries can be roughly measured, for their necessary expenditure is directly connected with the volume of the currency by means of which it is effected. The difference would be in favour of India, and on this ground so large a quantity of money in circulation might seem unnecessary. India, however, is a backward country, and therefore would use metallic money more and credit expedients less than would be used in France, *per capita*. Taking these circumstances into consideration, an amount of coin in circulation not very much less than 31,342 millions of rupees would be insufficient to meet all the requirements of the population, and after enough had been supplied to extinguish the customs of barter and of purchases of food and other necessaries on the credit of the coming harvest, and to allow of cash dealings becoming fairly general, the necessity for further supplies of currency would be constantly growing. It is, therefore, impossible to fix any figure as the limit to which the circulation may expand, but such a calculation as this, although it is from the nature of the case only approximate, serves to show how great a void must be filled before India is properly equipped with currency, and, therefore, how great the capacity of the country is for absorbing any supply of silver which it is likely to obtain. It is evident that if 30 millions of sovereigns were coined out of the gold now in India, and used as money, it would not diminish the demand for silver in any appreciable degree, and that there is besides ample field for the use of a gold currency of larger dimensions than this figure expresses.

There will subsequently appear reason for expecting that this quantity of gold money or more would come into circulation, were it made legal tender in India, within a short time after this were done; and this sum of gold would as easily have been taken up into circulation seventeen years ago as at the present day. If, therefore, only a fraction of the immense treasure of hoarded gold which India possesses had been brought into use immediately that silver began to decline in value, the demand for increased currency which the growing trade of India has during that time been making would have been partly met with gold, and for the reasons just given the demand for silver would not at the same time have fallen off.

In the ordinary course of commerce, goods exported by one country are exchanged against the produce of another and foreign country, and these being brought into a place of export and sold at a profit, the money so obtained is employed in the production and manufacture of another series of goods for sale, and so on. The peculiarity of the Indian trade is that that part of the price of Indian exportations which has been taken in gold bullion, and which should have been employed in setting industry in motion, has instead been buried out of sight, and rendered useless for the purposes of industry and trade. It has not gone towards raising a single quarter of wheat or of any other produce, or to maintaining any kind of manufacture. If this gold bullion had been coined and circulated as money, it would have gone to increase the capital fund of India, and would have been used in the reproductive employment of labour, with profit both to capitalist and workman. As the case stands, all the labour which it might have set in motion has been locked up and laid aside, and the country, instead of being the richer for the possession of this immense treasure of gold, is very much the poorer. Its actual wealth, which is its power of production, the activity of its industries, the creation of commodities for profitable sale, has been less than it would have been had the return to these exportations come back either in goods or in silver, which could have been coined into money. Every million of gold which has come into India to be hoarded has diminished the volume of the currency to the extent to which it would have been increased if the money metal had been the subject of importation; prices have in consequence been lowered below the point to which they would otherwise have risen, and the industrial competition of India with the West has been proportionately stimulated. The purchasing power of the currency of India has been enhanced by the money-monopoly thus bestowed on silver, and at the same time the withdrawal during the last fifty-four years of gold metal to the value of above 130 millions sterling from European sources of supply, has assisted to appreciate gold against commodities, to depress prices, and to aggravate the effects of over-production in gold-using countries.

It has been urged as a reason for withholding a gold currency from the people of India that they do not really need it as long as they have the gold wherewith to purchase silver which they can coin into money. But this argument overlooks the fact that silver money so coined would be burdened with the cost of its transportation from foreign parts into India in order to be sold for gold there; or with the double cost of the exportation of gold now in India to Europe or America for the purchase of silver, and of the importation of silver so procured into India. Gold coined out of the stock of metal existing in the country would obviously circulate at an advantage to silver thus imported for coinage. Furthermore, those who are in possession of the stock of gold in India, where it has for many years past been rising in value, would, if they had sent it abroad to buy silver which has been falling in value, have exchanged the dearer for the cheaper metal, and have lost by the exchange; whereas, if their gold had been coined and used as money, it would have earned the profits due to its increasing value, as well as those ordinarily arising from the use of money in trade—that is to say, the largest returns to its employment would have been secured by this means, instead of the smallest by the other.

The result of the monetary legislation of past years has been that in every Western nation the use of silver money has been more or less restricted. In the Latin Union sometimes silver sometimes gold has been partly excluded from circulation, and in

India gold money has been wholly discarded in favour of silver; thus, in regard to the exchange between different kinds of money and the commerce between gold and silver money circulating together and commodities, the principles of Free Trade have been entirely ignored, with the result that the natural laws of commerce have claimed the penalties they impose on those who set them aside. We have in consequence witnessed the collapse of the French bimetallic system, an immense activity of production with inadequate means of exchanging commodities, an unprecedented dislocation of values, disorder in the commercial system, prolonged depression of trade, with widespread poverty and much misery carried into many thousands of working homes. At the same time the drain of gold into India, and the prohibition of its use as money, has prevented its return through the courses of trade into Western markets, where it would have assisted to reduce the evils under which trade has so long languished. The same cause has secured to the silver currency of that country a factitious elevation of value, which has kept down prices, diminished the profits of industry, lessened the earnings of her working classes, and limited their capacity to produce and their ability to improve their condition by adding to their material wealth. This prohibition has thus in India hindered the expansion of industry and affected the conditions of production, and has made the whole labour of the country less effective, less remunerative, and therefore of less value in the exchange with foreign commodities than under more favourable circumstances it would have been. It has as a necessary result stimulated the competition between certain productions of India thus artificially cheapened with similar commodities of our own country, which had at the same time fallen in price from an appreciation in the value of gold, for which Indian legislation is partly responsible.

In order to circulate gold and silver money together in India, the plan has been discussed of reducing the silver rupee to a token coin, and thereby giving it an artificial value in gold when used in small sums, and making an unlimited coinage of gold the standard money. But there are some fatal objections to the use of money on these terms. The volume of the currency would be so diminished by the restriction which it would be necessary to place on the coinage of silver, in order to raise the value of rupees in the same manner that shillings and half-crowns are raised in value against sovereigns under the English system, that the machinery of commerce and administration would be seriously deranged. The country has indeed a large supply of gold, but in order that its beneficial uses may be brought home to the people, we have to consider the means which are best adapted for bringing it out of its hiding-places. There can be no doubt that any attempt on the part of the State to influence natural values by law would not be regarded by the owners of gold as made in their interests, and suspicion would be aroused among the people unfavourable to the motives of the Government. They would perceive that their gold, when coined and put into circulation, would exchange for a lesser bulk, and therefore for a lower value of silver at home than it would fetch abroad; they would anticipate, and with reason, an immediate exportation from the country of all the gold which speculators could obtain with silver thus over-valued, and therefore would withhold it. For the same reason that gold now in India would not be sent to the mints for coinage, none would come from abroad for that purpose either. Thus the diminution of currency arising from a restricted circulation of silver money would not be made up by gold money fabricated from bullion provided by the people themselves. Prices would fall considerably, every inconvenience and evil which has already been described as likely to result from an attempt to introduce the bimetallism of the Latin Union into the country would be experienced in this case also, and the industrial competition of India, from the increasing cheapness of her productions, would become more severe than ever.

If the coinage of silver were limited, with a view to raising its exchange rate with gold, another and equally probable eventuality might occur by which the amount of coin in circulation would be increased; but all system and method in the action of money on prices would be lost. The people would supply themselves with silver money without having recourse to the State mints. A legal fixation of the value of silver in gold money would be immediately defeated by an invasion of intrinsically good imitation coins from abroad, which speculators would put upon the market at a profit measured by the difference between the commercial and the rated value of the coins. The limitation on the supply of silver money by which an artificial valuation for a token currency is maintained, would cease to be effective, and the legal rating would be universally disregarded. Furthermore, the mints of the native states, and the owners of hoards of coin of the native currencies, would supply silver coins of recognized patterns commonly in use in every part of the country for circulation throughout British India. The bazaars would be full of legally issued coin nominally exchanging with gold at one rate, and silver pieces of pure metal which would not be legal tender actually exchanging with gold at another rate. The latter would be preferred in all kinds of business, because any particular gold coin would command a greater weight of silver metal in them than in British money, and the exchange would in one case be nearer the point of intrinsic value than in the other. Silver prices would be regulated by this intrinsic exchange as opposed to the legal exchange of silver for gold coins, and would be quoted in different rates in either kind of coin. The people would pay their revenue in British coin, which Government would be obliged to accept at its own valuation in gold, but in making payments, the State coins would only pass at their commercial value, calculated on the basis of that of the illicit coinage, in the gold currency. Government would take its dues in its own rupees at the dear rate as token money, and spend them in paying its obligations at the cheap rate, that is, at their bullion value. It would be impossible to keep coins fabricated at the mints of the native powers or elsewhere in imitation of them, out of British India, even if full-value imitations of British coins could be excluded, which is highly improbable. The former not being made in imitation of legal-tender coin, their circulation would not be illegal. In law the coins would be merely medals; passing by weight, they would everywhere be taken in preference to British silver coin passing by tale. This is only what happens on a small scale where British and native coins come into circulation together, and if such a state of things were to become general, the confusion and uncertainty of prices in the retail trade throughout the country would obviously be intolerable.

Silver must for many generations to come be the money of the people, from being more adapted than gold to the low-value transactions which constitute the daily business of the bazaar, and all legislation should be directed to enlarge rather than restrict its supply for coinage into money, and thereby foster the development of every kind of industry, and raise the value of Indian produce; and the principal objection to such a use of silver money in India, is that if the system were successful, it would have exactly the opposite effects, and be beyond calculation injurious to the commercial interests of the people and to the financial business of the Government. Gold monometallism, with a silver token money, is clearly not the kind of dual currency which India requires.

Dual currencies of gold and silver, exchanging with one another at their market valuation, have been commonly in use in India for many centuries, and are so to this day. It is only in British territory and since the year 1835, that gold has been demonetized. The re-employment of gold as money in British India has been from time to time matter for discussion, inquiry, and experiment. In 1866 a Gold-Currency Commission reported in its favour; in 1868 Colonel Ballard, R.E., then Master of the Mint at

Bombay, wrote a pamphlet (from which quotations have already been made), with the same object; on other occasions the payment of sovereigns in lieu of rupees has been invited by Government, but the gold coin having been improperly valued, no results were obtained. No gold coin, except the gold mohur, which contains as many grains of fine gold as the rupee contains of fine silver, has been for many years coined in the mints at Calcutta and Bombay. These coins are made for private individuals; they are few in number and are not legal tender; they are scarcely ever seen and are in no demand. The sovereign of the Tower Mint or of the Australian currency, on the other hand, is commonly to be met with in every large town throughout India.

The first occasion when the specific plan for the use of gold money, which we are now considering, was put before the public, was in 1879,* and again in 1884;† intermediately it has been discussed in English and American reviews, and was at some length explained by its author to the Institute of Bankers in 1886. The method of exchanging gold and silver money which the plan proposes, was suggested by the immemorial practice of the East, and it includes an arrangement under which the State would declare by notification in the Gazette of India what the existing market rate of exchange might be, and undertake to receive in gold coin any payment due to it in silver at that rate. In order the more completely to bestow on gold coin the quality of legal tender, it provides

* "Gold in the East" (London, Strahan and Co., 1879), by the author.

† "The Gold Treasure of India" (London, Kegan Paul, Trench and Co., 1884), by the author.

that any debtor should be at liberty to discharge a debt due in silver money to the amount of 5000 rs. and upwards, by the payment of an equivalent value of gold coin calculated at the rate of exchange thus declared to be the market rate found to prevail in India. The details for working this dual currency for India are as follows:—

PLAN FOR CIRCULATING GOLD MONEY.

1. That the Indian mints be open to the public for the free coinage of any amount of gold or silver bullion which may be brought to them for the purpose.

2. That the silver currency be coined and issued under the rules now in force, which are contained in the Indian Coinage Act, 1870.

3. That the Government of India shall coin a gold coin in all respects identical with the £1 sterling of the currency of the realm, out of the stock of gold now to be found in India, to any amount, in which the metal may be brought by its owners to the mints for that purpose.

4. That these gold coins shall be declared *legal tender* for the payment of *any sum of money due to the Government of India, at the option of the party making the payment;* and in other cases that they should be legal tender for the discharge of any obligation *amounting to 5000 rs. and upwards, at the option of the party making the payment.*

5. That the Government of India shall from time to time declare (but not more frequently than may be necessary and convenient) the rate at which the gold coin of its currency shall be accepted as legal payment of sums contracted to be paid in

silver coin; and this State rate of conversion shall be strictly regulated by the market value of the silver rupees of the British Indian currency in these gold sovereigns.

6. That the silver rupee shall still continue to be legal tender for all kinds of payments, and in any amount; except when payment in gold is stipulated; at the option of the party making the payment.

7. That no person (the Government excepted) shall be obliged to take payment in gold of a debt due to be paid in silver, which may be less in amount than 5000 rs., unless he shall previously have agreed with his debtor to do so.

8. Nothing in these rules shall limit the right of contracting parties to exchange gold and silver money, or to convert silver payments into gold payments, or *vice versâ*, at any rate which they may agree upon. Acceptance of a gold payment becomes obligatory upon a creditor under rule 4, when no agreement between him and his debtor to the contrary exists.

The effect of these rules is to open the mints of India to the coinage of rupees and sovereigns to any amount to which the public may bring bullion for coinage; to maintain silver money in its present position of legal tender in all amounts and under all circumstances; to make gold money legal tender in all cases in which the State's debtor may choose to employ it in payments made to Government, and in all cases in which private individuals may choose to use it in payment of debts exceeding 5000 rs. in value. It leaves the silver currency wholly unaffected, and maintains the right of the people to use gold and silver money on any terms they choose, and under any circumstances, in their dealings with one another. The Government at the same time undertakes to declare a rate for the conversion of silver payments due to itself into gold payments, and for the conversion of other payments of 5000 rs. and upwards in value as above mentioned, at a rate of exchange in strict conformity with the market rate of rupees in sovereigns. By accepting the conversion of payments due to itself in silver, however small, into gold payments, the Government gives a guarantee to the public that the State and the commercial rate shall go together; since if any variation arose between the two, and gold were overvalued, Government would be paid in gold at less than its value in silver, and if gold were undervalued, Government would receive no gold payments at all.

At the time when gold and silver money were both in use in the East India Company's territories, attempts were made from time to time, by recoining the gold and silver coins in conformity with what appeared to be their market value in one another, to make them exchange at a fixed rate, but it was never successful for a long time together. Among the authorized silver currencies two standards prevailed, and one of gold; and there were several—as many, it is said, as fifteen—different silver currencies, and more than one unauthorized gold currency commonly in use. They were, doubtless, provided by the mints of the native powers. The confusion, fraud, and loss prevailing throughout the petty commerce of the country was a serious grievance. But now we have quite a different state of things to deal with. We have one silver currency and an uncurrent gold coin, the £1 sterling of the British mint. The gold mohur, which is coined at the mints on the application of private parties, is not used as money in any way. The £1 sterling is a coin with which the people of India, and of many other countries besides, are familiar. It is daily sold for silver in all the ports, and is obtainable everywhere at a price quoted in the trade price lists and published in the newspapers. Its value in rupees is ascertainable with the most complete ease and certainty. Its use as legal-tender money is not contemplated except in transactions of high value. It will be especially useful in the foreign trade of India, and as only traders in a large way of business will carry on business on a gold basis, there is no risk of their incurring loss, or being put to inconvenience from ignorance of its value in exchange. If the gold sovereign circulates in the petty trade of the country, its use will be the result of mutual agreement among individuals, and arise from reasons connected with profit or convenience, and, except with his own consent, no one will be required to pay gold in preference to silver.

It is said that the idea of a legal ratio following that of the market ratio, and being published in an official notification, was a favourite idea of the older bimetallists, who never disputed that their legal ratio might not be the same as the market ratio, and that it might have to be altered from time to time. This is likely enough. The French currency legislation of 1803 was certainly based upon a *projet de loi*, which suggested the reminting of the gold money when circumstances might change its relation of value to the silver money from 1 to $15\frac{1}{2}$ to some other proportion; but no such provision was incorporated in the law. As, however, the expedient of altering the exchange rate of gold and silver money was obviously an easier solution of any difficulty arising from a divergence between the legal and the commercial rate of exchange than the recoinage of the whole gold currency, such a plan must, doubtless, have recommended itself to many on occasions when one kind of coin, from being undervalued, was withdrawn from circulation in France.

Lord Stanhope * reports a conversation which the Duke of Wellington held with him in 1839 (in a work published in 1888), in which the Duke expressed himself in favour of a method of this kind for working a full-value currency of gold and silver in this country. As the passage has been quoted by bi-metallists in support of their own system, while it really advocates another, proceeding upon a totally opposite principle, and provides an argument in favour of the plan just described, it is quoted at length. If this conversation took place (which appears to be the case) in 1839, it is not clear what is meant by the words, "In France the proportion is not settled by law;" yet there can be no doubt that the Duke recognized the ease with which the Government of a country can ascertain the market value of one kind of money in the other and declare that value for general information, and also that he had arrived at the conclusion that a rate of exchange fixed by law could not in practice be maintained, and that the equivalence of intrinsic values is the true basis for the interchange of full-value gold and silver

* "Notes of Conversations with the Duke of Wellington." London, 1888.

coins in the same currency. The Duke of Wellington had served in India, where he doubtless had witnessed the difficulty which the East India Company found in circulating gold and silver money at a fixed rate of exchange. Between 1769 and 1833 the currency of gold mohurs and rupees was remodelled four times. Almost as soon as a legal rate was settled, it was upset by the evolution of a different commercial rate. From 1793 to 1833 the gold coin of India was undervalued in the silver coin, if judged by the contemporary European price of one metal in the other, which perhaps accounts for the almost complete disappearance of gold money from circulation. "At the beginning of this century, and previously, the East India Company used to export gold to England, while the undervaluation at the Mint prevented the gold coinage from being replenished; at the same time the importations of silver went on increasing, and in 1835 the Company, giving up the attempt to keep two kinds of full-value coin in circulation together at a fixed rate of exchange, abandoned gold and made silver, which had become the predominant currency, the standard of value and money of account for India." * With this experience of the system in use in India during the first quarter of this century, of the system in use in France when he commanded the allied army in Paris, and our own system later on, it is remarkable that the Duke of Wellington should have found them all more or less wanting, and have favoured a particular kind of dual currency so closely similar to that which we are now discussing.

* "Remarks on a Gold Currency for India," by Colonel Ballard, R.E., Mint-master, Bombay. 1868.

The following is the conversation referred to :—

"I walked alone with the Duke on the ramparts, when he detailed to me the plan he had always entertained for the finances of the country.

"'It is not to effect any change whatever in the standard of value or allow of paper, but to revert to the ancient practice of this country and the present practice of the Continent, by making silver as well as gold a legal tender for large sums. This silver to be given by weight, and not by tale, and the Government to fix in the *Gazette* from time to time the precise rate at which the two metals should stand towards each other. The rate would be about 15 to 1—a little more at one time, a little less at another. In France the proportion is not settled by law, but it is left to the parties themselves to settle, under the name of *agio*; but then they have a police and a gendarmerie to prevent quarrels and outrages on that score in markets. But that would not do in England, and the Government should therefore determine the proportion for the public according to the relative supply of the precious metals.'

"'In this way,' I observed, 'the finance of the country would have two strings to its bow.'

"'Just so; or rather, would have two feet to stand on instead of one. It would prevent the drain of one metal alone at any sudden pressure, such as may be feared this very year, for the purchase of foreign corn. It would enable the country to rest on the supply of one metal, if the other failed, and would put it in the power of the great men who have such masses of plate in their possession to send their plate into the Bank at an extraordinary emergency of national credit. For my part,' continued the Duke, 'I was in the Cabinet in 1826, and I well remember that had it not been for most extraordinary exertions, above all on the part of old Rothschild, the Bank must have stopped payment. I have explained this plan of mine several times to Horsley Palmer, and other of the Bank Directors. Their objection is that it would oblige the Bank to have a deposit of silver as well as a deposit of gold. But I answer, So much the better for the country. If you choose to trust the financial affairs of this country to such a body as the Bank, the more security you have of their being able to perform their share of their contract the better.' " *

The reasons for Mr. Horsley Palmer's objection to the Duke of Wellington's proposal may have been good in respect of the business of the Bank of England, but under the system for circulating gold money in India above sketched out, they could have no force. If paper money were issued against a gold reserve, coin or bullion of gold would be kept in the Bank, and silver coin or bullion to support a paper currency issued in terms of silver, in such proportions to the paper issued as might be considered safe. There is no provision in the scheme, except that contained in rule 4, for the payment of silver notes with gold money; in the same way, a banker who had received a deposit of rupees would have the option of cashing a cheque for 5000 rs. and upwards with gold coin; in either case no such payment would be made unless gold had first been provided

* "Notes of Conversations with the Duke of Wellington," p. 158. 1888.

for the purpose. Bank-notes and cheques would be cashed, with this exception, with the coin inscribed on them, which in either case would have been reserved or deposited for the purpose. A bank-note or a cheque drawn in terms of gold, would predicate a stipulation that payment should be made in coin of that metal. There would be no sort of difficulty in making such payments.

CHAPTER XI.

PRACTICAL APPLICATION OF THE SCHEME.

This plan secures unrestricted supply of money to commerce—Use of gold will stimulate use of silver and improve the exchanges—Consequent stability of gold and silver prices and of the gold price of silver—Reasons why gold money will not be hoarded—Alleged hoarding of silver exaggerated—Causes of diminished hoarding of silver apply to gold—Effect on Indian commerce of double full-value standard—The £1 sterling and international currency—The Indian currency will secure ascertainment of relative values of gold and silver for all the world—Necessity for gold money being legal tender—State rate of conversion fixed by innumerable trade dealings—Alterations in the State rate of conversion will seldom occur—Conditions of maintenance of true value of the two kinds of money in one another—Indian system would be unaffected by any addition to either kind of coin—Instances of State valuations of gold and silver money—Facility of ascertaining the commercial value—Objections to a varying rate of exchange—Case of gold falling against silver—Case of silver falling against gold—Alleged loss of common measure of value—Indian system provides a better common measure than French system—Case of effect of system on retail dealings—Variations in exchange rate involve no loss on use of either money—Case of double accounts—Case of "cornering" gold could not occur—Apprehension that India will be drained of gold groundless—Theory that gold coin would be of no more use in India than gold bullion—Its unsoundness shown—Indian gold money a support to British commerce—Levy of a gold revenue—Objections thereto considered—Comparative advantages of a gold and silver revenue—Beneficial to all classes alike—Necessity for strengthening our commercial

INDUCEMENTS TO USE GOLD MONEY.

connection with India—Dependent on continued prosperity of India—Proposed currency reform especially suited to India—Beneficial results summed up—Diminished taxation—Substitution of silver by gold as financial basis—Returns to investments attainable in most profitable form—Indian currency the test of gold and silver values—Will cause a general diffusion of money and promote cash transactions in trade—Will raise prices of Indian productions abroad—Fallacy involved in the theory that high prices are injurious to Indian industry—Influence of system on foreign exchanges—Leaves silver currency of India unaffected—Avoids differentiation of values in respect of either metal—Excludes influence of law and promotes free trade in the precious metals—Is especially beneficial to commercial and financial business of England.

As the use of the gold money will secure to traders and investors payment in the metal which brings in the largest instead of the smallest returns, which has for some time past been increasing in purchasing power, and at present shows no signs of declining in value, the knowledge that payments on sales, dividends on investments, commissions, and various similar charges will be realizable in gold will induce all classes of men engaged in business to use every means in their power to promote the circulation of gold money, for that which is the interest of the whole body of mercantile men is in detail the interest of the individuals who compose it. Gold will become the medium of exchange between the domestic trade of India and the trade with gold-using communities; and the defect in the mechanism of the English trade with the East arising from its diversified and inharmonious details, consisting of gold money in one part and silver money in the other, will be cured; it will in future be a single and uniform apparatus. As the convenience of this uniformity is experienced, it will become more appreciated, and gold money will come into use in quantities increasingly great.

Reason is shown in another part of this paper for believing that the practice of hoarding silver for the sake of hoarding has almost disappeared under the influence of a secure and extensive trade; and therefore the expectation that hoarded gold will not be employed as hoarded silver has been, for the benefit of its owners, when it is once made convertible into legal-tender money, is opposed to all the probabilities of the case, and the experience of all who are acquainted with the business-like habits of the trading classes in India. Gold will run to any part of the world where it can be used with profit, as surely as water runs downhill, and it will be no matter for surprise if the loan fund on the London market is considerably enlarged, and the rate of interest permanently lowered by gold from India seeking employment here. Such an expectation is at least justified by all past experience of the effect of an increase in the supply of legal-tender gold money.

On the other hand, silver will long remain the popular money of India. The wealthy trader, the foreign capitalist, the professional classes, and rich men generally will use gold money; but wages, small salaries, the retail trade, dealings in produce and in the raw material for manufacture, the initial stages of husbandry and of every kind of production, and business in the interior of the country generally, will absorb more silver than ever under the stimulus which the circulation of gold will give to industry.

If, for instance, 10 millions sterling are subscribed in England for the construction of a railway in India, the gold money will be spent at home, the equivalent of some portion of the capital will be exported in the form of silver or remitted by bills payable in silver in India, because silver money will be required for the wages of workmen, the construction of works, salaries of clerks, engineers, and so forth. At the same time, part of the returns to the traffic will be taken in gold, and gold remitted to pay the shareholders their dividends. In much the same way, capital subscribed for all kinds of commercial undertakings in India will be gold capital, the intermediate expenditure will be in silver, and the returns will be received in gold. The local trader, the indigo-planter, the tea-planter, the produce merchant, while making their sales in gold, will all use silver for the purposes of production. The more, therefore, trade thrives, and the use of gold money increases, the greater will be the demand for silver for all kinds of expenditure antecedent to the presentation of increasing stocks of commodities in the markets, either for internal consumption or for foreign exportation.

Seventy years ago there were but few metalled and bridged roads, no railways or steamships, nor a strong and consolidated empire to assist in the development of the trade of India. Since then it has increased tenfold. If in the future the civilized world is opened out to India as a market, and the many millions of men who buy and sell with either gold or silver money become her customers on a common monetary basis—for under the system proposed the gold money of India will hold a par of exchange with that of all gold-using countries, and her silver money with that of all silver-using countries—it is scarcely possible to predict the limits to which her commerce may expand, or to calculate the extent to which the expenditure of silver money in India may grow in providing commodities sufficient to meet so extended a demand.

No one can say how far a demand of this kind may disclose hidden and unexpected stores of the metal in mines unexhausted, undeveloped, or unopened; it may happen that silver will be forthcoming in quantities equal to or exceeding the demand, the present value may not be maintained, and it may still further decline. If the use of gold money in India does not bring about a rise in the value of silver, it will be an abundance of supply, not the circulation of gold money, which pushes it further down the slope; in any other case it will serve to drag it up, which no other measure which can be devised for the purpose will in the same degree effect.

Those who wish to raise the value of silver for its own sake, who believe that there is some inherent virtue in dear silver, can do nothing better in order to bring their views to the test of experience than work for the remonetizing of gold in India under the plan suggested; for if circumstances connected with the production of silver are favourable, and the supply falls short of the demand, it will have a high exchanging power with gold. Silver in such a case would obtain this quality from the relation of value to commodities which commerce bestows upon it, and any enhancement of value which it might acquire would therefore be more permanent than if it were the result of the artificial support of a monetary law.

While, therefore, the expenditure of silver money in India will increase rather than diminish, the currency of gold will continually augment in volume, as experience is obtained of the advantage and convenience arising from its use. From both these causes commerce will be fed with as ample a supply of capital in the form of both gold and silver money, as any currency system can provide for it.

India has long been, in respect to England, the creditor country; the balance of trade is always in her favour. She exports more commodities than she imports. Those offering bills of exchange are more numerous than those asking for them. When once a gold currency is established, it will become evident that the exchange is in favour of India. If India had possessed a currency holding a par of exchange with that of England, this would have been seen to be the case in all these years in which the exchange has been against remitters from that country; but the fall in the value of silver has swept away the rise in exchange which the course of trade would have given to Indian money had it been gold money. Whatever, therefore, gold money may cost in silver money, the Indian sovereign will, if a similar distribution of trade between the two countries continues, command a premium in the exchange. How far this may be affected by the remittances made by the Government in India to meet the cost of the home expenditure, whether by means of commercial bills or otherwise, or by the Secretary of State drawing bills against the gold revenue of India for a similar purpose, it would be premature to discuss. As far as a gold currency is concerned, it would afford a better medium of exchange than a silver currency can.

That the remonetizing of gold in India under this plan which gives free action to the ordinary laws of commerce, will promote sound trading, continuity to industry, and steadiness of employment among the wage-earning classes, by inducing stability of prices and exchange, will appear evident from the following considerations.

The bimetallists claim for the system of the Latin Union that it not only declared the relative value of gold and silver, but actually fixed it alike in France, India, and many other countries. We have shown reasons for doubting the reality of this influence; but if an artificial rate of exchange arising out of the force of a monetary law can be asserted to create a commercial value (which commerce left to itself would not have created) in places lying far beyond the territorial range of the law, how much more efficient for the same purpose will a rate of exchange become, which is evolved out of the free circulation of gold and silver money in all those parts of the habitable globe where sovereigns on the one hand, and dollars, rupees, and various descriptions of silver money on the other, will be competing for employment in the exchanges of commerce?

It seems evident that, whatever influence can be claimed for the bimetallic system in past years in the direction of determining the values of gold and silver money, or bullion in one another, and of both kinds of money in respect of commodities, much more may safely be predicted for a system of exchange at intrinsic values in the future.

Of all the dual currencies in the world, in the Indian currency only will gold and silver money exchange at their true commercial value, therefore India alone will provide the necessary equilibrating apparatus for ascertaining for general and universal information what that value may be. The correct discharge of this function is of some importance, since all those commodities into the production of which the use of silver money enters, will find their value in gold to a great extent regulated by the value of silver money in gold money, and the greater the certainty with which this is ascertained the better for trade.

If the system works successfully, the mass of both gold and silver money which will daily be brought to the balance, and their value in one another determined by the action of the Indian currency, not only in India but in other parts of the world besides, will be enormous; this circumstance will contribute to the stability of values and thereby diminish fluctuations in the exchange rate to an extent which may be indefinitely great, and in a manner which is wholly unattainable under existing circumstances.

As the gold coin of India will be fabricated from metal now in the country, it will circulate at a slight advantage over imported gold coin of the London or Australian mints, and the currency will therefore be replenished from inside instead of from outside India. All the conditions of supply will be favourable to the circulation of the new gold money, unaffected by the cost of importation or other adventitious circumstances, and no drawback to its profitable use will exist; it may therefore be expected that just such quantities as trade requires will from time to time appear in the markets. More than this is neither desirable or necessary towards inducing owners of bullion to coin and circulate it as money, and less than this would involve risk of some derangement in the true commercial evolution of the value of the gold money either in goods or in silver.

As the cost of issuing the coin will only amount to a shilling or two in every hundred pieces, the price at which the public will obtain so great a benefit as a gold currency will be quite insignificant, and if the Government of India show the same solicitude for maintenance of the legal weight of their gold coin that they do in the case of their rupee coinage, the intrinsic value of the coin and therefore the stability of the standard will never be affected by attrition.

As the values of gold and silver money converge more and more under the influence of an extended use of both in the same markets, fluctuations in the exchange rate will move over a narrower range and become less severe; and they will also become less frequent as the stock of money increases and approaches more closely to the full amount which trade requires; that this should be so is a necessary result of the principle that the ratio of exchange depends on relative purchasing power, for the greater the certainty with which the requirements of commerce for money may be met, the fewer will be the occasions on which prices generally will vary from a normal point of value. Silver coin in this place may be regarded as a commodity since it will exchange with gold at a varying rate determined by the market, and its price in gold will in consequence be liable to alterations under similar conditions to those which regulate alterations in the prices of commodities, that is to say, that the instability of the gold price of silver will not be greater than the instability of the gold price of any other commodity, for which the demand is great and the supply continuous and ample,—in other words, variations in the exchange rate for gold and silver money will become much less frequent under the steadying influence of a free commerce in them, than under existing conditions is possible.

The objection, however, may be made that, owing to the propensity which the Indians show to hoard treasure, the continuity of the supply of gold for coinage, from within the country, cannot be depended upon, as the people, as fast as they coin their gold bullion, will replace it in their hoards. We can only judge of the extent to which this practice will be carried, in the case of gold, from what we know of the practice in the case of silver. The extent to which silver is hoarded is much exaggerated. That silver coin is hoarded to some extent in India may be assumed to be true, as it is in other countries, civilized and semi-civilized alike; but the statements made on the subject are for the most part conjectural, and we have no good reason for supposing that the practice in any way interferes with the flow of silver coin into the currency when it is wanted for use in trade. All the evidence of facts goes to show that while the principal native rulers and noblemen of lesser rank possess stocks of treasure which they put to little use, the mercantile classes keep no silver in reserve. The former hoard treasure with an eye to political contingencies, the latter use all the silver they can obtain for trade, because it is more profitable to use it so than to hoard it. These same causes will act in restraint of the practice of hoarding gold. For the objects which the native princes have in view, silver is as useful as gold, and this class of men will find their advantage in using gold for certain purposes rather than silver. Mercantile men will not hoard gold any more than they hoard silver now, when by doing so they injure their own business. They hoard gold now because it cannot be used as money, and because it is rising in value. If it were capable of use as money, the first reason would disappear, and the second would disappear with it; since the coinage of the gold treasure in India and its circulation as money would tend to depreciate the value of gold generally, the unused portion of the stock would diminish in value while the portion in use would earn a profit for its owners. Those who assert that gold will be hoarded in future because it has been hoarded in the past, look to the appearances rather than to the realities of things; they do not stop to inquire into the reasons for the practice, nor to reflect that it will die out when the reasons which justify it no longer exist (Qs. 1174, etc.). General Ballard, who, as Master of the Mint at Bombay, had excellent opportunities for forming an opinion on the prevalence of hoarding silver and gold in that part of India, writes as follows:—

"There is no reserve of silver bullion in India available for minting purposes. A considerable quantity of silver bullion is to be found scattered as ornaments among the poorer classes, who substitute gold for it whenever they can; but silver bars are never kept in store by bankers or merchants, and the greatest monetary pressure fails to bring local supplies of silver to the mint for coinage. The amount of gold bullion held as a reserve of wealth in the shape of bars and sovereigns is considerable; all this would be sent to the mint when it became profitable to do so. To gather up the silver reserve of bullion is like gleaning ears of wheat in a field, but a large portion of the gold reserve is stacked ready for the threshing-floor."

This opinion is corroborated by the facts of the coinage of silver in India, which show that during the first twenty years of the existence of the new currency, from 1835 to 1855, 324 millions and upwards of rupees were coined out of *new* silver (that is to say, out of silver held in other forms than that of coin) in excess of the value of *imported* silver; the difference must therefore have been supplied out of hoards of silver bullion existing in India. During the following thirty years, however, between 1855 and 1885 the figures changed places, and the coinage of *imported* silver exceeded the *new* silver coined by $12\frac{1}{2}$ millions of rupees, which shows that there were no hoards of silver left available for coinage. This $12\frac{1}{2}$ millions of rupees, or rather silver to that value, may during the thirty years in question have been buried in the ground, but it was more probably absorbed in coinage by the native powers, or used in the arts.

With reference to this alleged propensity of the people to hoard the precious metals, it is not irrelevant to remark that in times of scarcity and high prices no more silver is brought to the mint, from stocks existing in India, than in more prosperous times. If great hoards of silver existed, the pressure of poverty and the temptation of high prices would equally tend to unearth them, but no such result arises. Neither during the scarcity in the Deccan in 1845, nor again in 1854, nor during the famine in Northern and Western India in 1861, nor at the time of the scarcity in Eastern and Southern India in 1866, was there any unusual increase in the coinage of silver, of an extent to predicate such a resource as large stocks of hoarded metal. In the time of the Behar famine in 1874 the coinage of silver rose to 49 millions of rupees, and in the Madras famine of 1877, to 161 millions; but on both these occasions the imports of silver from abroad increased correspondingly. When the matter is looked into, the signs of hoarding silver are found wanting. The habit of withdrawing silver from circulation by melting down coined money is doubtless much exaggerated. That it prevails may be admitted, but not to an extent to diminish in any appreciable degree the quantity of money which but for the practice would be in use.

The reason why coined silver of the British currency is not withdrawn from circulation (putting aside the unprofitableness of doing so) is that, being mixed with alloy, it is too hard to be easily worked up into ornaments; soft unalloyed silver is more suitable for that purpose. The reason why coins are converted into ornaments is partly to satisfy the desire for personal adornment and partly in order to hold silver in a form in which it does not lose much of its value. The value of ornaments made of unalloyed silver is easily ascertainable, and they are sold at a better price than when made of alloyed silver. In the latter case, the circumstance that ornaments offered for sale were made of a composite metal would be a reason with the silversmith for putting their price even lower than the value of the fine silver in them might warrant, from its proportion in the composition being uncertain and difficult to test. Jewellery in the East is always valued more for its bullion than for its artistic value. For this reason, the belief that British coin is melted down into ingots, for exportation, for hoarding, or for recoinage has no foundation in a custom of general prevalence. Ingots of silver, either exported or offered for coinage, have come into the country in that form, or if they had previously been in the form of coin, the coin must have formed part of the currencies issuing from the mints of the native powers. To make ingots either for exportation or recoinage out of the hard alloyed coin of British India would be simply waste of time and money. The silver would be more valuable in the country as coin than it would be either at home or abroad as bullion.

This cessation of the practice of hoarding silver in India has been brought about by the security which good government gives to the profitable pursuit of every kind of industry. Fifty years ago, when internal war had hardly ceased, when the police were inefficient, brigandage common, and property comparatively insecure, there was some reason for hoarding; but there is none now, and consequently tens of millions of rupees worth of silver are annually coined and put into circulation, and the same would occur with gold bullion. If the practice of hoarding silver has diminished or nearly ceased, neither reason nor experience support the assumption that an exactly opposite result will arise from the liberation of the hoarded gold of India and its remonetization under exactly similar conditions. That gold, when the law allows, will be as freely used as silver is now as money for those transactions for which it is best fitted; and that the propensity to hoard gold which now prevails will disappear along with the circumstances out of which it has arisen, may be confidently predicted, and all the stability of values and exchanges which we may reasonably expect from a plentiful use of gold money in India will be secured.

The adoption of a coin identical with the £1 sterling of the English and Australian currencies has this to recommend it, that so far as gold may be hoarded, if it is hoarded in the form of this coin it will be more easily available for use than if it were kept in the shape of gold bars or gold ornaments. As General Ballard very truly remarks, " In the former case there is a greater chance that the hoard will be broken in upon. If a cultivator worth 100 rs. in gold ornaments has a bad season, and is in debt for his land-tax, or loses a bullock, or wishes to marry his daughter, he is reluctant to break up his golden treasure. If he does break it up he must submit to the imposition of the goldsmith, who is at once assayer and purchaser. In preference he borrows at 30 per cent. But if his hoard were in coined money he would have less scruple in paying away a portion."

Having once acquired the form of legal-tender money, it becomes immediately available for circulation. Gold in the form of bullion is in times of pressure useless as money, it has first to be sold for money before it can afford relief. In the one case, the presentation of hoarded money in the markets is an effective addition to the currency; in the other case, the presentation of hoarded bullion is no addition at all to the money in use, it only throws more work upon the coin in circulation than if it had not been offered for sale, and adds to rather than diminishes, a pressure for money.

A commerce which is conducted to too great an extent on credit is liable to be the victim of panics, sometimes of not altogether reasonable panics, arising from a real or an imaginary dearth of metallic money; the existence of abundant wealth in other forms than that of money does not prevent their occurrence from time to time, and the custom of holding in reserve large stocks of gold and silver money is the best preservative against them. As the commerce and trade of India expand, the necessity of such a reserve as a counterpoise to an extended system of credit, will not be denied, and the practice within limits is not to be deprecated. The cautious attitude of mind also, which is the origin of the propensity will tend to keep in check any undue inflation of prices from overtrading, and those who hoard money, while they are able to supply it for purposes of sound business, will confer a public benefit by withdrawing it from use in speculative adventures. The practice of hoarding either gold or silver money to the limited extent to which it is likely to prevail will have the effect of preventing or at least of mitigating violent fluctuations in prices.

As the commerce of India extends into all gold-using countries, the mercantile classes in every part of the country will be under a greater necessity than they are now to inform themselves about the prices ruling in foreign parts for commodities which India exports. This they can do by no means so easy and reliable as that provided by the use of a gold money identical with that in which quotations are made abroad, or, if not identical, at least holding with it a metallic par of exchange. That stability of prices, and with it stability of exchange rate, will be very much promoted by the trader in every considerable Indian market being able to compare daily the foreign and home values of the produce and manufactures of his own country, is too obvious to need argument for its proof. The stability of prices which the bimetallists seek can be assured in no way with which a dual currency is concerned so certainly as under this system, which secures to gold money its fullest returns either in commodities or in silver coin, which leaves prices and exchanges unaffected by any conditions but those arising out of the processes of a free commerce, both of the precious metals in one another, and of full-value money of both kinds in commodities, which gives free play to that capacity for mutual substitution which gold and silver, when used in quantities unrestricted by any but commercial limitations possess, and which removes all artificial hindrances to the natural evolution of price and the maintenance of a true level of value.

The introduction of gold legal-tender money into India would bestow upon the people of the country, as well as upon those they may be trading with abroad, the most efficient medium of exchange. It would complete the mechanism of the commerce of the whole empire by providing gold for the Indian trade with gold-using countries, in addition to silver for trade with silver-using countries. The inconvenience which mercantile men now complain of, arising from the necessity they are under of trading on the basis of two different sorts of money at the same time, would cease.

It is evident that if Indian staples—corn, jute, indigo, and many others—can be bought in Calcutta and Bombay by foreign merchants with gold current in those cities and exchanged elsewhere with other merchandise at a gold valuation, an impulse will be given to the trade of the country corresponding to the ease and the diminution of risk of loss, arising from variations in the standard of value, which such a reform in the currency will secure. If, for instance, a merchant in London finds that he can sell indigo at £30 a hundredweight, and telegraphs an order to Calcutta to purchase at £25, and his correspondent there can go to the indigo broker and give him a cheque for the price, say £1000, the manufacturer will in his turn take his price in sovereigns also, and there will be a complete transaction carried through in gold money only, instead of that which now takes place, when the broker sells indigo for silver, and pays the indigo planter silver, and the Calcutta merchant sells the produce for gold in London, and is paid by a silver bill—a council draft drawn on Calcutta. No silver under the system proposed will be made use of in this transaction from first to last. That which is now called "loss by exchange," and the complications arising from a varying gold price for silver, will have been eliminated before the produce comes to market. A gold price being quoted for indigo in London, the bidders at the indigo auctions will bid in gold, the planter will base his expenditure in manufacturing the indigo on the probable gold price, as he now does on the probable silver price; any silver money he may use in preparing his indigo for the market, will be taken account of in the cost of production, just as the rent of his land, the wages of his factory servants, and the copper money which he pays to the coolies who beat the plant in his vats are now. The silver equivalent of the gold price of the indigo in Calcutta will no more concern the exporting merchant than the details of the cost of the manufacture do now—which is not at all. The same will occur throughout the whole of the foreign trade of India with gold-using countries, and silver will be superseded by gold as its foundation.

The greater the facilities may be for exchanging Indian with foreign productions in all parts of the world, the wider will the market become which is open to India, and the more numerous will the customers be with whom she trades. The £1 sterling of the English mint is everywhere recognized as a common isobar, by which the relative values of all kinds of commodities in the commerce between civilized nations is ascertained with certainty. As many communities in the neighbourhood of India accept the rupee to a greater or less extent for their money, so in the course of time not only these people, but the inhabitants of more distant and more important countries in the further East, would take into use the Indian gold sovereign in common with that of England and Australia; and thus the gold money of India would in this form become part of a vast and increasing volume of currency circulating with different degrees of activity throughout half the habitable globe. The Indian trader is far too shrewd not to perceive the sources of profit which would be open to him, if he were to convert his hoard of gold into legal-tender money; by doing so he would be able to buy and sell in Europe, America, and India alike with the same coins, and under similar advantages to those which he obtains from the use of silver money in the trade with China, Japan, and Southern Asia. As price is fixed by the amount of commodities offered for sale compared with the volume of the currency used in exchanging them, the general value of Indian productions in one another would be more accurately ascertained, their prices would rise to their highest level and remain there with greater permanency than would be the case in a narrower market.

Regarded from the point of view of the world's commerce, such a reform of the Indian currency would go far to meet the widely expressed demand for an international coin and standard of value, by providing a single measure of value for all commodities, and a single equivalent with which men of all nations alike could exchange the goods they traffic in for one another. It is probably chimerical to expect that the use of a common coin will ever become universal, nor is it necessary that it should. If all the principal trading nations of the earth employ the £1 sterling of the British Empire as a common standard of value, the question of an international currency is practically settled.

The gold coin of India, circulating with full-value silver money, would constitute a currency which in the traffic in the precious metals would play the part in the future which the bimetallic system of the Latin Union played in the past, that of an equilibrating machine for ascertaining the relative value of particular quantities of gold and silver money. The French system threw out the cheaper and took in the dearer metal, and this went on until such a distribution of the two over different centres of commerce came about by the action of natural causes, that the equivalence of value returned to the point from which it had wandered. The process of reversion was sometimes long and spread over many years, during which France was practically monometallic. Under the system proposed for India, the operation of the machine will be so far different from that of the French system that it will affect a much greater volume of currency and more numerous populations; it will have the range of an international as compared with a domestic currency.

The rupee currency of India holds a natural parity of exchange with the silver currencies of all silver-using countries, and her gold currency will hold a similar parity of exchange with the gold currencies of all gold-using countries, because they have in each case a common metallic basis. As the late Mr. Bagehot put the matter, so will his words turn out to be true in respect of the Indian currency when it is perfected by the reform under discussion : " When two countries use the same metal for money, a certain weight of that metal, of a certain fineness in the currency of one of these countries, will always exchange for an equal weight of metal of like quality in the currency of the other."* Dollars and rupees have a parity of value, and sovereigns of the Indian, English, and Australian mints will have as amongst themselves, as well as relatively to all other gold coins, a parity of value also. Therefore, whatever value of silver in gold may be ascertained by the passage of rupees into sovereigns, or of silver payments into gold payments in the Indian markets and at the Indian State treasuries, it will serve as a guide obtained from actual exchanges of the rate at which dollars and other full-value silver currencies will exchange for sovereigns in other parts of the commercial world; and it follows that whatever rate of exchange may be found to subsist between the sovereigns and the rupees of the Indian currency, a rate of exchange at the same valuation will subsist between all full-value silver and all full-value gold coins circulating as money in other places. The evolution of values as between the monies made from the two precious metals, thus expressed by the Indian exchange rate, and by the action of the Indian currency, will not depend on the coin of India alone, but on that of the whole volume of similar coins in use throughout the world, because, as closely as time and distance allow, the rate of exchange for the Indian money will, for the reason just given, correspond with that prevailing elsewhere for coins made from the same metals.

In this way the actual commercial value of one kind of metallic money in the other will be ascertained more truly than it ever was under the system of the Latin Union, because it will be brought to the test of exchanges innumerable in number, either of one

* *Economist*, August 12, 1860.

metal for the other, or of the same commodity exchanged alternately for gold and silver coin. This is obviously a more accurate method of determining values than that under which money of one of the two metals was liable to be thrown out of use for long periods of time, until falling to a fixed point of value it returned to use again, and under which goods could only be sold for many years together, for money of one sort, to the exclusion of money of the other.

It is an important part of this scheme that the payment of gold money should constitute a legal acquittance of debt, for its circulation on any other terms would be confined to money received and paid away by Government, or to perhaps a little more. The circulation of gold money will not be large until every one who pays it away is assured that in the course of his business he will be able repossess himself of gold if he may desire to do so. The reasons which have induced men to bring gold to India, will not allow them to part with it as coin, if there is little or no chance of their seeing it again. If gold is in general circulation, it will pass with as much certainty in one transaction as in another of the same class. In such a case it can also be said with confidence that any given quantity of gold is worth so much silver or so much of any kind of merchandise, because the point of value struck by two considerable masses of coin in use at the same time is not quickly or easily altered, whereas the exact contrary is the case when a large quantity of silver and a small quantity of gold are circulating together. For the same reason that a small quantity of scarce pictures, books, jewels, or other curiosities command a fancy price which is measured not by their utility but by their rarity, so gold, when the supply is small and the demand great, will pass in silver at a scarcity price; but the true market price of gold in silver money, and its true commercial value in commodities is not its scarcity price, but its utility price, and this cannot be arrived at except the quantity in use corresponds with the extent to which traders find it convenient to use it.

To expect this complete correspondence between supply and demand may perhaps be considered utopian, but if gold money is as certain of being received again, as silver money now is, when once it has been given in exchange, the approximation thereto may be indefinitely great. This certainty cannot, however, be felt with any confidence unless gold money is made legal tender for payments of debts and obligations in those kinds of business where its use is ordinarily more convenient and profitable than the use of silver. The more general the use of gold may become, the larger will grow the demand for it; and the inducement to the owners of gold to put it to use as money will increase with the advantage indirectly arising to the community from its increasing circulation, and the use of gold legal-tender money in large contracts is obviously the surest means of obtaining this result. The community which pays in gold will command the markets of the world. India, by paying her public debt in gold rather than in silver, is able to draw upon a vastly larger loan fund, and to borrow money at a lower rate of interest than if she only paid in silver; for the same reason the merchant who pays in gold in preference to silver, will secure more customers and lower prices than his rival who has only silver coin to trade with. Among the causes which have contributed to the magnitude and universality of British commerce the use of gold standard money in preference to silver money is not the least potent. That which is true of British trade, will be true of Indian trade; but in order to this end it is necessary that gold money should be reasonably plentiful, and a constancy of value secured by its continuous and general circulation. Were the use of gold limited to small quantities and confined to State transactions, the money might serve as a theoretic standard of value, but it would fail to act as an actual and visible equivalent in exchange, and the currency of which it formed a part would be no more but perhaps less effective than without it, since its value would be artificially enhanced by its scarcity in the markets, and fluctuations in the exchange for gold and silver money would be no less than they are now.

One principal object of the scheme is that at least a portion of the vast treasure of gold which has been withdrawn from the West into India during many centuries should be rendered available for use, throughout the commerce of the world, by being coined and circulated as legal-tender money in India. Bearing this quality, some part of the new coinage would be carried into every city in the British Empire with which India might hold commercial relations, provided that a sufficient supply were forthcoming. If a mere fraction of this treasure, 10 or 12 millions, just so much as the Government might obtain by taxation and pay away again in the business of administration, were the limit of the circulation, this result would not in any degree be gained. The Western world would obtain no compensation for its past loss of gold as a money-metal by recovering its use in the future, and the drain of gold from Europe and America to India might go on unchecked. Thus, both on the ground of the interests of the people of India, no less than on that of the benefits which would accrue to the industrial classes in other parts of the world by a yearly augmentation of the stock of gold money in general circulation, it is necessary that the discharge of debts in the new gold money should, under certain conditions, be legalized by the law of India.

The novelty of the scheme consists in the provision under which the State fixes a rate of conversion for the gold and silver money current among the people, that is, declares what the market value of one may be in the other at any given time. In doing this there are two difficulties to be overcome, one the manner of ascertaining what the point of value may be at which exchanges are taking place, and the other the reluctance of official persons to make themselves responsible for a declaration of value which bestows on gold money the quality of legal tender for use in the discharge and the fulfilment of contracts. At present, when gold is not in use as money, its value in silver money is sufficiently notorious to be daily published in the newspapers; and in future there would be no real difficulty, certainly less than there may be now, in ascertaining the same fact. Gold would be used in two ways: in small sums below legal-tender limit by mutual agreement, and in larger sums of a value equivalent to or exceeding 5000 rs. The one would concern the petty commerce of the country, and the other its wholesale trade, both domestic and foreign. The provision that the rupee currency should remain under all circumstances legal tender—save in the case of the gold revenue, to be afterwards stated—would also secure the undiminished use of silver as money, and leave that sort of money unaffected except for the better. That the values of sovereigns and rupees will, under this reform, tend to converge and become more stable with every increase in the gold currency, is shown in another part of this paper; and the difficulty of ascertaining the rate of exchange will be proportionately diminished by the extent to which the frequency and the range of its fluctuations may be reduced.

The popularity of gold for certain kinds of payments may be depended upon, and as the use of silver money for general purposes would remain undiminished, there would be no lack of dealings in the sale and purchase of the same commodities, throughout the principal centres of trade, for which money of both kinds would be used alike, although in sums below the legal-tender limit.

Such transactions as these fix the commercial rate of exchange; they would be watched by chambers of commerce, by the local banks in the interior of the country, and by leading firms, both native and European, engaged either in banking or in the trade in produce. That, with the information thus made available, any mistake would be made in declaring, for State and legal-tender purposes, a valuation in accurate agreement with that evolved by commerce, is highly improbable. Government would have every reason to be careful, as it would be the first to suffer by its own error, and due publicity being given to the method of ascertainment, every possible safeguard against loss to individuals arising from a difference between the State rate and the commercial rate of conversion would be provided.

The popularity of gold as a means of payment would lead to contracts being drawn in terms of gold, and the practice would become increasingly common every year, and thus make resort to a State rate of conversion for silver into gold payments less and less frequent. Those who feared that variations in the gold price of silver would make their returns uncertain, would do business on a gold basis only, and gold would become, in the course of no long time, the money used in supercession of silver in all business of importance. The rupee would be used in all the processes of production up to the act of sale in the market, and if at different times a different number of rupees were, in consequence of variations in the silver price of wages or materials, used in the manufacture of any staple, that circumstance would be reckoned, just as the same incidents in trade are reckoned now, as elements of uncertainty in the cost of bringing the article to market, and would be discounted in the gold price with no more disadvantage to the producer than occurs every day. If cotton for use in a Bombay mill goes up a fraction of an anna in the seer, the manufacture will go on exactly as it would now in a similar case, and the increased price of the raw material will be reproduced in the gold price of the calico, in the same way that it is reproduced now in the silver price; and if concurrently with this (and in consequence of it) a corresponding fluctuation occurs in the gold price both of raw cotton and of silver, no one will attribute it to any but its real, that is to say, its commercial, cause, or complain that a change in the rate of exchange has made cotton dearer. But this is by the way.

There can be no doubt that in a very short time the general interchange of gold and silver money in free commerce throughout India will elicit a ratio of value which, if not permanent, would be but little liable to disturbance, because it would be accepted throughout a commerce sufficiently vast to extend through Europe to America on one side, and to Japan and Australia on the other side of the globe. No conditions out of which a ratio of value can anywhere else arise will at all approach in magnitude and importance those which will determine the Indian rate of exchange, and therefore no other can be expressed with equal authority or obtain more general acceptance. Any other rate elsewhere prevailing will prove to be temporary and occasional; while the Indian rate, resting on a sounder and a wider foundation, will stand firm, the other will yield. Those therefore who undertake the duty of declaring the true commercial rate of exchange for the purposes of the Indian currency, will find their task neither onerous or difficult.

Having shown that variations in the rate of exchange will not be excessive, and will move within a narrow field, it is not irrelevant to this part of the argument to explain why they will seldom occur, and that occasions for altering the State rate of conversion will only arise at long intervals of time.

As in a free commerce it is the real and not the nominal value of the current money in which goods are priced and values described, and as it is the sale and purchase of commodities in either kind of money which regulates the rate of exchange for one into the other, it follows that the greater the freedom given to the circulation of both kinds of money, the more exactly will the relative values of gold and silver money coincide with variations in the values of goods as expressed in terms of either kind of coin. The values of all commodities vary very slowly against the whole stock of money in circulation, so slowly that it is very difficult to find out, except by comparing the prices of many commodities through a long course of time, whether the purchasing power of money has increased or diminished or stood still.

It will be found that prices, in a dual currency of full-value money constantly exchanging at their market value in one another, will alter no more frequently than where one standard money is in use; and if any variation in the exchange rate is brought about by an addition to the stock of one kind of money, it must be so large as to affect the prices of all the principal commodities in the market, and to cheapen them, before it can cause a fall of its own value in the other kind of money. Experience tells us that even very large additions to the stock of money, when diffused over a wide area, do not materially raise prices—witness the influx of gold from Australia and California into the European and American currencies since 1850, and the enormous increase which has taken place in the silver currency of India during the same period compared with the trifling effect on prices, either in the West or in the East, which those additions have respectively produced.

Gold and silver money, exchanging at their market value and used indifferently for the purchase of goods, ordinarily rise and fall together in their purchasing power; were it not so and were the two kinds of money circulating at proportionate values, each to possess its peculiar efficiency for purchase without reference to the other, we should see £100 of gold money efficient to buy given quantities of goods and of silver, and the given quantitity of silver purchasing a different quantity of goods, which is impossible. Provided that the currency is open to the circulation of any amount of gold and silver money which the public may choose to supply, an identity of purchasing power is maintained between both kinds of money, by the volition of the people acting under the impulse of self-interest. They continuously supply the metal which may show an inclination to rise in value, in preference to the cheaper metal, as long as this tendency lasts; there is thus a force in hourly operation equalizing the values of the two metals circulating together in any given proportions, and this keeps the rate of exchange more constant (because it maintains an equilibrium of prices) than any other force that can be brought to bear on the determination of their relative values. For this reason the apprehension that under the plan proposed alterations in the State rate of conversion for silver into gold payments will be frequent is deprived of probability.

Men see silver coin and gold bullion or gold coin and silver bullion, varying in price against one another with some frequency, but at the same time take no note of the fact that these two metals are not used together as full-value legal-tender money in the same markets. Their relative values as money are therefore never brought under the levelling influence of use in the purchase of the same quantities of the same commodities, in given sums of either, in innumerable transactions in the commerce of millions of men. As matters now stand, this principal and dominant factor in the fixation of a true rate of exchange is wholly lost; and therefore no argument against the future stability of rupees in sovereigns under the proposed plan can be drawn from the existing instability of the value of the Indian in the English money. An absolutely free interchange between full-value gold and silver money in unlimited quantities, and between both in the merchandise of trade, is the single condition under which their true value in one another can be with certainty maintained at any given point of value, because that will coincide with the true commercial par of exchange. When this condition is fulfilled, the rate of exchange prevailing between the gold and silver money of the Indian currency will become as permanent as the nature of things allows. It follows from this that alterations in the rate of exchange notified by the Government will only occur at long intervals, and that the necessity of such alterations, arising as they will from natural causes, gradual and progressive in their action, can never take the public by surprise; and being foreseen and calculable, and dependent on ascertained prices evolved out of the daily business of the markets, will meet with general acceptance, and impose upon Government no more serious responsibility than attaches to every administrative act.

It may be objected that alterations in the exchange rate for the Indian currency may unexpectedly be occasioned by a sudden invasion of one metal—say, silver—such as occurred when Germany attempted to discharge a great quantity of her own silver currency into that of France. But the constitution of the system proposed for India is such that this cannot occur. The French system permitted the exchange of the silver coming from Germany, when coined into five-franc pieces, into French gold money at a valuation which had no reference to the fall in its commercial value induced by its rejection from the German currency, and the choice offered to the managers of the bimetallic currencies was to accept the silver at a higher than its commercial value, or to refuse it altogether. They naturally chose the latter alternative, but paid the penalty in the collapse of their system, which professed to receive and to coin any amount of silver at a fixed proportionate value to gold. Under the Indian system no such fixed proportionate value will be recognized, and therefore no silver can be offered for circulation except at its market value; only so much would be offered as might be capable of finding its way into circulation through the purchase of goods or of gold, and as no one owning silver would part with it for either purpose, except at the ordinary trade profit, the additions made to the stock of silver would, like those made to the stock of any other commodity, be spread over a long time, and no sudden and violent disturbance of the rate of exchange would occur. An attempt to force a market for a large quantity of silver excavated from the mines at a very low cost, might under certain circumstances occur, and if the amount were so large and its value so low as to affect the general level of prices by raising the silver price of every description of commodity in the market, a case would be made out for an alteration in the State rate of conversion, because silver would necessarily fall against gold to the same degree that it had fallen, *ex hypothesi*, against goods. But there could in this case be no such collapse of the system as the bimetallism of the Latin Union experienced in 1873. Prices would probably rise slightly from a greater abundance of money, silver would purchase less gold, but there would be more of it in the pockets of the purchasers, the exchange rate would stand at a new figure, trade would go on as usual with the use of both kinds of money, and no one would be better or worse off than before.

The idea of exchanging gold and silver money at varying rates is one with which, although from long desuetude Englishmen are not familiar, is habitual with the populations of Asia. In parts of Eastern Europe, in the Levant, and in Northern Africa, such a use of money is common enough, and it does not in the least diminish the amount of business in the city of London with which the foreign exchanges deal. In the Austro-Hungarian Empire certain payments for custom duties and rates of carriage on the State railways, which are due to be made in gold coin, can be, according to law, converted into silver coin at a rate of exchange fixed by the average of the exchange during the preceding month. Where questions arise as to the market rate of exchange for silver into gold money among persons agreeing to use a gold price in their private business, the courts of law would be guided in the ascertainment of the real market rate of exchange by the official quotation of the Bourse Stock Exchange of Vienna or Buda-Pesth, according to locality. There is therefore at least one country of high rank and importance where an official declaration of an actual market price is not considered a matter of difficulty. In America a similar experiment is proposed for trial in the issue of notes against a reserve of silver, the value of silver being reckoned at its gold price for the day at the market. The Government of the United States evidently considers itself capable of exactly valuing one metal in the other, and undertakes a serious obligation in connection with the redemption of these notes on the strength of its ability to do so.* What these States can do the Government of India can do equally well.

* The objections made to Mr. Secretary Windom's plan (proposed to Congress at the end of 1889) for the use of silver in this manner have no connection with the question of accuracy in fixing the valuation, but arise from an absence of any adequate precaution against the United States Treasury being swamped with unsaleable silver. It is not irrelevant to notice in this place a plan, published by the author of this book in January, 1886, for the use of silver by means of an issue of notes against a reserve of equal values of gold and silver. In this plan any such risk as is involved in Mr. Windom's scheme is obviated by the condition that all persons contributing silver to the reserve, in order to obtain notes, would be required to pay in an equal value of gold at the same time. By this arrangement deposits of silver would be limited to such amounts as could be profitably used in trade, and as the gold

It is expected by some that under this plan the difficulty of following the commercial rate of exchange will be insurmountable, except by changes in the legal rate, of almost daily occurrence; and that the exchange rate will be one in one place and another in another. But these apprehensions are groundless. An exchange rate for currency purposes would be a rate for all India, deduced from an average of the rates prevailing in those places where the largest business was being done and most money of each kind was in circulation. The rate in such places would naturally dominate that prevailing in less important centres, and in practice the authorized rate would probably follow that which might at the time be ruling in the two or three largest commercial cities in India. As it is, the rate for bills on England and the price of sovereigns in rupees never varies for many hours together between Calcutta and Bombay, nor would it vary any more if sovereigns were money instead of being bullion in those cities. The ruling influence of the Bank of England's rate of discount over the rate of interest for the day throughout the city is of much the same character as that which the exchange rate prevailing in those two cities would exercise over that of less considerable markets. The former would reflect the latter, and to some extent be guided by it, but when once declared would dominate the

placed in the reserve would, to a great extent, have been previously bought with silver, an element of steadiness would be given to the gold price of silver, which is not obtainable except by means of frequent sales across the counter of one metal for another. An outline of this scheme, extracted from Appendix No. III., " Report of the Gold and Silver Mission," will be found in the Appendix to this book.

local rates, and bring these rates, slightly varying from one another, into harmony and agreement with itself. Lesser cities would take their exchange rate from Calcutta and Bombay, and this would be so for the reason that the seaborne trade, which would be chiefly concerned with the use of gold money, centres in those ports, and the Indian prices of both imports and exports are mainly settled and declared in those places for the information of the country generally.

The case for an alteration of the State rate of conversion would not necessarily arise at every trifling variation, but only when it had become evident that a new trade valuation for money of one metal in the other, different from that expressed in the Government rate last declared, had been worked out and was maintained with some stability.

It may be said that if the ratio of value were a fixed ratio, any aberration therefrom in trade dealings which indicated a rise in the value of one metal would bring in an additional supply of the metal most in demand, and so restore the rate to its original point of equivalence; but that in the case of the Indian currency the public would wait for the State rate of conversion to bring the legal and commercial rates into unison, and that in consequence the fresh supply of money would be withheld, and the natural action of supply and demand would be checked. But this will not be the case. If the declaration of an alteration in the State rate of conversion were made in consequence of transactions, which in number and value might only be a minute fraction of all the dealings daily taking place in gold and silver money, and therefore indicated an exceptional instead of a general variation, it could not create a fresh value, and would be disregarded by commerce. If in such a case a rate were declared at variance with the market rate, it would be immediately falsified by a fresh divergence between the two. The currency rules will not be found to interfere in any way with the terms of exchange for gold and silver money, which the trade in merchandise of all kinds will determine. Whatever may be the State rate of conversion, buying and selling will go on at just such prices in silver and gold as considerations of cost and profit may fix. The business of the Government will be to watch the movements in the gold price of silver, and acting on the best advice and information procurable, only to change its rate when that movement ceases at a fresh point of constancy. Such alterations, for reasons already explained, will only rarely occur.

Another objection to the exchange of gold and silver money at a varying market rate is stated in the following words: "If a man has so many rupees to pay away for rent, wages, etc., it is not possible to imagine that he will buy his gold for 2s. in order at once to pay it away for a debt of 1s. 6d., and yet if we are to accept Mr. Clarmont Daniell's doctrine that is what would happen. To suppose that the operation would be otherwise would be to admit that the rupee would rise to and remain at 2s., and that bimetallism would be successful" (Q. 4461). We fail to see how the conclusion is arrived at by this argument; but it may be admitted that no one would intentionally buy gold in a falling market, or pay 2s. for a piece of gold knowing that he could get it next day for 1s. 6d.; but the criticism thus stated misses the characteristic of a system of exchange on the basis of commercial values. It would, however, be as well, even when stating a hypothetical case, to use terms which have some reference to probability, and not to argue upon a fall in gold at the rate of 1 per cent. per hour. Let us then suppose that a piece of gold, say £1, which may be worth 15 rs. one day, falls to $14\frac{15}{16}$ rs., or by about 1d. in the £1, the next day it will be found to purchase proportionately less of any merchandise which had before been selling for 15 rs., because when full-value gold and silver money are exchanging together in unrestricted quantities, both silver money and commodities rise and fall together as against the standard coin, gold. Neither those holding gold nor those holding silver will have reason for parting with either because of this variation in value. The £1 will buy less goods than before, but it will buy as much as $14\frac{15}{16}$ rs. can buy, and, therefore, nothing will be gained by exchanging one kind of coin for the other. If a man has to pay away rupees in wages or rent, he will be just as well off, whether he uses gold or silver in doing so. If, however, gold money appears to be still falling, a purchaser will naturally part with that which is the cheaper of the two; everybody else will do the same; silver money being therefore rather neglected, will be less in demand for the moment, and being slightly dear in gold, will come into the market in fresh supplies. Both these causes acting together, one to relieve silver money of part of its work and the other to increase the supply, will speedily restore gold to its former point of value. To this extent only will there be a general reluctance to use silver, and there will be no reluctance to use gold, which in the kind of case stated in the objection will be preferred for making payments, to silver. A man will, it is true, not *buy* gold, under such circumstances in order to get rid of it at a loss, but he will pay it away if he has it, rather than pay away silver. This objection, therefore, has no reality in it, and discloses no defect either in the principle or practice of the system.

This criticism (Q. 4461), which is intended to prove the impossibily of exchanging gold and silver money at a varying rate, is very serviceable to our argument, for reducing the case it puts to practical limits; it shows that at every variation of value from a normal point the propensity of purchasers and debtors to use the cheap and hold the dear metal, as long as they can, will immediately operate to rectify a temporary disparity of value, and bring money of both kinds into their true relation of value towards commodities and towards one another.

Furthermore, it is an instance of the inability sometimes shown by bimetallists, to get away from certain ideas which appear to dominate their minds; such as that commerce exists for currency and not currency for commerce, that the object of trade is to exchange gold and silver, that some intrinsic advantage would be gained for trade if a particular piece of gold money and a particular piece of silver money always had the same value in one another, that the exchanges regulate the values of commodities, whereas it is the values of commodities which fix the exchanges. Two men may go on exchanging silver for gold, and gold for silver all their lives, and be no richer than when they began. It is only when the money-metal is used in trade that the potentiality of wealth becomes reality, and it follows that while the rate of exchange is immaterial, a facility of exchange between the precious metals in the form of legal-tender money, and commodities, is of the highest importance to the expansion of trade. The more free the exchange of the one for the other may become, the larger will be the volume of capital supplied to trade, and the greater will be the number of exchanges of commodities in commerce, and wider and more numerous will be the avenues to wealth.

That the trade of two countries flourishes as well under one rate of exchange as under another is an economic maxim the truth of which is as clearly proved by reason as it is by experience, and never more fully proved than by the growth of our Eastern trade during the period of the decline in the value of silver. This maxim affords an invincible presumption against the success of any scheme for fixing the rate of exchange of full-value money upon any but a commercial basis. It rests upon immutable natural laws, the operation of which is wholly in favour of that system of exchange which the criticism we are considering condemns.

It has been made an objection to this plan for circulating gold and silver money, that all the gold brought into use would displace a corresponding value of silver, and therefore lower its value in gold. It has already been shown that India can use in the progress of no long time, tenfold the amount of silver coin which is in use now, and any amount of silver money which may be displaced by the use of gold money will only serve towards filling a void, and substituting cash payments for barter, and for credit dealings carrying interest in the purchase of the merest necessaries of life. It is because silver money has during many years served this purpose, that prices have been so little affected by the enormous additions which have been made to the currency of the country. The influence of gold money in attracting silver to India for coinage and use in trade, and thereby increasing rather than diminishing the demand for the metal, has already been discussed. The tendency of both these causes acting at the same time will be to raise not to lower the value of silver. Other causes, such as the production of silver in large quantities at a low cost, would have an opposite effect, but that effect on the gold price of silver would not be felt in any greater degree in consequence of gold being used as legal-tender money. Both the first-mentioned causes would then operate to keep the value of silver in gold steady, and it is more probable that this reform in the currency of India will cause a rise instead of a fall in the gold price of silver.

This objection also takes another form, but, stated in any terms, it is not difficult to show that with a gold standard in use for pricing commodities, a fluctuation in the silver price of goods or in the gold price of silver is equally immaterial.

The system under discussion has been described as creating a fluctuating standard, because it recognizes the fact that silver fluctuates in value against gold. The complaint against it is that it has "all the evils of a radical change without bringing us back to that state of the common measure of value which was lost when the French mint prices were given up. The use of a standard is, that if the unit be a pound, a dollar, a mark, a rupee, a franc, the persons having any number of these written against their names may know, as exactly as possible, what their debt is, and what quantity of what substance will suffice to free them from it. Now, with a varying price between gold and silver, notwithstanding that both would be used as 'instruments of exchange between nations,' the above advantage would be lost."

This is an entire mistake; the standard is identical with the £1 sterling of the realm, and this is acknowledged to be the most constant and reliable that mankind possesses, and is the coin which serves as standard money for the larger part of the British Empire, and for many other parts of the world besides. Goods will be valued by that standard, and they will be paid for in varying proportions of gold and silver money under the ordinary action of the law of supply and demand, and variations in the gold price of silver, for the same reason, will indicate the changes which its value in commodities is undergoing.

It is physically impossible that silver can remain at one figure in the gold valuation while it varies through a series of figures in a valuation by commodities. If it is asserted that under the system of the Latin Union such a stability was secured, it has been clearly shown that the contrary was the case, and that frequently there was not stability sufficient to insure the circulation of both kinds of money. The monetary law, furthermore, did not guarantee the exchange of gold and silver money at the rate fixed for coinage, which it might have done, if the alleged stability had not been wanting. It is the case that if a depositor had 1000 frs. entered against his name in his banker's books, he could not know for certain that he had 50 napoleons to his credit, because his banker was under no obligation to repay the deposit in gold coin at that rate, although he may have received gold money from his customer. Silver being unlimited legal tender, all that the depositor could claim was repayment in silver coin, while he might be obliged to take less gold than he had paid into the bank, if he insisted on payment in that form. The system of exchange at market values can provide as much stability of standard as this, because no banker would refuse to take a deposit of gold on condition of repaying the same sum in gold at any date, however distant, nor would he refuse to pay silver for gold, or gold for silver, at the market rate of the day of demand, because he could not lose by doing so, and the French banker would do less in the one case and could do no more in the other than this. So far from this system being a defective bimetallism, or inferior to a mere fixed-ratio-mintage system, it is a perfect bimetallism, because it provides for the use of both the metals as money on the basis of their actual commercial value in one another under all circumstances and in any amount; and whatever the changes in the equivalence of value may be, they are produced by the action of trade, and therefore any sum of money composed of gold and silver coins in any proportions, becomes a measure of value common to all commodities. It uses gold as a standard instead of silver, the standard under the French system; and its dual currency is a "common measure of value" superior to that constituted by the currencies of the Latin Union. Reasons have been given which show that as great (if not greater) stability of prices would be attained under its use as the system of the Latin Union secured, among them, not the least cogent, is the encouragement which a completely free trade in the precious metals holds out to capitalists to supply both kinds of money in just such quantities as can be profitably used in commerce. Their interchange at market values guarantees their joint exchange with commodities at just what they are worth, and no more sound or certain a "common measure of value" than this can in the nature of things be devised.

The varying rate of exchange for gold and silver money is also the ground of another objection, which is stated as follows: "No man," it is said, "will know what change he is to get for a sovereign." Again, "If a man pays his servant a sovereign for his wages, calculated at 15 rs., the servant may change the coin a month after for only 14 rs. 15 ans." Putting aside the improbability, already dwelt upon, that frequent and wide alterations will occur in the exchange rate; the scheme is so constituted as to escape the complaint (wholly without reason as it would be), that it affects prices and wages paid in small sums in silver, as it only gives to gold money the quality of legal tender when used to liquidate silver payments in large sums of 5000 rs. and upwards. In changing a single sovereign into silver coin, any one in a position to do so would have no difficulty in ascertaining its value, no more difficulty than the poorest class of working people now find in exchanging rupees for country pice,* for which the rate of exchange varies quite as much as that for rupees into sovereigns would in the case in hand. The other objection connected with the payment of wages could never arise, as gold would never be used in paying small sums, such as 15 rs., except by agreement among the parties, in which case a mutual advantage must be presumed, and no ground for making it would exist. But no real loss would result to a purchaser from, say, a hat costing £1 or 15 rs. in one month, and £1 or 15 rs. 1 an. in the next; nor would a servant, accepting a sovereign in lieu of his wages of 15 rs. in one month, and exchanging it for 14 rs. 15 ans. the next month, be a loser. In each case the silver money would buy as much as the gold coin, and by no device can it be made to buy more. This would immediately become evident from the gold coin instead of the silver being used for purchases.

The principle that no loss or gain can accrue from the use of either kind of money in preference to the other, under this plan, is equally good for dealings in tens of thousands of pounds or lakhs of rupees, as in dealings in single sovereigns or tens of rupees. Let us take the case of a debtor electing to pay 6000 rs., in discharge of a debt contracted when the £1 was at 15 rs., with £400. If the rupee had fallen ½ an. in the £1, the value of the gold money would have risen correspondingly, and as £400 would in that case procure 6012 rs. 8 ans., the

* The unauthorized currency of copper coin, in general use throughout British India.

6000 rs. becomes repayable with 399 sovereigns and 2 rs. and 8 ans. in silver money. If the creditor thinks that he has suffered a loss of 12 rs. 8 ans., and that £399 2 rs. 8 ans. will buy less of any goods than he can get for 6000 rs., he will, by paying away the latter sum, find that he is mistaken. To take the opposite case of a rise in the value of silver to a similar extent, and £400 to become the equivalent of 5987 rs. 8 ans., either of those sums of money would purchase as much of any kind of goods as the other. In the one case the gold money would buy more of silver and more of commodities, and in the other less of either; but whatever quantity the gold money would buy, its silver equivalent would procure as much. If, however, it were the case that two sums of gold and silver exchanging together commanded different quantities of the same kind of goods, such a condition of prices would only be momentary, and the silver price of commodities would follow its gold price, as quickly as time and space would allow an adjustment; that is to say, in a few hours. Gold being accepted as a standard of value, commodities and silver alike must take their values from gold, and that which appears as a variation in the exchange rate, is really brought about by a variation in the purchasing power of silver in respect both of commodities and of gold. Were it the case that alterations in the gold price of silver depended on any other cause than this; if it were possible that under this plan the owners of either sort of coin would be the better or the worse off, at any time, by holding one and getting rid of the other; or that they could make a profit by the use of one in preference to the other; then Euclid would have taught in vain, and things which are equal to the same thing would *not* be equal to one another.

It may not be unnecessary to repeat, that if under this plan a purchaser finds his silver and his gold money purchases more or purchases less of goods than was the case before, such a fall or rise in prices will depend on circumstances connected with the demand and supply of money and the quantity of commodities under sale in the markets, and not in any degree on the rate of exchange for gold and silver money; any more than is now the case when a fall in the value of commodities in gold money is erroneously attributed to a fall in the exchange rate of silver into gold.

In considering the practical working of the scheme, it will not escape notice that bankers will be under the necessity of keeping double accounts of deposits made in gold money, and those made in silver money. A banker in his own interest will secure to a customer depositing gold, payment of his cheques in gold, just as he will cash cheques in terms of silver against a deposit of silver. There will be no trouble in keeping accounts in both kinds of coins, or, if either kind of deposit is used by a banker for purposes of his business, in providing for the return of similar money into his till on due dates. This method of keeping accounts would only amount to an extension of that which every banker has now to keep up for his own and his customers' convenience in respect of remittances which they have to make to Europe or to parts of India outside British territory. There is an apprehension that combinations may be formed to engross the gold coin in circulation, and raise its value against those who are obliged to use it in making payments. But combinations only succeed when the supply is limited, and a certain quantity of gold is required by a particular date. If the Government of India or a mercantile firm were bound to convert a silver into a gold payment in a very large amount, say, many millions, on a particular day, and the gold money of the country were in a few hands, such a combination might be tried, but this condition of things could never arise in India, where the stock of gold would be manifold greater than the money in circulation, and would be held by an innumerable number of persons in all parts of the country, and would, from the nature of the case, be more accessible to the bankers whose interests were attacked than to the speculators who might try to form a "ring" against them. It will also not be forgotten that silver money will under all circumstances be legal tender, and those against whom such a combination were directed could at once defeat it, by using silver for their payments instead of gold money. For the rest, bankers and traders generally will not promise to pay gold unless they have the means at command for doing so.

The operation of the system will no doubt tend to keep the banks well supplied with gold money. Professional men, such as doctors and lawyers, tradespeople, wholesale traders, and various other classes of men, will take as large a part of their incomes in gold as they can, which they will pay into their accounts at their bankers'. Their expenditure, on the other hand, will be almost entirely, if not altogether, in silver, thus the gold deposits will become the property of the bankers to any extent to which silver has been paid away against them, or if remittances abroad have been made against them, to the extent to which bills have been drawn in the depositors' favour. Thus the bankers will be the class who will be large holders of gold coin, and as no other class will be under a necessity to pay gold away, they need fear no combination of the kind we are considering. The Government of India may of course arrange to make its own gold payments in England, it need make none in India, but it will not do this until it has provided itself with a gold revenue sufficiently large for the purpose.

Among the reasons for apprehending that the coinage of gold for use as legal-tender money in India will prove abortive, there are two which, although they are mutually destructive, it is desirable to anticipate and disarm. One is, that as fast as the coinage goes on the money will be drained away to Europe. The other is that the gold money thus fabricated will prove no addition to the world's supply, because no more of it would be dispersed abroad outside India, as coined money, than is now exported as gold bullion and is or can be coined into money in Europe and America. The people of India, it is said, if they want more money, can use their gold bullion to buy silver for coinage, and they will be no better off by using their gold coin in future for the same purpose.

Ordinarily, money moves from country to country in settlement of international balances; the creditor countries on the whole receive more than they part with to the debtor countries. England, which produces no gold, replenishes her stock of the money-metal in this way; contracts with English traders can only be discharged in gold, and as this country has to receive more than she has to pay away her stock of gold money is maintained. The same is the case with India. The silver currency is supplied with many millions of rupees, principally by traders in foreign countries who have to find silver to pay for produce or manufactures which they import from India; these exportations are partly paid for in gold, and this kind of payment will continue to be made just as regularly after gold becomes legal-tender money as it is now. The balance of trade, as long as it is in favour of India, will be paid partly in gold and partly in silver. Gold bullion will leave India, that is, will be re-exported, as it is now, for storage or coinage abroad in the ordinary movements of the precious metals which commerce sets up, and while one current is flowing westward, another will be flowing eastward, and the volume of the latter, owing to the prosperous condition of Indian trade, will be the larger of the two.

Among civilized nations, gold is not the object of trade, currency is merely the mechanism by which commerce moves. No such nation keeps more gold than it wants for the exchanges of its trade; every £1000 of gold which becomes redundant immediately goes elsewhere where it is more wanted. No country can procure a continuous supply of gold, except by creating commodities for the exchange of which it may be required; every ounce of gold therefore taken from India must be obtained in exchange for English goods manufactured for export and sold there; and it is not possible that the industries of Europe and America will undergo so great and sudden a development as to draw away from India, and permanently retain, any considerable part of the stock of gold now in that country; whatever quantity may leave in one season will come back in another.

Without the advantage of a gold currency, India has been accumulating gold for centuries; the same causes will act in the future as in the past, and although the gold supply of India may, when the trade of the country is more valuable and more widely diffused than it is now, become increasingly great, its use will be shared with other nations, it will be in constant movement instead of being, as is now the case, locked up and laid aside from use altogether. There is nothing in the nature of the trade between the West and the East, as it is at present conducted, which could produce such a phenomenon as a continuous and uninterrupted flow of gold from India to Europe without a compensating current in the reverse direction. When gold leaves the Bank of England for New York or Paris, there is no cry raised that England is being drained of her gold; when it goes to India there is some reason for saying so, because as a matter of fact to some extent it is the case. Give India a common monetary basis with England for the trade between the two countries, and they will then be as nearly on a footing of equality in currency matters as the difference between their systems will allow; and the use of her own gold money will be as fully secured to India as that of her silver currency is at present. The only case in which the gold stock of India could disappear, would be that of her entering into contracts to pay gold as interest on a public debt or otherwise, without having the power of producing wealth wherewith to buy the money-metal. If the industrial, the commercial, and the financial position of India were ever reduced to that which now prevails in the South American republics, and she were to owe a debt to a gold-using country, upon which she could not pay the interest without continually borrowing in order to do so, gold might become as scarce in India as it is in the Argentine Republic and other States in that part of the world; but this is a contingency which it is the business of political foresight to provide against, and which this reform in the Indian currency would, if such an eventuality were in prospect, greatly help in averting. In the absence of such a condition of affairs the apprehension that the gold of India, if once made available as money for the world's commerce will be totally or even partially lost to that country, is wholly groundless.

Next it is asserted that, because gold bullion can always be used for the purchase of silver in order to the coinage of rupees, gold money, when made legal tender, will be of no more use than gold bullion; that so far as commerce would assist in the dispersion of the store of gold in India, if it were coined money, it could do so equally well now when the metal is uncoined. Both these objections arise from the same mistake. Those who put them forward overlook the advantage which coined money has, as a legal and established standard of value, over bullion of the same metal. To make them good it is first necessary to account for the circumstance that the one step in the development of currency progress is always a substitution of a gold standard for one of inferior metal. Civilized mankind may be making a mistake in this respect, but it is more probable that they are not, and that the comparative rarity of gold, the improbability of the supply exceeding the demand for it, the superior stability of value which it possesses over every other money-metal, the high value which can be held in a small compass, and other reasons which have contributed to make it the best medium of exchange which we possess, will operate in its favour with the people of British India when their laws allow its circulation as money, and will induce them to use it as readily (and more readily, because with a keener commercial intelligence and insight) as their forefathers did during more than two thousand years.

That which occurred in England during the last century will recur in India. Among us the use of gold became so popular as the trade of the country expanded and daily life demanded increasing monetary conveniences, that it was substituted for silver in response to a national exigency, and it seems to be the height of contradiction and equally opposed to experience and to reason to argue that the public requirement in India, under similar conditions, will be exactly the reverse of that which has always come into existence everywhere else. If this anticipation is verified, and the people of their own motion and with a view to their own profit and advantage, convert their gold into money, and several millions of sovereigns come into circulation, the currency of India will then hold the same or nearly the same relation to that of England and other gold-using countries that they hold to one another. In the country the money will be in use among tradesmen and their customers, it will be held by the banks and by the numerous mercantile firms which, according to the custom of India combine trade and banking. It will always be in movement from those parts of the country where it is least wanted to those where it is most wanted, a certain portion of the supply will be available at a few hours' notice for the purposes of international business, for export if required or for use in discounting foreign bills. The difference between the gold of India as it is now, and as it may be in future will be all the difference between money and no money. Bullion is not money, and although it may answer one of the purposes of money as an ultimate reserve and support to credit, it does this less efficiently than if it were reserved as legal-tender coin, and other purposes of money it fails to answer altogether.

The financial supremacy of London over all other commercial cities in the world depends partly on its ability to pay gold under all circumstances, and partly on its banking system, which practically concentrates the supply of gold money for commerce under the control of a single institution. As gold comes more and more into use, banking business in India will become as highly organized as it is in England, and the owners of gold will obtain facilities for applying their resources in the most profitable manner correspondingly extended. At present any progress in that direction is wholly impossible, because gold in India is not money, but is scattered over the country in a thousand hiding-places, in forms which prevent its being immediately utilized, under circumstances in which a prompt supply at a few hours' notice of demand is essential to its profitable employment. When however it is in circulation, and held by banks and mercantile firms for business purposes, it will become to an extent indefinitely great available for the internal trade of the country, and a real addition to the world's supply of gold money.

The currency of India, as applied to use abroad, will be subject to one disqualification which, from the nature of a dual currency worked on the basis of the commercial exchange, is unavoidable. Those making payments (as has above been stated) of sums over 5000 rs. in value are to have the option of paying in either metal, in the absence of specific contract to pay in gold. A bill for £1000 drawn on Calcutta (unless drawn against gold previously deposited by the drawer) will therefore not necessarily be paid in gold, or if it is paid in gold the acceptor may demand a favourable rate as a compensation for giving up his option to pay with silver, and to meet a possible rise in the silver price of gold which an increase in the number of bills payable in gold might occasion. In this respect the English currency will stand in much the same position to the gold currency of India that it holds to the gold currency of France, where both gold and silver are unlimited legal tender, and payment of a bill of exchange in gold cannot be assured beforehand. In order to secure payment in gold of bills drawn on India, a special rate for gold would become customary in the foreign exchanges, varying with fluctuations in the supply of gold money in the market. Gold would always be procurable at a price, and that price might, *ceteris paribus*, be higher than if gold money were sole legal tender for large payments, and at the same time abundant in supply. This circumstance would somewhat interrupt the export of gold from India, but it will by no means stop or interfere with its return thither in due course of business. It will induce larger accumulations of gold in the Indian banks than might otherwise be the case, which for the domestic trade of the country would not be disadvantageous. In its application to foreign commerce with gold-using countries the system would be less complete, and the movement of gold less free than if it were not tied to silver; but on an emergency, upon one of those occasions when the city of London is turned upside down for want of a million of money, the assistance of the Indian gold currency may prove most seasonable.

As a tentative scheme which affords the only possible initiative towards endowing India with a gold currency it secures results which are certainly beneficial; it involves no risk of loss to the public which both supplies the material for the gold currency and need only use it in substitution for silver as individual discretion or convenience may dictate; while the correspondence between the State rate and the commercial rate of exchange will prevent those using either metal from benefiting at the expense of those using the other; it does not attempt impossibilities, or pretend to cure in some heroic manner the various inconveniences which are laid to the door of cheap silver. It cannot, nor can any currency system, make the rupee more valuable by the gold standard than it is now, but it can assist commerce to bring such a change about, which no other plan dealing with the money of the country can succeed in doing.

Such a scheme as this for circulating gold money would be incomplete if it were not intimately connected with the revenue as well as with the trade of the country. First, because the rate accepted by Government for converting silver payments due to it into gold payments should be a sure guide to the market value of one kind of money in the other, and serve as a guarantee that the rate of conversion was one which no private person would suffer by using; and also because the levy of a revenue in gold and its immediate expenditure for State purposes would maintain the circulation of gold in a far greater state of activity than would be the case without such assistance. It is sought by this scheme to secure a fund of gold money at the disposal of the Government of India upon which the Secretary of State can draw, and thus procure gold for use in England; and to provide a currency which will serve for the encashment of ordinary mercantile bills drawn in terms of gold by traders in foreign parts on banks and mercantile firms in India. Without a gold revenue the circulation of gold would be sluggish, and the latter of these objects be only partially attained, while the former would not be attained at all. A gold revenue would indirectly assist in putting some portion of the hoarded gold treasure of India back into the channels of commerce from which it has been withdrawn, and thus incorporating the gold money of the country with the general stock of such money in use in international trade. It cannot be doubted that when this is accomplished the drain of gold to the East which is of such moment to commerce generally will be checked, and that the supply of that money-metal in the West will be increased by contributions from India, thus the world in general will gain to the extent to which the continuous depletion of the stock of gold available for money may be lessened, while at the same time the supply is replenished from a source hitherto untapped.

The Government of India has sources of revenue which are not properly speaking derived from taxation, and some, which although reckoned as taxes, can be levied in gold for the same reasons that they are now levied in silver. The most important of these sources of revenue are those derived from the sale of opium, the duties on salt, from customs, and from railway receipts. By accounts made up either to the end of the year 1887, or to the end of the first quarter of 1888, the figures for these heads of revenue are as follows.

	Rupees.
Opium	85,154,620
Salt	66,707,280
Sea customs	13,205,910 *
Railways	44,000,000
Total	209,067,810

Those who would pay the opium and salt revenue are men in a large way of business, and could provide

---

* Making a deduction of about 25,000 rs. for articles severally yielding less than 10,000 rs.

themselves with gold for the purpose without difficulty. Customs are taken compulsorily in gold in other countries, such as the United States of America, and Austria, and could be levied in the same way in India. The railway receipts taken on the Imperial and Provincial State Railways, were in 1887 approximately 106¼ millions of rupees. Those taken on the "guaranteed" railways are not taken into account, as it is not certain how far under existing arrangements the receipts of these railways would be available for providing gold money for the home charges, or could be fairly expected to assist in doing so. If out of the railway receipts which are the property of the State one quarter of those derived from "coaching" traffic, and one half of those derived from the carriage of goods could be levied in gold, a revenue equivalent in value to 44 millions of rupees might be secured. The total estimated gold revenue thus converted into gold from silver receipts would amount to 209 millions of rupees;* and the home charges during the year just closed (1888-89), amounted to £15,041,000. Provision would thus be made for meeting the expenditure of the Indian Government which is incurred in England to nearly its whole extent, the remainder, if there is any, being obtained by bills drawn in terms of silver.

In support of this contention it is necessary to examine the arguments against any levy of a gold revenue in India at all. To levy a gold revenue in India will, it is said, be tantamount to an increase

* Stated in terms of gold this revenue of 209 millions of rupees would yield, at 15 rs. to the £1 sterling, within a few thousand pounds of £14,000,000 sterling.

in the taxation of the people; the taxpayer (so runs the argument) will gain nothing by the conversion of silver into gold payments at market rates, and as gold appreciates he will only be able to procure it at a sacrifice of more and more of the proceeds of his industry. This, however, is not correct. If gold appreciates from scarcity in the supply, a smaller amount of gold will be obtained every year corresponding with the fall in the gold price of silver at which the conversion is effected. In fact, that which happens now will happen then, the taxation of the country will be increased as the cost of laying down gold in England increases; but this result will in no degree be attributable to the conversion of silver into gold payments as taxes, but to causes connected with the relation of value existing between commodities and silver on the one hand, and gold on the other.

Of the sources of revenue above indicated three, if not all four, might be fixed in gold, and then no question would arise of converting silver payments into gold payments. Whether a continued appreciation of gold results in the gold revenue yielding less than the silver revenue yields now or only as much or more, will not depend on the gold price of silver apart from the gold price of commodities. The prices paid for opium will be governed by the circumstances of the trade; railway freights, sea customs, and salt duties will be regulated partly by competition and partly by the ability of the people to pay the charges fixed by Government without the risk being run of a diminished revenue. Whether the gold revenue will be a heavier burden than a silver would be a financial not a currency question, as will appear from the following consideration. The gold revenue in this case would be levied compulsorily without option of payment in silver.* It would be analogous to the levy of customs duties in the United States and in Austria, where they are taken either wholly or in part in gold to the exclusion of silver money. It may be argued that if the gold revenue were fixed at a time when 10 rs. were the equivalent of £1, and silver were afterwards to fall and 12 rs. to become equal to £1, then the taxpayer would pay ⅕th more revenue than he did before. This eventuality may be set forth as follows. Let us suppose that a taxpayer produces 100 maunds of produce, valued at £100, and that his taxes amount to £1 per annum, and that 10 rs. = £1, then 1 maund = 10 rs.; and that later on, silver falls to 12 rs. to £1. The maund of produce would then be priced at 12 rs. In each case 1 maund of produce would be surrendered to pay the tax, but in one case 10 rs. and in the other case 12 rs. of silver value. The taxpayer parts in the latter case with 2 rs. more of silver in order to pay his tax, but the remaining 99 maunds of produce sell for £99, each maund will fetch as much gold money as it did before, and 2 rs. more silver money. He parts with no more of his produce to pay his tax, as gold has not risen against commodities, while their increased silver value, being discounted by the fall in value of that kind of money, brings him in no gain. He is not better or worse off.

Then, to take the case in which gold may have risen against silver and against commodities likewise.

* In this case only will an exception arise to the provision in rule 6. p. 198.

£1 will (let us suppose) buy $1\frac{1}{5}$ maunds of the produce instead of 1 maund, and 12 rs. instead of 10 rs. Will the taxpayer be a loser? The answer is, "Yes," because he will be obliged to surrender $1\frac{1}{6}$ maunds more of his produce to pay his taxes than before. He will get more silver as in the other case, but it will go no further than the proceeds of the sale of his produce at 10 rs. per. maund; but the remaining $98\frac{2}{6}$ maunds of his produce will not fetch so much gold as before by $\frac{1}{6}$th of £1 per maund. Then will arise the consideration whether the tax is not too heavy, and this, as has been just said, is a purely fiscal question; the increase in the burden of the impost having been brought about by commercial, and not in any way by currency causes. Such a revenue would be exposed to no greater vicissitudes of productiveness than a silver revenue, and in the case of a continued appreciation of gold arising from a scarcity of supply, it would go as far as a silver revenue in paying the home charges, and for general purposes its purchasing power would be increasingly greater. In the case of gold continuing to appreciate from this cause, the taxpayer will be no worse off than before, and as far as a gold revenue serves to promote commercial progress he will share in the general advantages it brings with it.

But the arguments already used will, we hope, have established the proposition that the introduction of a gold currency into India will cause gold to become rather less than more valuable, and prices to rise rather than to fall. If commodities rose, as they would in that event, this would be the consequence of a general rise of all values, an accompaniment of increasing prosperity, and of a wider diffusion of material wealth and comfort among the whole people. Evidently in this case a gold revenue would become a lighter burden every year, each individual taxpayer would surrender a continually decreasing proportion of his goods to meet his taxes, and the receipts of revenue would increase by increasing numbers of the taxpayers becoming rich enough to fall under the impost.

As regards the particular sources of income above mentioned, the home charges would be met at a decreasing cost to the individual taxpayer; and this certainly would not be the case if they were obtained as they are now, in silver. Let us suppose that in five years a gold revenue increases by reason of an improvement in the general prosperity of the people to the extent of 5 per cent. from £1,000,000 to £1,050,000. If, however, the tax had been levied in silver, although its yield might from the same cause have increased absolutely, yet from silver continuing to fall against gold, its efficiency for the purchase of gold would have decreased in a greater proportion than the returns to the tax had increased. A tax yielding 15 millions of rupees in 1890, might yield 15¾ millions, or, say, 16 millions of rupees in 1895, but its value in gold would have fallen in the five years 10 per cent., which is about the average rate of the decline in the gold price of silver for some years past; the larger sum of revenue (16 millions) would purchase considerably less than 1 million sterling, that is, less gold than the 15 millions, would have purchased at the beginning of the period. The gold revenue, once obtained, would grow in value every year; the silver revenue would decline.

If at the same time the expectation were realized that with the use of a gold currency the metal would slightly depreciate against both commodities and silver, an absolute increase in the returns to a gold revenue would not only be obtained from the increasing means of the whole people to support taxation, but also by reason of an appreciation of silver. Any tax which might be not merely fixed in gold but be converted from a silver into a gold payment at market rates, would from this cause become more and more productive; 15 millions of rupees converted into sovereigns would not have lost 10 per cent. of their value, but something less. If rupees had risen in value in sovereigns from 15 rs. to 14 rs., then a tax of 15 millions of rupees would yield £71,425 more than it did before. By the levy of a gold instead of a silver revenue the country would, under these circumstances, be a considerable gainer.

If India continues to advance in material prosperity, as she is doing now, her productions will have a rising value in those of foreign countries, and for this reason also a gold revenue will not be a heavier but a lighter burden on those who pay it; it will be provided by goods sold abroad in increasing proportions, the labour of the people will be more remunerative, while that part of it which they hand over to the tax-gatherer will be no greater than it was in times past.

Looking at the matter from the point of view of the exchanges, whether silver were to rise in value against gold from being more largely used than before, or whether it were to fall from increasing supplies coming from the mines, the interests of the people would remain unaffected. In the former case, as the value of silver drew nearer to that of gold from being more in demand for money, it would command a higher value in commodities, silver prices would fall, a smaller sum of silver (because it would exchange for the same value of gold as the larger sum) would procure the same value of goods as before. In the latter case, if in spite of an increased use of silver the gold price of silver were to fall from an abundance of supply, or if the gold price of silver money declined, from its use diminishing as a consequence of the circulation of gold money, silver prices would rise, but gold prices would, as far as the rate of exchange was concerned, remain unaltered, and a gold revenue would be as efficient for all its purposes as it was before the rate of exchange altered. £100 would pay for gold in England, or pay for Commissariat stores in India equally well, were it worth 1000 rs. or 990 rs.

In any view of the case, therefore, the taxpayer, the investor, the capitalist, the merchant, the official and Government alike will be better off as each fresh million of gold taxes is substituted for its silver equivalent. Each will be nearer the consummation which all desire, that gold may become so commonly used, that taxes, incomes, dividends, and returns of all kinds will be paid in gold. In this form both private incomes and the public revenue will buy as much as money can buy; in the form of silver they will buy less and less each succeeding year.

The military resources of England, as a means of maintaining our connection with India, although ostensibly of primary importance, really take rank after the political and commercial considerations upon which the physical part of our power rests. Numerically, the English army in India would be wholly inadequate to the support of British power were it not for the much larger army which is composed of natives of the country. The military strength of England in India rests on the willing acquiescence of the people in her rule, a feeling which sends volunteer recruits into the ranks in any required numbers either in time of peace or war, and which places at the disposal of the Queen-Empress the armies of the native powers. This general contentment is largely owing to the prosperity which pervades all classes, and to the prospect of its indefinite increase. The Sepoy would bring the discontent of his village into "cantonments" if there were any to bring, and a widespread irritation produced by financial misadventures acting on the fortunes of the masses would sap this source of our power as surely as military disaster. The English people are trying in India the most extraordinary political experiment which the world has ever seen. It is only an experiment, it is not finished, nor is success achieved, nor will it be until the commercial centres of India stand in the same relation to London and Liverpool, as one of those cities stands to the other—until Lancashire ceases to regard the gains of Bombay as so much lost to Manchester.

It has been remarked, as a characteristic of the modern age, " that a larger type of State is springing up in the world than has hitherto been known," and that this " becomes a serious consideration for those States which only rise to the old level of magnitude." * England, if she is not to sink into the

* "Expansion of England." Macmillan. 1884.

position of Venice or Spain, and find her part in the drama of history played out, must rely on her Colonial and Indian Empire to redress the disparity of size between the island home of the race and the territories of such powers as the North American Republic, Russia, and Germany. The separation of our great dependency in the East from the dominions of the Queen-Empress would be irrecoverably calamitous, and one way of averting such a catastrophe is to draw more closely the bonds of a common interest and common fortune which happily unite India to England so closely now. Were England to lose the dominion of India, she would lose her place with it in the councils of Europe, and whatever power succeeded her would hasten to extinguish the English trade. At present India stands third in rank, next to the United States and France, in the value of her exportations to England, and as an importer from England stands only second to the United States. Under proper management, the political union which this commerce implies will in the next generation become infinitely stronger, and be to the people of India material proof of the fact that their prosperity is so closely interwoven with that of England that the two cannot be disengaged without tearing the fabric of empire to shreds, and dissipating for ever the fair prospect of political and social amelioration which is now clearly in their view.

Indian trade being open to all the world, it will flow to the ports of those countries whose fiscal laws give India the greater chances of profit. There is not much in the political connection which induces the trade of India to come to England rather than to go to America or the shores of the Mediterranean. The establishment of English houses of business a century old is an advantage, but it is not one which can for certain be retained, or which it would be at all difficult to supersede. There is no reason why Germans, Greeks, Americans, or Parsees should not divert the course of trade into other countries than England, unless the English make it more advantageous to the Indians to trade with them than with other people. The ability of England to retain the Indian trade rests on other grounds than the political connection. India and England sell to each other because they can sell freely; their goods are not made dearer than they need be in each other's markets by the imposition of protective duties, and as these exchange at their true commercial values in one another, the two countries trade together at a greater advantage than either can with many other countries. It is of importance to each country to retain the markets of the other; but having regard to Continental and American competition it is of the greatest importance to England to extend her trade. In order to succeed in doing this she must find more customers, or customers able to pay a higher price for her goods. She can find these in India, she cannot be sure of finding them in other quarters where "Protection" closes the ports to her trade. India can fulfil these two conditions in favour of English trade, only so long as she is growing richer, and wealth becoming more widely diffused among her people, and their capacity to purchase English goods increasing, and the number of possible purchasers increasing also.

A sound currency system which withholds no facilities of wealth from the people promotes the growth of these conditions more than any fiscal measure which can be devised. We already carry on free trade in goods with India, to complete the system we must bestow upon her free trade in money also. By this means England is secured to some extent against the risk of India finding better customers elsewhere, and in such an event England would necessarily find fewer customers in India. It is therefore of vital necessity to England to make the trade as profitable to the people of India as circumstances allow, especially at a time when the principal commercial nations of the world are combined in a protective league against her, when they, to a considerable extent, exclude her wares from their markets and undersell her in her own markets with "bounty-paid" manufactures or commodities of which the cost has been covered by the sale at high prices of the portion reserved for consumption at home.

India being an Oriental country, with institutions and methods of administration very dissimilar to our own, it is no objection to any detail of administration that it is un-English. This consideration is especially relevant to such a scheme as this proposed reform of the currency, which, while it has no counterpart in our own financial system, is exactly consonant in respect of the exchange of money with immemorial custom in India, and in the matter of State interference in declaring the rate of exchange, could not otherwise command the confidence of the people or secure their acceptance in any appreciable degree. The estimate of the duties of a ruler which an Oriental makes is sometimes the exact reverse of that which public opinion sanctions in Europe, and not among the least important of the duties which Eastern polity assigns to Government, is that of providing the people with sound money, and enforcing such regulations for its use that all classes of people shall benefit alike. The employment of this particular method of currency would not be at variance with the fiscal or commercial customs of India, while it would be a further adaptation of the methods of English administration to Indian ideas, to which so much of the success and popularity of British rule in India is to be traced.

It has been already stated that the principle of the measure is believed to have been the resource upon which the early bimetallists relied for correcting aberrations in the rate of exchange from a normal point of value, and it is only to be expected that any special application of the principle to practice, should be viewed in different ways by men whose experience of public affairs has been gained in different fields of work. While in England the interference of a State department in the manner suggested, not to fix or determine but to declare the present prevalence of a particular condition of prices, would not be favourably received, the very opposite would be the case in India. In that country—and the reader will not fail to observe that this plan for circulating gold money is recommended for use in India only—no public body exists which can compete with the Government in its claim to public confidence. The custom of the Government always is, to get the best information it can on the possible effects of any administrative project under consideration, and to take all possible care that the sources of its information are of a representative character. For this reason legislative action in India is singularly successful in practice, an abortive measure, or a law becoming a dead letter, being almost if not entirely unknown.

The moral strength of the British Government in India consists in the confidence in the honesty of its aims, and in the singleness of its desire to promote the interests of the people, which pervade all classes, and secure for its rule a willing and universal acceptance. There is nothing in the principle or practice of this reform in the currency which is otherwise than consistent with these conditions, or which is likely to induce any consequences but such as would be wholly beneficial to the country at large. These results we may summarize as follows :—

It gives the State a gold revenue of moderate amount which may in the progress of time be much enlarged; for the present, this is sufficient to meet a pressing want, the means of making the expenditure of the Government in England, in a manner which places no heavier burden on the taxpayers, but on the contrary will year by year make it lighter.

It lays the foundation of a sound financial system by supplying a gold instead of a silver basis, both for the commerce and revenues of the country, under conditions which admit of indefinite expansion as the people advance in material prosperity.

From the point of view of Indian commerce it should be regarded with favour, because it directly facilitates the purchase of Indian productions abroad, and the importation of foreign productions into India, by placing her commerce, whether with silver or gold-using communities, under the same valuation as that in use in each different country with which her merchants are trading. The Lancashire merchant and the London broker may ask what his cotton goods will sell for, or what his indigo or tea may cost in India. The Chinaman will inquire the price he can get for his silk, and the price he will have to pay for the saltpetre he imports from India in exchange. The one will get his answer in terms of gold, and the other in terms of silver. That the Indian currency should provide a common measure of value for her own and foreign productions in every commercial country in the globe is an advantage of no slight importance to the people, and will most certainly be obtained under this scheme.

As the Indian currency will be a machine for certifying the true values of the precious metals in one another, and will secure their interchange in accordance therewith, it will attract capital to India by the security it affords that the returns to investments will be made in the coin which every class of investor may find most profitable to himself.

If a return to the bimetallism of the Latin Union ever becomes possible in Europe, the dual currency of India will have cleared the ground for the fixation of a ratio by ascertaining what the point is from which the relative values of gold and silver money will least diverge.

It will have the effect of diffusing coined money in increasing quantities among the largest possible number of people, and thereby promote cash dealings to the diminution of barter and credit transactions. By making money more common, it will lower the rate of interest and release the working man from dependence on the money-lender, and will allow the farmer to hold his crop, and the village craftsman his manufacture, for better prices and thus secure to each of them a larger share than they now get of the fruits of their own industry, and give a corresponding impulse to every sort of production, and raise the general level of prices.

It will secure a higher value to Indian exportations in the goods of foreign countries than they now hold, because they will be more valuable at home. The larger may be the prices which these command abroad, the greater will be the support they give to foreign industries employed in procuring the means of paying for them, and the more profitable will the foreign labour become which they will serve to set in motion. Whether India will sell more of her productions thus enhanced in value abroad than she did when they were cheaper will depend on her foreign customers' ability to pay the higher price. If her produce becomes too valuable to be profitably exported, she may sell less in some foreign markets, but will sell more at home; for the prevalence of high prices in the country itself would prove that the people were able and willing to pay more than they used to pay for the same article. To any extent to which this may take place, it will only amount to a change of customers, an Indian substituted for an European purchaser, and will be one obviously beneficial to the people themselves, as it would predicate a permanent advance in their material prosperity.

The rise in prices, which the use of gold money in India will set in motion, is that which the country requires more than anything else to stimulate improvements in the methods of production and manufacture, and give activity to the ways of doing business which have come down to the present generation with very little change, from a remote antiquity. It will foster competition as contrasted with combination, the movement of the West as compared with the stagnation of the East. The richer the country becomes, the more easily will she pay her way, the lighter will be the burden of taxation, and the more easily will the cost of government be borne.

The expansion which the export trade of India has experienced during the last five and twenty years, has been largely the result of improved means of communication with foreign countries; the next step in progress is that further expansion which industry obtains by providing luxuries for the richer classes, as well as necessaries for all; and a richer class is formed by the general diffusion of moderate wealth among vast numbers. This is the peculiar result of the commercial economy of this country during the last fifty years, and to produce a similar distribution of wealth ought to be the aim of currency legislation in India. The remonetizing of gold on the plan proposed would mark a distinct advance in that direction, which cannot be made in any other way. It is not to be denied that the result will be to make everything dearer, but to say that, is to say nothing against it. Those who take up the opposite line of argument and assert that India must sell cheap to sell at all, and that it is better for her to do this than to lose her trade, overlook the compensations which the growth of domestic wealth affords, and if they were to follow their argument to its logical conclusion, would find that it led them to the self-evident fallacy, that as cheap production means poor producers, so it is better that a people should sell its productions for little than for much, and that it is better for a country to be poor than to be rich.

Looking further afield than India, this scheme provides a true bimetallism which will encourage the accumulation of either kind of coin indifferently as convenience may dictate; for as in India any value of either will be exchangeable without loss into the other, the Indian rate of exchange will serve as an authoritative exponent of the values of the precious metals for foreign countries, while the currency itself will afford an ever-present and unfailing test of what that value in practice is.

It establishes an equilibrium of value for gold and silver money without the enormous expense of re-coinage, and without resort to the device of taking into the currency the cheaper and throwing out the dearer metal, which was an unavoidable necessity in securing the same object under the French system. That method of dealing with currency, more or less limited the employment of money to one kind, by the partial exclusion of the other, and thus restricted the volume of metallic capital supplied to trade; whereas this system, by maintaining the circulation of a dual currency at market values, allows gold and silver money to be employed in any quantity, and in proportions regulated by the volition of the people, and therefore in exact correspondence with the requirements of commerce.

It leaves the efficiency of silver money as full legal tender unimpaired, and the coinage of rupees unrestricted.

It overcomes the objection which some make to a resumption of the use of silver, on the ground that such a resumption would unfairly benefit the owners of silver by raising its value ; and meets the argument of others, that as silver has become depressed in consequence of a political measure, so it should be restored in value by a legislative act; for as the scheme gives no advantage to the owners of one metal over those owning the other, it leaves existing contracts unaffected, and gives fair play to both.

It excludes the influence of law and the artificial or arbitrary valuation of money; and by securing the evolution of natural values, as well for gold and silver money in one another as for both in commodities, it gives as much stability to prices as freedom of commerce can provide.

This method of using gold money involves no restraint on trade or restriction on the supply of capital to trade, it promotes the movement of money between one country and another, assists to maintain a general level of prices, and to reduce fluctuations in the exchanges, and administers in every way to the freedom and expansion of commerce. It would be followed by no disadvantageous results such as attend upon the arbitrary valuations of a fixed-ratio system, and upon the artificial enhancement which the purchasing power of gold obtains under our own system. It induces no consequences which are in themselves undesirable, while it meets the necessities of the people of India, and as far as it affects the rest of the commercial world would prove wholly beneficial in its action, and in an especial manner advantageous to the foreign trade of the empire, and to that sphere of international finance which has its centre in London.

APPENDIX.

(*Referred to at p. 341.*)

APPENDIX III. TO FINAL REPORT OF THE ROYAL COMMISSION APPOINTED TO INQUIRE INTO THE RECENT CHANGES IN THE RELATIVE VALUES OF THE PRECIOUS METALS.

(III.) A Plan for remonetizing silver in Europe, by circulating silver and gold money together, without variation in the rate of exchange; by means of a Paper Currency issued against a Reserve of gold and silver Bullion, by Clarmont Daniell, F.S.S., late of the Indian Civil Service.

The plan for the remonetizing of silver in Europe, which I published in "Discarded Silver" (Kegan Paul, Trench, and Co., 1886), consists of the following provisions:—

1. That any State desiring to use silver money at an unvarying rate of exchange with gold should constitute a reserve of equal values of gold and silver bullion—

(*a*) To be supplied by private persons wishing to use their hoards of silver as money; or

(*b*) By the State if possessed of hoards of discarded silver; or

(*c*) By both.

2. The equation of value regulating the relative supply of either metal to be that determined by the market rate of the day for gold and silver in one another.

3. As the silver constituent in the reserve would vary against the gold constituent, the State would maintain the equilibrium of value by making additions to the stock of silver in a falling market and by withdrawing silver in a rising market. The demand made on the market for silver by the constitution of this reserve would give an upward tendency to the price of silver in gold, and the State (or managers of the reserve) would acquire a constantly increasing stock of silver bullion, which would be laid aside to pro-

2 C

vide contributions to the reserve when the market for silver might fall, and the necessity of purchasing silver would never be serious or last over any length of time.

4. It follows that any value of mixed gold and silver bullion would always be of the same value in the standard gold coin of the country as twice that of the gold constituent, and would always be maintained at that value.

5. Against this reserve would be issued notes drawn in terms of the standard gold coin of the country, which would circulate at par with that class of coin.

6. The State or managers of the reserve acting for the Government would open the reserve to a fixed amount of contributions calculated on the requirement of the people for silver money. As this limit need never be too high, and would only be enlarged as occasion might require, and as the notes in circulation would be limited by the bullion in the reserve, and as this bullion would be supplied by the free action of those contributing the bullion of both kinds to the reserve, no artificial inflation of prices would arise from an excess of currency.

7. The limit set on the contributions to the reserve would prevent any foreign nation discharging its spare silver into such a reserve opened in a neighbouring country; and at the same time the action of the demand for silver on the part of several governments using this system, would raise the value of silver to a point at which it would become unprofitable for any State not using it to get rid of its silver by means of a neighbouring nation's reserve.

8. The success of such a system would be ensured by several States agreeing to circulate notes issued against gold and silver bullion on these terms. This agreement would only extend to the adoption of the principle involved, all details being left to the individual action of the several States.

9. By this means any value of silver bullion placed in the reserve would become effective money, and as the notes issued against the reserve would always circulate at par with standard gold money, the inconvenience of a varying rate for the exchange of gold and silver money would be overcome.

10. Depositors putting bullion in the reserve could always withdraw it on presenting notes, the bullion they would receive would be equal values of gold and silver to the aggregate value inscribed on the notes, which would be payable to "bearer" "on demand."

11. The gold bullion in the reserve would not amount to a diminution on the supply of gold money to the currency, as its place in the circulation would be taken by the notes issued against

the reserve, and these notes would at the same time circulate an equal value of silver money.

12. Such a system might be introduced without conflicting with or disorganizing any system in use in the country to which it might be applied. It could be used in England, in India, or in countries using the "fixed-ratio" system of the Latin Union (as it was at work up to 1873), *pari passu* with the existing currency. In gold-using countries it would supply the people with any quantity of silver money they might choose to circulate in this way, and in silver-using countries with any quantity of gold money, money being paper money circulating to the full metallic value of the bullion in the reserve.

13. I argue that as silver has fallen in value, with all its resulting losses and prospective dangers from disuse, so these results are to be obviated by bringing the metal again into its most profitable field of employment as money, in quantities only limited by the requirements of the people. This effect the *above-described plan will secure*.

FINIS.

www.ingramcontent.com/pod-product-compliance
Lightning Source LLC
Chambersburg PA
CBHW020106010526
44115CB00008B/713